AN INTRODUCTION TO APPLIED PHYSICS

AN INTRODUCTION TO APPLIED PHYSICS

By

Dr. Ajit Kumar Sharma

M.Sc., Ph.D.

Head

Department of Physics

D.A.V. (P.G.) College, Bulandshahr (U.P.)

(India)

DPH

DISCOVERY PUBLISHING HOUSE PVT. LTD.

NEW DELHI-110 002

Published by:
Tilak Wasan
DISCOVERY PUBLISHING HOUSE PVT. LTD.
4383/4B, Ansari Road, Darya Ganj
New Delhi-110 002 (India)
Phone : +91-11-23279245, 43596064-65
Fax : +91-11-23253475
E-mail : discoverypublishinghouse@gmail.com
sales@discoverypublishinggroup.com
parul.wasan@gmail.com
web : www.discoverypublishinggroup.com

***First Edition:* 2014**

ISBN: 978-93-5056-403-5

An Introduction to Applied Physics

Printed at:
Dynamic Printers
Delhi

Preface

Applied physics implies physics which is intended for a particular technological or practical use. Applied is distinguished from 'pure' by a subtle combination of factors such as the motivation and attitude of researchers and the nature of the relationship to the technology or science that may be affected by the work. An applied physics prospectus frequently contains a few classes in an applied discipline, like geology or electrical engineering. It usually differs from engineering in that an applied physicist may not be designing something in particular, but rather is using physics or conducting physics study with the aim of developing new technologies or solving a problem.

Physical properties of elements and compounds which supply conclusive evidence of chemical composition include odour, colour, volume, density, melting point, boiling point, heat capacity, physical form and shape at room temperature, hardness, porosity, index of refraction and many others. The mechanical properties of materials explain characteristics such as their strength and resistance to deformation. For example, steel beams are used in construction because of their high strength, meaning that they neither break nor bend significantly under the applied load.

A crystalline solid is a substance which is composed of a basic unit which is repeated in three dimensions (3D) in an ordered fashion. The basic 3D repeating pattern is called the unit cell and can be composed of atoms, ions, or molecules. One of the controlling aspects of the packing of spheres is how they are arranged within each layer. In some layers all of the spheres are touching and each sphere is surrounded by six others. This is the most efficient way to pack spheres and is called closest packing. Layers can also be fashioned from spheres which do not make such efficient use of the available space; in these layers one sphere will be in contact with only four other spheres. The least efficient packing of sphere layers occurs when no contact at all exists between the spheres. The arrangement of the spheres in two dimensional sheets represents only one aspect of the overall crystal structure; how the two dimensional sheets are stacked must also be considered. Two different types of closest packed structures can be generated depending on how close-packed layers of spheres are stacked.

The theory of quantum mechanics is built upon the fundamental concepts of wave-functions and operators. The wave-function is a single-valued square-integrable function of the system parameters and time which provides a complete description of the structure. Linear Hermitian operators act on the wave-function and correspond to the physical observables, those dynamical variables which can be measured, e.g. position, momentum and energy.

This book is planned to serve as a textbook of applied physics. Thorough treatment of topics in Bonding in Solids, Units and Dimensions, Crystal Structures, Motion, Work, Energy and Power, Principles of Quantum Mechanics, Electron Theory of Metals, Semiconductors, Superconductivity, Crystal Structures and Lasens. The book will also be useful for the students taking various competitive examinations.

—Author

Contents

Chapter 1

Units and Dimensions

INTRODUCTION

By international agreement a small number of physical quantities such as length, time etc. are chosen and assigned standards. These quantities are called 'base quantities' and their units as 'base units'. All other physical quantities are expressed in terms of these 'base quantities'. The units of these dependent quantities are called 'derived units'. The standard for a unit should have the following characteristics:

- It should be well defined.
- It should be invariable (should not change with time)
- It should be convenient to use.
- It should be easily accessible.

The 14th general conference on weights and measures (in France) picked seven quantities as base quantities, thereby forming the International System of Units abbreviated as SI (System de International) system.

Base Quantities and their Units

Table 1.1 : The Seven base Quantities and their Units are:

Base Quantity	*Unit*	*Symbol*
Length	Metre	M
Mass	Kilogram	Kg
Time	Second	Sec
Electric current	Ampere	A
Temperature	Kelvin	K

Contd...

Base Quantity	*Unit*	*Symbol*
Luminous intensity	Candela	Cd
Amount of substance	Mole	Mole

Derived Units

Derived units are those units which can be uttered in terms of base units. For example, speed is defined to be the ratio of distance to time.

Unit of Speed = (unit of distance (length))/(unit of time) = m/s = ms^{-1} (Read as metre per sec.)

Table 1.2 : Some Derived SI Units and their Symbols

Quantity	*Unit*	*Symbol*	*Expressed in base Units*
Force	newton	N	Kg-m/sec^2
Work	joules	J	Kg-m^2/sec^2
Power	watt	W	Kg-m^2/sec^3
Pressure	pascal	Pa	Kg m^{-1}/S^2

Important

The following conventions are adopted while writing a unit:

- Even if a unit is named after a person the unit is not written IN capital letters. i.e. we write joules not Joules.
- For a unit named after a person the symbol is a capital letter e.g. for joules we write 'J' and the rest of them are in lowercase letters *e.g.* seconds is written as 's'.
- The symbols of units do not have plural form *i.e.* 70 m not 70 ms or 10 N not 10Ns.
- Punctuation marks are not written after the unit *e.g.* 1 litre = 1000 cc not 1000 c.c.

It has to be borne in mind that SI system of units is not the only system of units that is followed all over the world. There are some countries (though they are very few in number) which use different system of units. For example: the FPS (Foot Pound Second) system or the CGS (Centimeter Gram Second) system.

Dimensions Express

The unit of any derived quantity depends upon one or more fundamental units. This dependence can be expressed with the help of dimensions of that derived quantity. In other words, the dimensions of a physical quantity shows how its unit is related to the fundamental units.

To express dimensions, each fundamental unit is represented by a capital letter. Thus the unit of length is denoted by L, unit of mass by M. Unit of time by T, unit of electric current by I, unit of temperature by K and unit of luminous intensity by C.

Remember that speed will always remain distance covered per unit of time, whatever is the system of units, so the complex quantity speed can be expressed in terms of length L and time T.

Now, we say that dimensional formula of speed is LT-1. We can relate the physical quantities to each other (usually we express complex quantities in terms of base quantities) by a system of dimensions.

Dimension of a physical quantity are the powers to which the fundamental quantities must be raised to represent the given physical quantity.

Units and Dimensions

Units

Most physical quantities include a unit, but not all - some are dimensionless. Neither the name of a physical quantity, nor the symbol used to denote it, implies a particular choice of unit, though SI units are usually preferred and assumed today due to their ease of use and all-round applicability. For example, a quantity of mass might be represented by the symbol m, and could be expressed in the units kilograms (kg), pounds (lb), or Daltons (Da).

Dimensions

The notion of *physical dimension* of a physical quantity was introduced by Joseph Fourier in 1822. By convention, physical quantities are organized in a dimensional system built upon base quantities, each of which is regarded as having its own dimension.

PHYSICAL QUANTITIES

A physical quantity is a quantity in physics that can be measured or a physical quantity is a physical property that can be quantified. Examples of physical quantities are mass, volume, length, time, temperature, electric current.

Basic and Derived Quantities

Quantities can be divided into two types *i.e.* basic quantities and derived quantities.

Basic Quantities

Basic quantities are the fundamental quantities that are not related to each other and that are use to derive all other quantities.

There are seven basic quantities. They are:

- Length
- Time
- Mass
- Thermodynamic temperature
- Electric current
- Amount of substance and
- Luminous intensity.

Derived Quantities

Derived quantities are just quantities that are derived from one or more basic quantities. For example area is a derived quantity because it is derived from the basic quantity length:

Area = length * length

Volume is a derived quantities because it is derived from the basic quantity length:

Volume = length * length * length

Density is a derived quantity because it is derived from length and mass, two basic quantities:

Density = mass/(length * length * length)

As you can see all other quantities apart from the seven basic quantities are derived from the seven basic quantities and it can easily be shown as in the example above.

Can you show what are the basic quantities that are used to derive the following derived quantities:

- Force
- Kinetic energy
- Power
- Pressure.

Definition of a Physical Quantity

Property of a phenomenon, body, or substance, where the property has a magnitude that can be expressed as a number and a reference.

Hence the value of a physical quantity q is expressed as the product of a numerical value N_q and a unit of measurement u_q;

$Q = N_q \times u_q$

Quantity calculus describes how to do maths with quantities.

Examples

If the temperature T of a body is quantified as 300 kelvin (in which T is the quantity symbol, 300 the value, and K is the unit), this is written

$T = 300 \times \text{K} = 300\ \text{K}$,

If a person weighs 120 pounds, then "120" is the numerical value and "pound" is the unit. This physical quantity mass would be written as "120 lb", or

$m = 120$ lb

If a person travelling with a yardstick, measures the length of such yardstick, the physical quantity of length would be written as

$L = 36$ inches

An example employing SI units and scientific notation for the number, might be a measurement of power written as

$P = 42.3 \times 10^3$ W,

In practice, note that different observers may get different values of a quantity depending on the frame of reference; in turn the coordinate system and metric. Physical properties such as length, mass or time, by themselves, are not physically invariant. However, the *laws of physics* which include these properties *are* invariant.

Extensive and Intensive Quantities

Extensive Quantity: Its magnitude is additive for subsystems (volume, mass, *etc.*)

Intensive Quantity: The magnitude is independent of the extent of the system (temperature, pressure, *etc.*)

There are also physical quantities that can be classified as neither extensive nor intensive, for example angular momentum, area, force, length, and time.

Symbols, Nomenclature

General: Symbols for quantities should be chosen according to the international recommendations from ISO 80000, the IUPAP red book and the IUPAC green book. For example, the recommended symbol for the physical quantity 'mass' is m, and the recommended symbol for the quantity 'charge' is Q.

Subscripts and Indices

Subscripts are used for two reasons, to merely attach a name to the quantity or associate it with another quantity, or represent a specific vector, matrix, or tensor component.

Name Reference: The quantity has a subscripted or superscripted single letter, a number of letters, or an entire word, to specify what concept or entity they refer to, and tend to be written in upright roman typeface rather than italic while the quantity is in italic.

For instance E_k or $E_{kinetic}$ is usually used to denote kinetic energy and E_p or $E_{potential}$ is usually used to denote potential energy.

Quantity Reference: The quantity has a subscripted or superscripted single letter, a number of letters, or an entire word, to specify what measurement/s they refer to, and tend to be written in italic rather than upright roman typeface while the quantity is also in italic. For example c_p or $c_{isobaric}$ is heat capacity at constant pressure.

Note the difference in the style of the subscripts: k and p are abbreviations of the words kinetic and potential, whereas *p* (italic) is the symbol for the physical quantity *pressure* rather than an abbreviation of the word "pressure".

Indices: These are quite apart from the above, their use is for mathematical formalism.

Scalars: Symbols for physical quantities are usually chosen to be a single letter of the Latin or Greek alphabet, and are printed in italic type.

Vectors: Symbols for physical quantities that are vectors are in bold type, underlined or with an arrow above. If, *e.g.*, *u* is the speed of a particle, then the straightforward notation for its velocity is **u**, u̲, or $\vec{u}$.

Numbers and Elementary Functions

Numerical quantities, even those denoted by letters, are usually printed in roman (upright) type, though sometimes can be italic. Symbols for elementary functions (circular trigonometric, hyperbolic, logarithmic *etc.*), changes in a quantity like Δ in Δy or operators like d in $\mathrm{d}x$, are also recommended to be printed in roman type.

Examples

Real numbers are as usual, such as 1 or $\sqrt{2}$,
e for the base of natural logarithm,
i for the imaginary unit,
π for 3.14152658...
δx, Δy, dz,
sin α, sinh γ, log x

Base Quantities

The seven base quantities of the International System of Quantities (ISQ) and their corresponding SI units and dimensions are listed in the following table. Other conventions may have a different number of fundamental units (*e.g.* the CGS and MKS systems of units).

International System of Units Base Quantities				
Quantity name/s	**(Common) Quantity symbol/s**	**SI unit name**	**SI unit symbol**	**Dimension symbol**
Length, width, height, depth	$a, b, c, d, h, l, r, w, x, y, z$	metre	m	[L]
Time	t	second	s	[T]
Mass	m	kilogram	kg	[M]
Temperature	T, θ	kelvin	K	[Θ]
Amount of substance, number of moles	n	mole	mol	[N]
Electric current	i, I	ampere	A	[I]
Luminous intensity	I_v	candela	Cd	[J]
Plane angle	$\alpha, \beta, \gamma, \theta, \phi, \chi$	radian	rad	dimensionless
Solid angle	ω, Ω	steradian	sr	dimensionless

The last two angular units *i.e.*; plane angle and solid angle are subsidiary units used in the SI, but treated dimensionless. The subsidiary units are used for convenience to differentiate between a *truly dimensionless* quantity (pure number) and an *angle*, which are different measurements.

Description of Units and Physical Quantities

Physical quantities and units follow the same hierarchy; *chosen base quantities* have *defined base units*, from these any other *quantities may be derived* and have corresponding *derived units*.

Colour Mixing Analogy

Defining quantities is analogous to mixing colours, and could be classified a similar way, although this is not standard. Primary colours are to base quantities; as secondary (or tertiary *etc.*) colours are to derived quantities. Mixing colours is analogous to combining quantities using mathematical operations. But colours could be for light or paint, and analogously the system of units could be one of many forms: such as SI (now most common), CGS, Gaussian, old imperial units, a specific form of natural units or even arbitrarily defined units characteristic to the physical system in consideration (characteristic units).

The choice of a base system of quantities and units is arbitrary; but once chosen it must be adhered to throughout all analysis which follows for consistency. It makes no sense to mix up different systems of units. Choosing a system of units, one system out of the SI, CGS etc., is like choosing whether use paint or light colours.

In light of this analogy, primary definitions are base quantities with no defining equation, but defined standardized condition, "secondary" definitions are quantities defined purely in terms of base quantities, "tertiary" for quantities in terms of both base and "secondary" quantities, "quaternary" for quantities in terms of base, "secondary", and "tertiary" quantities, and so on.

Motivation

Much of physics requires definitions to be made for the equations to make sense.

Theoretical Implications: Definitions are important since they can lead into new insights of a branch of physics. Two such examples occurred in classical physics. When entropy S was defined – the range of thermodynamics was greatly extended by associating chaos and disorder with a numerical quantity that could relate to energy and temperature, leading to the understanding of the second thermodynamic law and statistical mechanics. Also the action functional (also written S) (together with generalized coordinates and momenta and the lagrangian function), initially an alternative formulation of classical mechanics to Newton's laws, now extends the range of modern physics in general – notably quantum mechanics and particle physics.

Analytical Convenience: They allow other equations to be written more compsier mathematical manipulation.

Example

As an example consider Ampère's circuital la (with Maxwell's correction) in integral form for an arbitrary current carrying conductor in a vacuum (so zero magnetization due medium, i.e M = 0):

$$\oint_S \mathbf{B}\cdot d\mathbf{l} = \mu_0 \oint_S \left(\mathbf{J} + \epsilon_0 \frac{\partial \mathbf{E}}{\partial t} \right) \cdot d\mathbf{A}$$

using the constitutive definition

$$\mathbf{B} = \mu_0 \mathbf{H},$$

and the current density definition

$$I = \oint_S \mathbf{J}\cdot d\mathbf{A},$$

similarly for the displacement current density

$\mathbf{J}_d = \epsilon_0 \frac{\partial \mathbf{E}}{\partial t}$ leading to the displacement current

$$I_d = \oint_S \mathbf{J}_d \cdot d\mathbf{A},$$

we have

$$\oint_S \mathbf{B}\cdot d\mathbf{l} = \mu_0 \oint_S \mathbf{J}\cdot d\mathbf{A} + \mu_0 \oint_S \mathbf{J}_d \cdot d\mathbf{A},$$

$$\oint_S \mathbf{H}\cdot d\mathbf{l} = I + I_d,$$

which is simpler to write, even if the equation is the same.

Ease of Comparison: They allow comparisons of measurements to be made when they might appear ambiguous and unclear otherwise.

Example

A basic example is mass density. It is not clear how compare how much matter constitutes a variety of substances given only their masses or only their volumes.

Given both for each substance, the mass m per unit volume V, or mass density ρ provides a meaningful comparison between the substances, since for each, a fixed amount of volume will correspond to an amount of mass depending on the substance.

To illustrate this; if two substances A and B have masses m_A and m_B respectively, occupying volumes V_A and V_B respectively, using the definition of mass density gives:

$\rho_A = m_A/V_A$, $\rho_B = m_B/V_B$

following this can be seen that:

if $m_A > m_B$ or $m_A < m_B$
and $V_A = V_B$, then $\rho_A > \rho_B$ or $\rho_A < \rho_B$,
if $m_A = m_B$ and $V_A > V_B$ or $V_A < V_B$, then $\rho_A < \rho_B$ or $\rho_A > \rho_B$,
if $\rho_A = \rho_B$, then $m_A/V_A = m_B/V_B$ so $m_A/m_B = V_A/V_B$,

demonstrating that if

$m_A > m_B$ or $m_A < m_B$, then $V_A > V_B$ or $V_A < V_B$.

CONSTRUCTION OF DEFINING EQUATIONS

SCOPE OF DEFINING EQUATIONS

Defining equations are normally formulated in terms of elementary algebra and calculus, vector algebra and calculus, or for the most universal applications tensor algebra and calculus, depending on the level of study and presentation, complexity of topic and scope of applicability. Functions may be incorporated into a definition, in for calculus this is necessary.

Quantities may also be complex-valued for theoretical advantage, but for a physical measurement the real part is relevant, the imaginary part can be discarded. For more advanced treatments the equation may have to be written in an equivalent but alternative form using other defining equations for the definition to be useful. Often definitions can start from elementary algebra, then modify to vectors, then in the limiting cases calculus may be used. The various levels of maths used typically follows this pattern.

Elementary Algebra

Operations are simply multiplication and division. Equations may be written in a product or quotient form, both of course equivalent.

	Angular Momentum	*Electric Current Density*
Quotient form	$p = \frac{L}{r}$	$J = \frac{\Delta I}{\Delta A}$
Product form	$L = pr$	$\Delta I = J\Delta A$

Vector Algebra

There is no way to divide a vector by a vector, so there are no product or quotient forms:

	Angular Momentum	*Electric Current Density*
Quotient form	N/A	$J \cdot \hat{n} = \frac{\Delta I}{\Delta A}$
Product form	Starting from $L = pr,$ since L = 0 when p and r are parallel or antiparallel, and is a maximum when perpendicular, so that the only component of p which contributes to L is the tangential $\lvert p \rvert \sin \theta$, the magnitude of angular momentum L should be re-written as $L = pr\sin\theta.$ Since r, p and L form a right-hand triad, this leads to the vector form $L = r \times p.$	$J \cdot \hat{n}\Delta A = \Delta I,$ $J \cdot \Delta A = \Delta I,$

Elementary Calculus

The arithmetic operations are modified to the limiting cases of differentiation and integration. Equations can be expressed in these equivalent and alternative ways.

Current Density	
Differential form	$J = \lim_{\delta A \to 0} \frac{\delta I}{\delta A} = \frac{dI}{dA}$
Integral form	$I = \lim_{\delta A_i \to 0} \sum_i J\delta A_i = \int_S J dA$ Alternatively for integral form $dI = J dA,$ $I = \int_S J dA.$

Vector Calculus

Current Density	
Differential form	$J \cdot \hat{n} = \frac{dI}{dA}$
Integral form	$L_i = \varepsilon_{ijk} r_j p_k$

Tensor Analysis

Vectors are rank-1 tensors.

The formulae below are no more than the vector equations in the language of tensors.

	Angular Momentum	Electric Current Density
Differential form	N/A	$J_i n_i = \frac{dI}{dA}$
Product/integral form	Starting from $L = r \times p$ the components are L_i, r_j, p_i, where i, j, k are each dummy indices each taking values 1,2,3, using the identity from tensor analysis $a = b \times c, \quad a_i = \int_{ijk} b_j c_k,$	Using the Einstein summation convention, $J_i n_i dA = dI$ $\int_S J_i dA = I$

Contd...

where ε_{ijk} is the permutation/Levi-Cita tensor, leads to

$$L_i = \varepsilon_{ijk} r_j p_k$$

Multiple Choice Definitions

Sometimes there is still freedom within the chosen units organization, to define one or more quantities in more than one way. The situation splits into two cases:

Mutually Exclusive Definitions: There are a number of possible choices for a quantity to be defined in terms of others, but only one can be used and not the others.

Choosing more than one of the exclusive equations for a definition leads to a contradiction – one equation might demand a quantity X to be *defined* in one way *using another* quantity Y, while another equation requires the *reverse*, Y be defined using X, but then another equation might falsify the use of both X and Y, and so on. The mutual disagreement makes it impossible to say which equation defines what quantity.

Equivalent Definitions: Defining equations which are equivalent and self-consistent with other equations and laws within the physical theory, simply written in different ways.

There are two possibilities for each case:

1. *One Defining Equation – One Defined Quantity:* A defining equation is used to define a single quantity in terms of a number of others.
2. *One Defining Equation – A Number of Defined Quantities:* A defining equation is used to define a number of quantities in terms of a number of others. A single defining equation shouldn't contain *one* quantity defining *all other* quantities in the *same equation*, otherwise contradictions arise again. There is no definition of the defined quantities separately since they are defined by a single quantity in a single equation. Furthermore the defined quantities may have already been defined before, so if another quantity defines these in the same equation, there is a clash between

definitions.

Contradictions can be avoided by defining quantities *successively*; the *order* in which quantities are defined must be accounted for.

Examples spanning these instances occur in electromagnetism, and are given below:

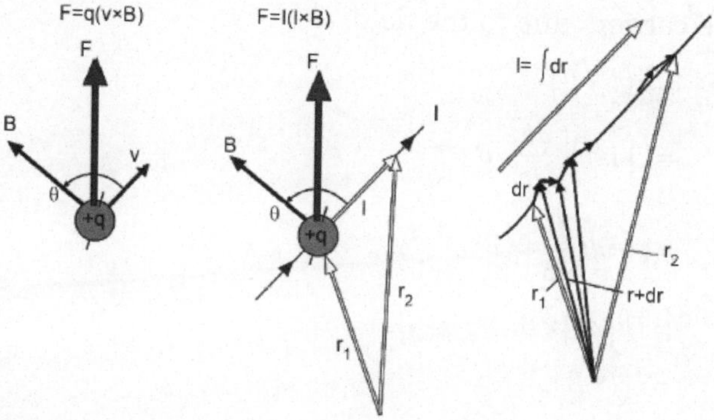

Magnetic Force

The electric current shown here is conventional. The vector l is the integral (sum) of all infinitesimal vectors *dr* from entry position r_1 to exit position r_2.

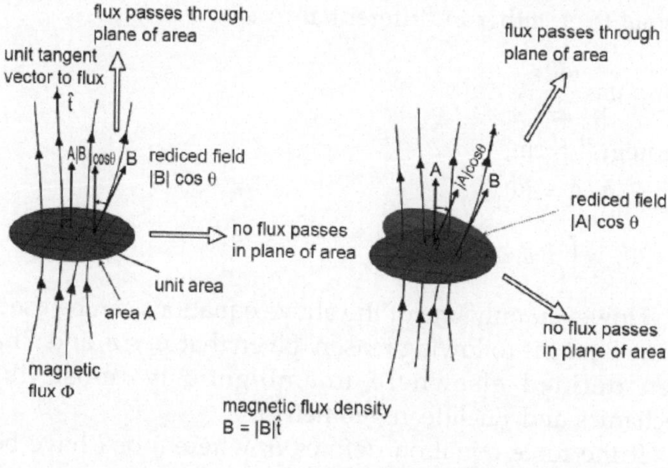

Figure 1.1: Magnetic Field and Flux. Note the Analogy with

the Current Density and Current Above.

Examples

Mutually Exclusive Definitions: The magnetic induction field B can be defined in terms of electric charge q or current I, and the Lorentz force (magnetic term) F experienced by the charge carriers due to the field,

$$\begin{aligned} F &= q(v \times B) \\ &= \left(\int I dt\right)\left(\frac{dr}{dt} \times B\right) \\ &= \left(\int I dt \frac{dr}{dt}\right) \times B \\ &= I\left(\int dr\right) \times B \\ &= I(l \times B), \end{aligned}$$

where $l = \int dr$ is the change in position traversed by the charge carriers (assuming current is independent of position, if not so a line integral must be done along the path of current) or in terms of the magnetic flux Φ_B through a surface S, where the area is used as a scalar A and vector: $A = A\hat{n}$ and $\hat{n}$ is a unit normal to A, either in differential form

$$B \cdot \hat{n} = \frac{d\Phi_B}{dA},$$

or integral form,

$$B \cdot \hat{n} dA = d\Phi_B,$$

$$\Phi_B = \int_S B \cdot dA.$$

However, only one of the above equations can be used to define B for the following reason, given that A, r, v, and F have been defined elsewhere unambiguously (most likely mechanics and Euclidean geometry).

If the force equation defines B, where q or I have been previously defined, then the flux equation defines Φ_B, since B has been previously defined unambiguously. If the flux equation defines B, where Φ_B, the force equation may be a defining equation for I or q. Notice the contradiction when B both equations define B simultaneously and when B is not a base quantity; the force equation demands that q or I be defined elsewhere while at the same time the flux equation demands that q or I be defined by the force equation, similarly the force equation requires Φ_B to be defined by the flux equation, at the same time the flux equation demands that Φ_B is defined elsewhere. For both equations to be used as definitions simultaneously, B must be a base quantity so that F and Φ_B can be defined to stem from B unambiguously.

Equivalent Definitions

Another example is inductance L which has two equivalent equations to use as a definition.

In terms of I and Φ_B, the inductance is given by

$$L = N\frac{d\Phi_B}{dI},$$

in terms of I and induced emf V

$$V = -L\frac{dI}{dt}.$$

These two are equivalent by Faraday's law of induction:

$$V = -N\frac{d\Phi_B}{dt},$$

$$Vdt = -Nd\Phi_B,$$

substituting into the first definition for L

$$L = -V\frac{dt}{dI}$$

$$V = -L\frac{dI}{dt}$$

and so they are not mutually exclusive.

One Defining Equation – A Number of Defined Quantities

Notice that L cannot define I and Φ_B simultaneously - this makes no sense. I, Φ_B and V have most likely all been defined before as (Φ_B given above in flux equation);

$$V = \frac{dW}{dq}, \quad I = \frac{dq}{dt},$$

where W = work done on charge q. Furthermore there is no definition of either I or Φ_B separately – because L is defining them in the same equation. However, using the Lorentz force for the electromagnetic field

$$F = q\left[E + (v \times B)\right],$$

As a single defining equation for the electric field E and magnetic field B is allowed, since E and B are not only defined by one variable, but *three*; force F, velocity v and charge q. This is consistent with isolated definitions of E and B since E is defined using F and q:

$$E = F / q.$$

and B defined by F, v, and q, as given above.

Limitations of Definitions

Definitions vs. Functions

Defining quantities can vary as a function of parameters other than those in the definition. A defining equation only defines how calculate the defined quantity, it *cannot* describe how the quantity varies as a function of other parameters since the function would vary from one application to another.

Examples

Mass density ρ is defined using mass m and volume V by but can vary as a function of temperature T and pressure p, $\rho = \rho(p, T)$

The angular frequency ω of wave propagation is defined using the frequency (or equivalently time period T) of the oscillation, as a function of wavenumber k, $\omega = \omega(k)$. This is the *dispersion relation* for wave propagation. The coefficient of restitution for a object colliding is defined using the speeds of separation and and approach with respect to the collision point, but depends on the nature of the surfaces in question.

Definitions vs. Theorems

There is a very important difference between defining equations and general or derived results, theorems or laws. Defining equations *do not find out any information* about a physical system, they simply re-state one measurement in terms of others. Results, theorems, and laws, on the other hand *do* provide meaningful information, if only a little, since they represent a calculation for a quantity given other properties of the system, and describe how the system behaves as variables are changed.

Examples

An example was given above for Ampere's law. Another is the conservation of momentum for N_1 initial particles having initial momenta p_i where $i = 1, 2 \ldots N_1$, and N_2 final particles having final momenta p_i (some particles may explode or adhere) where $j = 1, 2 \ldots N_2$, the equation of conservation reads:

$$\sum_i^{N_1} p_i = \sum_j^{N_2} p_j$$

Using the definition of momentum in terms of velocity:

$$p = mv$$

so that for each particle:

$$p_i = m_i v_i \quad \text{and} \quad p_j = m_j v_j$$

the conservation equation can be written as

$$\sum_i^{N_1} m_i v_i = \sum_j^{N_2} m_i v_i.$$

It is identical to the previous version. No information is lost or gained by changing quantities when definitions are substituted, but the equation itself does give information about the system.

Pseudo-defining Equations

Some equations, typically results from a derivation, contain quantities which may already be base quantities or have a definition, but be labelled in a different way with respect to the context of the result. These are not defining equations since they are results which apply to a physical situation– they are not quantity constructions, but can be used in the same way for calculations of the specific quantity within its scope of application.

Examples

Two examples in special relativity follow:

1. Mass could be at rest or in motion (relativistic mass), relativistic mass can be pseudo-defined by

   $$m = \gamma m_0$$

   where m_0 = rest mass, m = relativistic mass and γ is the Lorentz factor.

2. The invariant mass of a system could be pseudo-defined by the same equation as mass-momentum-energy invariance,

   $$m = \frac{1}{c^2}\sqrt{E^2 - (p \cdot p)c^2}$$

   where E = Total energy, p = Total 3-momentum of the system.

Two examples in electromagnetism follow, neglecting relativistic effects for simplicity.

Using SI units – not CGS or Gaussian which are fairly common in this field, the vacuum luminal speed c has the exact value c = 299 792 458 ms^{-1} (this in itself is the definition of the metre), and so does the vacuum permeability μ_0 (another defined value, cannot be obtained from experiment), where $\mu_0 = 4\pi \times 10^{-7}$ Hm^{-1}, so the value of the vacuum permittivity can be found from the pseudo-definition

$$\epsilon_0 = \frac{1}{c^2\mu_0}.$$

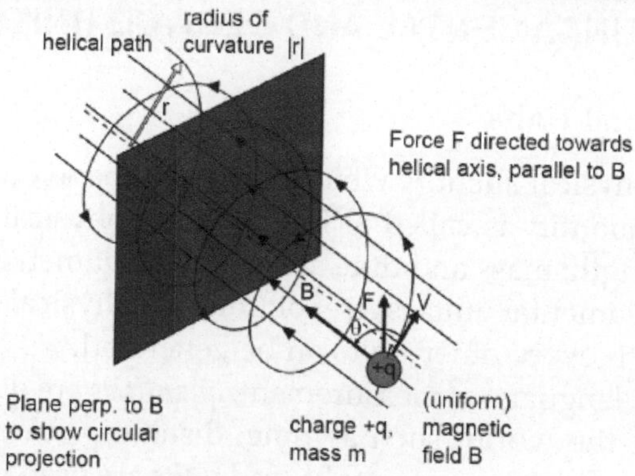

Figure 1.2: Magnetic Field Deflecting a Charged Particle, Pseudo-defining Magnetic Rigidity for the Particle.

For a charged particle (of mass m and charge q) in a uniform magnetic field B, deflected by the field in a circular helical arc at velocity v and radius of curvature r, where the helical trajectory inclined at an angle θ to B, the magnetic force is the centripetal force, so the force F acting on the particle is

$$F = -\frac{m(v \cdot v)\hat{r}}{|r|} = q(v \times B),$$

reducing to scalar form and solving for |B| |r|;

$$\frac{m|v|^2}{|r|} = q|v||B|\sin\theta,$$

$$\frac{m|v|}{|r|} = q|B|\sin\theta,$$

$$|B||r| = \frac{m|v|}{q\sin\theta},$$

serves as a pseudo-definition for the *magnetic rigidity* of the particle. Notice that these are all derived results from their respective theories – not proper definitions.

FUNDAMENTAL AND DERIVED UNITS

Fundamental Units

The physical quantity which does not depend on any other physical quantity is called a 'fundamental physical quantity' such as length; mass and time are called fundamental units. A set of fundamental units is a set of units for physical quantities from which every other unit can be generated.

In the language of measurement, *quantities* are quantifiable aspects of the world, such as time, distance, velocity, mass, momentum, energy, and weight, and *units* are used to describe their measure.

Many of these quantities are related to each other by various physical laws, and as a result the units of some of the quantities can be expressed as products (or ratios) of powers of other units (*e.g.*, momentum is mass times velocity and velocity is measured in distance divided by time). These relationships are discussed in dimensional analysis. Those that cannot be so expressed can be regarded as "fundamental" in this sense. There are other relationships between physical quantities which can be expressed by means of fundamental constants, and to some extent it is an arbitrary decision whether to retain the fundamental constant as a quantity with dimensions or simply to define it as unity or a fixed dimensionless number, and reduce the number of fundamental constants by one.

For instance, time and distance are related to every other by the speed of light, c, which is a fundamental constant. It is possible to use this relationship to eliminate either the fundamental unit of time or that of distance.

Similar considerations apply to Planck's constant, h, which relates energy (with dimensions of mass, length and time) to frequency (dimensions of time). In theoretical physics it is customary to use such units (natural units) in which $c = 1$ and $\hbar = 1$.

Slightly different considerations apply to the so-called permittivity of free space, which historically has been regarded as a separate physical constant in some systems of measurement but not in others.

In the SI system, there are seven fundamental units: kilogram, meter, candela, second, ampere, kelvin, and mole. In theory, a system of fundamental quantities (or sometimes fundamental dimensions) would be such that every other physical quantity (or dimension of physical quantity) can be generated from them:

- One could eliminate any two of the metre, kilogram and second by setting c and h to unity or to a fixed dimensionless number.
- One could then eliminate the ampere either by setting the permittivity of free space to a fixed dimensionless number or by setting the electronic charge to such a number.
- One could similarly eliminate the mole as a fundamental unit by reference to Avogadro's number.
- One could eliminate the kelvin as it can be argued that temperature simply expresses the energy per particle per degree of freedom which can be expressed in terms of energy (or mass, length, and time). Another way of saying this is that Boltzmann's constant could be expressed as a fixed dimensionless number.
- Similarly, one could eliminate the candela as that is defined in terms of other physical quantities.
- That just leaves one fundamental dimension and one fundamental unit, but we still have plenty of fundamental constants left to eliminate that too - for instance one could use *G*, the gravitational constant, or m(e), the electron rest mass.

A widely used choice is the so-called Planck units, which are defined by setting $\hbar = c = G = 1$.

That leaves every physical quantity expressed simply as a dimensionless number, so it is not surprising that there are also physicists who have cast doubt on the very existence of incompatible fundamental quantities.

Derived Units

The units that can be obtained from fundamental units are called derived units.

Fundamental (Primary) Units

Quantity	*Name of Unit*	*Definition*
Length	Metre (m)	
Mass	Kilogram (kg)	
Time	Second (s)	
Electric current	Ampere (A)	Coulomb/ second
Thermodynamic temperature	Kelvin (K)	
Amount of substance	Mole (mol)	
Luminous intensity	Candela (cd)	

Derived Units

Quantity	*Name of Unit*	*Definition*
Capacitance	Farad (F)	Coulomb/volt, (amp * second/volt)
Charge, quantity of	Coulomb (C)	(amp * second)
Energy (work)	Joule (J)	Newton-meter, (kg * m^2/ sec^2)
Force	Newton (N)	Joules/meter, kg * m/sec^2
Inductance	Henry (H)	volt * second/Ampere
Magnetic flux	Weber (Wb)	volt * second,
Magnetic flux density	Tesla (T)	(Webers/$meter^2$); (joules * second)/ (Coulomb * $meter^2$); (Note: 1 tesla = 1×10^{-4} Gauss = 1Newton/ (amp * meter))
Potential difference (electromotive force)	Volt (V)	joules/Coulomb, (kg * m^2/(sec^2 * Coulomb)), watts/Ampere
Power	Watt (W)	joules/second, (volts * Ampere)
Resistance	Ohm	volts/Ampere

Fundamental Constants

Constant	*Symbol*	*Value*
Speed of light	c	2.99792458×10^{8} m/s, Halliday
Charge, elementary	e	$1.60217738 \times 10^{-19}$ C, Halliday
Electric permittivity constant (in vacuum)	ε_0	8.85418781762E-12 F/m, Halliday
Planck's constant	h	$6.6260754 \times 10^{-34}$ j-s, Halliday
Planck's constant/ (2.0 π)	$\hbar$	1.055×10^{-34} joules-sec
Complex number	i	$\sqrt{-1}$
Magnetic permeability constant (in vacuum)	μ_0	$4.0\ \pi\ 1.0 \times 10^{-7}$ H/m (Newton/ amp^2)

SYSTEMS OF UNITS (FPS, CGS, MKS AND SI UNITS)

Different Systems of Units

There are a number of different systems of units. Most people become aware of these different systems while in elementary school when faced with the dreaded set of conversions from English units to metric units. Actually, there are more than two. Table 1.3 below provides information on five systems of units.

Table 1.3 : Systems of Units

System of Units	*Length*	*Mass*	*Force*	*Time*
Centimeter-gram-second (cgs)	cm	gram	dyne[1]	sec
International System of Units (SI)	meter	kilogram	newton[1]	sec
English Absolute	foot	pound	poundal[1]	sec
British Engineering	foot	slug[1]	pound weight	sec
American Engineering	foot	pound mass	pound force	sec

Note: These units are devided from the other three basic units

The first three systems of units presented in Table 1.3 have three defined units (length, mass, and time) and one (force) which is based on the other three. However, the American Engineering System has four different defined units, length, mass, force, and time. The word "pound" is used for both mass and force even though these are clearly not the same concept. Accordingly, some caution is needed when performing calculations in the American Engineering System, which remains the dominant system in the United States despite attempts to change to the cgs or SI systems of units.

Systems of Units of Measurement

Though the fundamental units are independent of all other units, there are different fundamental units accepted in different countries or the regions of the world. The group of fundamental units followed in different regions along with the derived units forms the systems of units. There are four categories of systems of units as described below:

- *The CGS (centimetre, gram, second) System:* In the CGS system of measurement length is measured in centimeters, the mass of the body or substance is measured in grams and time is measured in seconds. Thus centimeter, gram and seconds are the fundamental units of measurement in the CGS system.
- *MKS (meter, kilogram, second) System:* In MKS system or metric system, the unit of measurement for length is meter, for mass it is kilogram and for time it is seconds. Thus in this system meter, kilogram and seconds are fundamental units of measurement. This system was used in France and number of other European countries.
- *FPS (foot, pound, second) System:* In this system the unit of measurement for length is foot, for mass it is pound and for time it is second. This system is used commonly in Britain and the countries that were under its rule.
- *SI System:* The SI system or the International system of standards has now replaced all the systems of measurement. It is the improved metric system of measurement. In SI system length is measured in meter, mass in kilogram and time in seconds.

In the above systems we saw that different fundamental units are used in different systems. Since the derived units depend on the fundamental units, they also change in different systems of measurement. Let s consider the example of the speed or velocity of the body. In MKS system its unit of measurement is meter/second, in CGS system it is centimeter/second, in FPS system it is foot/second and in SI system it is meter/second.

FOOT-POUND-SECOND SYSTEM

The foot-pound-second system or FPS system is a system of units built on the three fundamental units foot for length, (avoirdupois) pound for either mass or force and second for time.

Pound as Mass Unit

When the pound is used as a unit of mass, the core of the coherent system is similar and functionally equivalent to the corresponding subsets of the International System of Units (SI), using kilogram, metre and second (MKS), and the earlier centimetre-gram-second system of units (CGS). In this sub-system, the unit of force is a derived unit known as the poundal.

$$1\text{pdl} = 1\text{lb}_m \cdot 1\frac{\text{ft}}{\text{s}^2}$$

In the context of the absolute FPS system, the pound-mass (lb_m) is usually referred to simply as the pound (lb).

Everett (1861) proposed the metric dyne and erg as the units of force and energy in the FPS system.

Latimer Clark's (1891) "Dictionary of Measures" contains *celo* (acceleration), *vel* or *velo* (velocity) and *pulse* (momentum) as proposed names for FPS absolute units.

Variants

Collectively, the variants of the FPS system were the most common system in technical publications in English until the middle of the 20th century.

Errors can be avoided and translation between the systems facilitated by labelling all physical dimensions consistently with their units. Especially in the context of the FPS system this is sometimes known as the Stroud system after William Stroud, who popularized it.

Pound-force as Force Unit

The technical or gravitational FPS system, is a coherent variant of the FPS system that is most common among engineers in the United States. It takes the pound-force as a fundamental unit of force instead of the pound as a fundamental unit of mass.

In this sub-system, the unit of mass is a derived unit known as the slug.

$$1 \text{ slug} = 1\text{lb}_F \cdot 1\frac{\text{s}^2}{\text{ft}}$$

In the context of the gravitational FPS system, the pound-force (lb_F) is almost universally simply referred to as the pound (lb).

Pound as Mass and Force Unit

Another variant of the FPS system uses both the pound-mass and the pound-force, but neither the slug nor the poundal. The resulting system is not coherent, lacking electrical or molar units, and is sometimes also known as the British engineering system, although rarely used nowadays in the United Kingdom.

Other Units

Molar Units

The unit of substance in the FPS system is the lb-mol = 273.16×10^{24}. Until the SI decided to adopt the gram-mole, the mole was directly derived from the mass unit as (mass unit)/(atomic mass unit).

The unit ($\text{lb}_F\cdot\text{s}^2/\text{ft}$)-mol also appears in a former definition of the atmosphere.

Electromagnetic Units

Electromagnetic units were formerly derived as an extension of the mechanical units, so any length-mass-time

(LMT) system has units in the manner of the CGS Gaussian theory, complete with three-dimensional analysis.

The 1929 "International Critical Tables" gives in the symbols and systems *fpse = FPS electrostatic system* and *fpsm = FPS electromagnetic system*. Under the conversions for charge, the following are given:

Electromagnetic FPS (EMU, stat-)
1 fpsm unit = 117.58 cgsm unit
Electrostatic FPS (ESU, ab-)
1 fpse unit = 3583.9 cgse unit
1 fpse unit = 1.1952×10^{-6} abs coulomb

Units of Light

The *candle* and the *foot-candle* were the first defined units of light. The foot-candle is the intensity of light at one foot from a *standard candle*. The units were internationally recognised in 1881, and adopted into the metric system.

Conversions

Together with the fact that the term "weight" is used for the gravitational force in some technical contexts (physics, engineering) and for mass in others (commerce, law), and that the distinction often does not matter in practice, the coexistence of variants of the FPS system causes confusion over the nature of the unit "pound". Its relation to international, metric units is expressed in kilograms, not newtons, though, and in earlier times it was defined by means of a mass prototype to be compared with a two-pan balance which is agnostic of local gravitational differences.

In July 1959 the various national foot and avoirdupois pound standards were replaced by the international foot of precisely 0.3048 m and the international pound of precisely 0.45359237 kg, making conversion between the systems a matter of simple mathematics. The conversion for the poundal is given by 1 pdl = 1 lb·ft/s^2 = 0.138254954376 N (precisely).

To convert between the absolute and gravitational FPS systems one needs to fix the standard acceleration g which connects the pound and the pound-force.

$1lb_F = 1lb_m \cdot g$

While g strictly depends on one's location on the Earth surface, since 1901 in most contexts it is fixed conventionally at precisely g_0 = 9.80665 m/s^2 ≈ 32.17405 ft/s^2. Therefore the slug is about 32.17405 lb$_m$ or 14.593903 kg.

CENTIMETRE-GRAM-SECOND (CGS) SYSTEM OF UNITS

The centimetre gram second system (abbreviated CGS or cgs) is a variant of the metric system of physical units based on centimetre as the unit of length, gram as a unit of mass, and second as a unit of time. All CGS mechanical units are unambiguously derived from these three base units, but there are several different ways of extending the CGS system to cover electromagnetism.

The CGS system has been largely supplanted by the MKS system, based on metre, kilogram, and second. MKS was in turn extended and replaced by the International System of Units (SI). The latter adopts the three base units of MKS, plus the ampere, mole, candela and kelvin. In many fields of science and engineering, SI is the only system of units in use. However, there remain certain subfields where CGS is prevalent.

In measurements of purely mechanical systems (involving units of length, mass, force, energy, pressure, and so on), the differences between CGS and SI are straightforward and rather trivial; the unit-conversion factors are all powers of 10 arising from the relations 100 cm = 1 m and 1000 g = 1 kg. For example, the CGS derived unit of force is the dyne, equal to 1 g·cm/s^2, while the SI derived unit of force is the newton, 1 kg·m/s^2. Thus it is straightforward to show that 1 dyne=10^{-5} newtons.

On the other hand, in measurements of electromagnetic phenomena (involving units of charge, electric and magnetic fields, voltage, and so on), converting between CGS and SI is much more subtle and involved. In fact, formulas for physical laws of electromagnetism (such as Maxwell's equations) need to be adjusted depending on what system of units one uses. This is because there is no one-to-one correspondence between electromagnetic units in SI and those in CGS, as is the case for mechanical units. Furthermore, within CGS, there are several plausible choices of electromagnetic units, leading to different unit "sub-systems", including Gaussian, "ESU", "EMU", and Heaviside-Lorentz. Among these choices, Gaussian units are the most common today, and in fact the phrase "CGS units" is often used to refer specifically to CGS-Gaussian units.

History

The CGS system goes back to a proposal in 1832 by the German mathematician Carl Friedrich Gauss. In 1874, it was extended by the British physicists James Clerk Maxwell and William Thomson with a set of electromagnetic units.

The sizes of many CGS units turned out to be inconvenient for practical purposes. For example, many everyday objects are hundreds or thousands of centimetres long, such as humans, rooms and buildings. Thus the CGS system never gained wide general use outside the field of science. Starting in the 1880s, and more significantly by the mid-20th century, CGS was gradually superseded internationally for scientific purposes by the MKS (metre kilogram second) system, which in turn developed into the modern SI standard. Since the international adoption of the MKS standard in the 1940s and the SI standard in the 1960s, the technical use of CGS units has gradually declined worldwide, in the United States more slowly than elsewhere. CGS units are today no longer accepted by the house styles of most scientific journals, textbook publishers, or standards bodies, although they are commonly used in astronomical journals such as the *Astrophysical Journal*.

The CGS units are still occasionally encountered in technical literature, especially in the United States in the fields of material science, electrodynamics and astronomy. The continued usage of CGS units is most prevalent in magnetism and related fields, as the primary MKS unit, the tesla, is inconvenienently large, leading to the continued common use of the gauss, the CGS equivalent. The units gram and centimetre remain useful *as prefixed units* within the SI system, especially for instructional physics and chemistry experiments, where they match the small scale of table-top setups. However, where derived units are needed, the SI ones are generally used and taught instead of the CGS ones today. For example, a physics lab course might ask students to record lengths in centimetres, and masses in grams, but force (a derived unit) in newtons, a usage consistent with the SI system.

Definition of CGS Units in Mechanics

In mechanics, the CGS and SI systems of units are built in an identical way. The two systems differ only in the scale of two out of the three base units (centimetre versus metre and gram versus kilogram, respectively), while the third unit (second as the unit of time) is the same in both systems.

There is a one-to-one correspondence between the base units of mechanics in CGS and SI, and the laws of mechanics are not affected by the choice of units. The definitions of all derived units in terms of the three base units are therefore the same in both systems, and there is an unambiguous one-to-one correspondence of derived units:

$$v = \frac{dx}{dt} \text{ (definition of velocity)}$$

$$F = m\frac{d^2x}{dt^2} \text{ (Newton's second law of motion)}$$

$$E = \int \vec{F} \cdot \overrightarrow{dx} \text{ (energy defined in terms of work)}$$

$$p = \frac{F}{L^2} \text{ (pressure defined as force per unit area)}$$

$$\eta = \tau / \frac{dv}{dx}$$ (dynamic viscosity defined as shear stress per unit velocity gradient).

Definitions and Conversion Factors of CGS Units in Mechanics

Thus, for example, the CGS unit of pressure, barye, is related to the CGS base units of length, mass, and time in the same way as the SI unit of pressure, pascal, is related to the SI base units of length, mass, and time:

1 unit of pressure = 1 unit of force/(1 unit of length)^2 = 1 unit of mass/[(1 unit of length·(1 unit of time)^2)]

1 Ba = 1 g/(cm·s^2)

1 Pa = 1 kg/(m·s^2).

Expressing a CGS derived unit in terms of the SI base units, or vice versa, requires combining the scale factors that relate the two systems:

1 Ba = 1 g/(cm·s^2) = 10^{-3} kg/(10^{-2} m·s^2) = 10^{-1} kg/(m·s^2) = 10^{-1} Pa.

Derivation of CGS Units in Electromagnetism

CGS Approach to Electromagnetic Units

The conversion factors relating electromagnetic units in the CGS and SI systems are much more complex – so much so that formulae expressing physical laws of electromagnetism are different depending on what system of units one uses. This illustrates the fundamental difference in the ways the two systems are built:

- In SI, the unit of electric current, the ampere (A) was historically defined such that the magnetic force

Quantity	Symbol	CGS unit	CGS unit abbreviation	Definition	Equivalent in SI units
Length, position	*L, x*	centimetre	cm	1/100 of metre	= 10^{-2} m
Mass	*m*	gram	g	1/1000 of kilogram	= 10^{-3} kg
Time	*t*	second	s	1 second	= 1 s
Velocity	*v*	centimetre per second	cm/s	cm/s	= 10^{-2} m/s
Acceleration	*a*	gal	Gal	cm/s^2	= 10^{-2} m/s^2
Force	*F*	dyne	dyn	g·cm/s^2	= 10^{-5} N
Energy	*E*	erg	erg	g·cm^2/s^2	= 10^{-7} J
Power	*P*	erg per second	erg/s	g·cm^2/s^3	= 10^{-7} W
Pressure	*p*	barye	Ba	g/(cm·s^2)	= 10^{-1} Pa
Dynamic Viscosity	*μ*	poise	P	g/(cm·s)	= 10^{-1} Pa·s
Kinematic viscosity	*ν*	stokes	St	cm^2/s	= 10^{-4} m/s
Wavenumber	*k*	kayser	cm^{-1}	cm^{-1}	= 100 m^{-1}

exerted by two infinitely long, thin, parallel wires 1 metre apart and carrying a current of 1 ampere is exactly 2×10^{-7} N/m. This definition results in all SI electromagnetic units consistent (subject to factors of some integer powers of 10) with the EMU CGS system described in further sections. The ampere is a base unit of the SI system, with the same status as the metre, kilogram, and second. Thus the relationship in the definition of the ampere with the metre and newton is disregarded, and the ampere is not treated as dimensionally equivalent to any combination of other base units. As a result, electromagnetic laws in SI require an additional constant of proportionality to relate electromagnetic units to kinematic units. (This constant of proportionality is derivable directly from the above definition of the ampere.) All other electric and magnetic units are derived from these four base units using the most basic common definitions: for example, electric charge q is defined as current I multiplied by time

$$t,\ q = I \cdot t,$$

therefore the unit of electric charge, the coulomb (C), is defined as 1 C = 1 A·s.

- The CGS system avoids introducing new base units and instead *derives* all electric and magnetic units directly from the centimetre, gram, and second based on the physical laws that relate electromagnetic phenomena to mechanics.

Alternate Derivations of CGS Units in Electromagnetism

Electromagnetic relationships to length, time and mass may be derived by several equally appealing methods. Two of them rely on the forces observed on charges. Two fundamental laws relate (independently of each other) the electric charge or its rate of change (electric current) to a mechanical quantity such as force. They can be written in system-independent form as follows:

- The first is Coulomb's law,

$$F = k_C \frac{q \cdot q'}{d^2},$$

which describes the electrostatic force F between electric charges q and q', separated by distance d. Here k_C is a constant which depends on how exactly the unit of charge is derived from the CGS base units.

- The second is Ampère's force law,

$$\frac{dF}{dL} = 2k_A \frac{II'}{d},$$

which describes the magnetic force F per unit length L between currents I and I' flowing in two straight parallel wires of infinite length, separated by a distance d that is much greater than the wire diameters. Since $I = q/t$ and $I' = q'/t$, the constant k_A also depends on how the unit of charge is derived from the CGS base units.

Maxwell's theory of electromagnetism relates these two laws to each other. It states that the ratio of proportionality constants k_C and k_A must obey $k_C / k_A = c^2$, where c is the speed of light in vacuum. Therefore, if one derives the unit of charge from the Coulomb's law by setting $k_C = 1$, it is obvious that the Ampère's force law will contain a prefactor $2/c^2$. Alternatively, deriving the unit of current, and therefore the unit of charge, from the Ampère's force law by setting $k_A = 1$ or $k_A = ½$, will lead to a constant prefactor in the Coulomb's law.

- Indeed, both of these mutually-exclusive approaches have been practiced by the users of CGS system, leading to the two independent and mutually-exclusive branches of CGS, described in the subsections below. However, the freedom of choice in deriving electromagnetic units from the units of length, mass, and time is not limited to the definition of charge. While the electric field can be related to the work performed by it on a moving electric charge, the magnetic force is always perpendicular to the velocity of the moving charge, and thus the work performed by the magnetic field on any charge is always zero. This leads to a choice between two laws of magnetism, each relating magnetic field to mechanical quantities and electric charge:

- The first law describes the Lorentz force produced by a magnetic field **B** on a charge **q** moving with velocity **v**:

  $\mathbf{F} = \alpha_L q\, \mathbf{v} \times \mathbf{B}$.

- The second describes the creation of a static magnetic field **B** by an electric current *I* of finite length **dl** at a point displaced by a vector **r**, known as Biot-Savart law:

  $d\mathbf{B} = \alpha_B \frac{Id\mathbf{l} \times \hat{\mathbf{r}}}{r^2}$, where **r** and $\hat{\mathbf{r}}$ are the length and the unit vector in the direction of vector r respectively.

These two laws can be used to derive Ampère's force law above, resulting in the relationship: $k_A = \alpha_L \cdot \alpha_B$. Therefore, if the unit of charge is based on the Ampère's force law such that $k_A = 1$, it is natural to derive the unit of magnetic field by setting $\alpha_L = \alpha_B = 1$. However, if it is not the case, a choice has to be made as to which of the two laws above is a more convenient basis for deriving the unit of magnetic field.

Furthermore, if we wish to describe the electric displacement field **D** and the magnetic field **H** in a medium other than vacuum, we need to also define the constants ε_0 and μ_0, which are the vacuum permittivity and permeability, respectively. Then we have (generally)

$$\mathbf{D} = \varepsilon_0\mathbf{E} + \lambda\mathbf{P} \text{ and } \mathbf{H} = \mathbf{B} / \mu_0 - \lambda'\mathbf{M},$$

where **P** and **M** are polarization density and magnetization vectors. The factors λ and λ′ are rationalization constants, which are usually chosen to be $4\pi k_C \epsilon_0$, a dimensionless quantity. If λ = λ′ = 1, the system is said to be "rationalized":

the laws for systems of spherical geometry contain factors of 4π (for example, point charges), those of cylindrical geometry - factors of 2π (for example, wires), and those of planar geometry contain no factors of π (for example, parallel-plate capacitors). However, the original CGS system used $\lambda = \lambda' = 4\pi$, or, equivalently, $k_C \epsilon_0 = 1$. Therefore, Gaussian, ESU, and EMU subsystems of CGS are not rationalized.

Various Extensions of the CGS System to Electromagnetism

Table 1.4 below shows the values of the above constants used in some common CGS subsystems:

Table 1.4

System	k_C	α_B	ϵ_0	μ_0	$k_A = \frac{k_C}{c^2}$	$\alpha_L = \frac{k_C}{\alpha_B c^2}$	$\lambda = 4\pi k_C \cdot \epsilon_0$	λ'
Electrostatic CGS (ESU, esu, or stat-)	1	c^{-2}	1	c^{-2}	c^{-2}	1	4π	4π
Electro-magnetic CGS (EMU, emu, or ab-)	c^2	1	c^{-2}	1	1	1	4π	4π
Gaussian CGS	1	c^{-1}	1	1	c^{-2}	c^{-1}	4π	4π
Lorentz–Heaviside CGS	$\frac{1}{4\pi}$	$\frac{1}{4\pi c}$	1	1	$\frac{1}{4\pi c^2}$	c^{-1}	1	1
SI	$\frac{c^2}{b}$	$\frac{1}{b}$	$\frac{b}{4\pi c^2}$	$\frac{4\pi}{b}$	$\frac{1}{b}$	1	1	1

The constant b in SI system is a unit-based scaling factor defined as:

$$b = 10^7\ \mathrm{A}^2/\mathrm{N} = 10^7\ \mathrm{m/H} = 4\pi/\mu_0 = 4\pi\epsilon_0 c^2.$$

Also, note the following correspondence of the above constants to those in Jackson and Leung:

$$k_C = k_1 = k_E$$

$$\alpha_B = \alpha \cdot k_2 = k_B$$

$$k_A = k_2 = k_E / c^2$$

$$\alpha_L = k_3 = k_F$$

In system-independent form, Maxwell's equations in vacuum can be written as:

$$\vec{\nabla}\cdot\vec{E} = 4\pi k_C \rho$$

$$\vec{\nabla}\cdot\vec{B} = 0$$

$$\vec{\nabla}\times\vec{E} = -\alpha_L \frac{\partial \vec{B}}{\partial t}$$

$$\vec{\nabla}\times\vec{B} = 4\pi\alpha_B \vec{J} + \frac{\alpha_B}{k_C}\frac{\partial \vec{E}}{\partial t}$$

Note that of all these variants, only in Gaussian and Heaviside Lorentz systems α_L equals c^{-1} rather than 1. As a result, vectors $\vec{E}$ and $\vec{B}$ of an electromagnetic wave propagating in vacuum have the same units and are equal in magnitude in these two variants of CGS.

Electrostatic Units (ESU)

In one variant of the CGS system, Electrostatic units (ESU), charge is defined via the force it exerts on other charges, and current is then defined as charge per time. It is done by setting the Coulomb force constant $k_C = 1$, so that Coulomb's law does not contain an explicit prefactor.

The ESU unit of charge, franklin (Fr), also known as statcoulomb or esu charge, is therefore defined as follows:

> two equal point charges spaced 1 centimetre apart are said to be of 1 franklin each if the electrostatic force between them is 1 dyne.

Therefore, in electrostatic CGS units, a franklin is equal to a centimetre times square root of dyne:

$$1\,\text{Fr} = 1\,\text{statcoulomb} = 1\,\text{esu charge} = 1\,\text{cm}\sqrt{\text{dyne}} = 1\text{g}^{1/2}\cdot\text{cm}^{3/2}\cdot\text{s}^{-1}.$$

The unit of current is defined as:

$$1\,\text{Fr/s} = 1\,\text{statampere} = 1\,\text{esu current} = 1(\text{cm/s})\sqrt{\text{dyne}} = 1\text{g}^{1/2}\cdot\text{cm}^{3/2}\cdot\text{s}^{-2}.$$

Dimensionally in the ESU CGS system, charge q is therefore equivalent to $m^{1/2}L^{3/2}t^{-1}$. Neither charge nor current are therefore an independent dimension of physical quantity in ESU CGS. This reduction of units is an application of the Buckingham π theorem.

ESU Notation

All electromagnetic units in ESU CGS system that do not have proper names are denoted by a corresponding SI name with an attached prefix "stat" or with a separate abbreviation "esu".

Electromagnetic Units (EMU)

In another variant of the CGS system, Electromagnetic units (EMU), current is defined via the force existing between two thin, parallel, infinitely long wires carrying it, and charge is then defined as current multiplied by time. (This approach was eventually used to define the SI unit of ampere as well). In the EMU CGS subsystem, this is done by setting the Ampere force constant $k_A = 1$, so that Ampère's force law simply contains 2 as an explicit prefactor (this prefactor 2 is itself a result of integrating a more general formulation of Ampère's law over the length of the infinite wire). The EMU unit of current, biot (Bi), also known as abampere or emu current, is therefore defined as follows: The biot is that constant current which, if maintained in two straight parallel conductors of infinite length, of negligible circular cross-section, and placed one centimetre apart in vacuum, would produce between these conductors a force equal to two dynes per centimetre of length. Therefore, in electromagnetic CGS units, a biot is equal to a square root of dyne:

$$1\,\mathrm{Bi} = 1\,\mathrm{abampere} = 1\,\mathrm{emu\ current} = 1\sqrt{\mathrm{dyne}} = 1\,\mathrm{g}^{1/2}\cdot\mathrm{cm}^{1/2}\cdot\mathrm{s}^{-1}.$$

The unit of charge in CGS EMU is:

$$1\,\mathrm{Bi{\cdot}s} = 1\,\mathrm{abcoulomb} = 1\,\mathrm{emu charge} = 1\,\mathrm{s}\cdot\sqrt{\mathrm{dyne}} = 1\,\mathrm{g}^{1/2}\cdot\mathrm{cm}^{1/2}.$$

Dimensionally in the EMU CGS system, charge q is therefore equivalent to $m^{1/2}L^{1/2}$. Neither charge nor current are therefore an independent dimension of physical quantity in EMU CGS.

EMU Notation

All electromagnetic units in EMU CGS system that do not have proper names are denoted by a corresponding SI name with an attached prefix "ab" or with a separate abbreviation "emu".

Relations between ESU and EMU Units

The ESU and EMU subsystems of CGS are connected by the fundamental relationship

$$k_C / k_A = c^2$$

where c = 29,979,245,800 ≈ 3×10^{10} is the speed of light in vacuum in cm/s. Therefore, the ratio of the corresponding "primary3 electrical and magnetic units (*e.g.* current, charge, voltage, *etc.*– quantities proportional to those that enter directly into Coulomb's law or Ampère's force law) is equal either to c^{-1} or c:

$$\frac{1\,\text{statcoulomb}}{1\,\text{abcoulomb}} = \frac{1\,\text{statampere}}{1\,\text{abampere}} = c^{-1}$$

and

$$\frac{1\,\text{statvolt}}{1\,\text{abvolt}} = \frac{1\,\text{stattesla}}{1\,\text{gauss}} = c.$$

Units derived from these may have ratios equal to higher powers of c, for example:

$$\frac{1\,\text{statohm}}{1\,\text{abohm}} = \frac{1\,\text{statvolt}}{1\,\text{abvolt}} \times \frac{1\,\text{abampere}}{1\,\text{statampere}} = c^2.$$

Other Variants

There were at various points in time about half a dozen systems of electromagnetic units in use, most based on the CGS system. These also include Gaussian units, and Heaviside–Lorentz units. Further complicating matters is the fact that some physicists and engineers in the United States use hybrid units, such as volts per centimetre for electric field. In fact, this is essentially the same as the SI unit system, by the variant to translate all lengths used into cm, *e.g.* 1 m = 100 cm.

Electromagnetic Units in Various CGS Systems

Conversion of SI units in electromagnetism to ESU, EMU, and Gaussian subsystems of CGS $c = 29{,}979{,}245{,}800 \approx 3 \cdot 10^{10}$					
Quantity	**Symbol**	**SI unit**	**ESU unit**	**EMU unit**	**Gaussian unit**
electric charge	q	1 C	$= (10^{-1}\, c)$ statC	$= (10^{-1})$ abC	$= (10^{-1}\, c)$ Fr
electric current	I	1 A	$= (10^{-1}\, c)$ statA	$= (10^{-1})$ abA	$= (10^{-1}\, c)$ $\mathrm{Fr \cdot s^{-1}}$
electric potential voltage	ϕ V	1 V	$= (10^{8}\, c^{-1})$ statV	$= (10^{8})$ abV	$= (10^{8}\, c^{-1})$ statV
electric field	**E**	1 V/m	$= (10^{6}\, c^{-1})$ statV/cm	$= (10^{6})$ abV/cm	$= (10^{6}\, c^{-1})$ statV/cm
magnetic B field	**B**	1 T	$= (10^{4}\, c^{-1})$ statT	$= (10^{4})$ G	$= (10^{4})$ G
magnetic H field	**H**	1 A/m	$= (4\pi\, 10^{-3}\, c)$ statA/cm	$= (4\pi\, 10^{-3})$ Oe	$= (4\pi\, 10^{-3})$ Oe
magnetic dipole moment	μ	1 $\mathrm{A \cdot m^2}$	$= (10^{3}\, c)$ $\mathrm{statA \cdot cm^2}$	$= (10^{3})$ $\mathrm{abA \cdot cm^2}$	$= (10^{3})$ erg/G
magnetic flux	Φ_m	1 Wb	$= (10^{8}\, c^{-1})$ $\mathrm{statT \cdot cm^2}$	$= (10^{8})$ Mw	$= (10^{8})$ $\mathrm{G \cdot cm^2}$
resistance	R	1 Ω	$= (10^{9}\, c^{-2})$ s/cm	$= (10^{9})$ abΩ	$= (10^{9}\, c^{-2})$ s/cm
resistivity	ρ	1 Ω·m	$= (10^{11}\, c^{-2})$ s	$= (10^{11})$ abΩ·cm	$= (10^{11}\, c^{-2})$ s
capacitance	C	1 F	$= (10^{-9}\, c^{2})$ cm	$= (10^{-9})$ abF	$= (10^{-9}\, c^{2})$ cm
inductance	L	1 H	$= (10^{9}\, c^{-2})$ $\mathrm{cm^{-1} \cdot s^2}$	$= (10^{9})$ abH	$= (10^{9}\, c^{-2})$ $\mathrm{cm^{-1} \cdot s^2}$

In this table, $c = 29{,}979{,}245{,}800 \approx 3 \times 10^{10}$ is the speed of light in vacuum in the CGS units of cm/s. One can think of the SI value of the Coulomb constant k_C as:

$$k_C = \frac{1}{4\pi\epsilon_0} = \frac{\mu_0 (c/100)^2}{4\pi} = 10^{-7} \times 10^{-4} \times c^2 = 10^{-11} \times c^2.$$

This explains why SI to ESU conversions involving factors of c^2 lead to significant simplifications of the ESU units, such as 1 statF = 1 cm and 1 statΩ = 1 s/cm: this is the consequence of the fact that in ESU system $k_C = 1$. For example, a centimetre of capacitance is the capacitance between a sphere of radius 1 cm in vacuum and infinity. The capacitance C between two concentric spheres of radii R and r in ESU CGS system is:

$$\frac{1}{\frac{1}{r} - \frac{1}{R}}.$$

By taking the limit as R goes to infinity we see C equals r.

Physical Constants in CGS Units

Table: Commonly Used Physical Constants in CGS Units

Constant	*Symbol*	*Value*
Atomic mass unit	u	$1.660\,538\,782 \times 10^{-24}$ g
Bohr magneton	μ_B	$9.274\,009\,15 \times 10^{-21}$ erg/G (EMU, Gaussian)
		$2.780\,278\,00 \times 10^{-10}$ statA·cm² (ESU)
Bohr radius	a_0	$5.291\,772\,0859 \times 10^{-9}$ cm
Boltzmann constant	k	$1.380\,6504 \times 10^{-16}$ erg/K
Electron mass	m_e	$9.109\,382\,15 \times 10^{-28}$ g
Elementary charge	e	$4.803\,204\,27 \times 10^{-10}$ Fr (ESU, Gaussian)
		$1.602\,176\,487 \times 10^{-20}$ abC (EMU)
Fine-structure constant	$\alpha \approx 1/137$	$7.297\,352\,570 \times 10^{-3}$
Gravitational constant	G	$6.674\,28 \times 10^{-8}$ cm³/(g·s²)
Planck constant	h	$6.626\,068\,85 \times 10^{-27}$ erg·s
	$\hbar$	$1.054\,5716 \times 10^{-27}$ erg·s
Speed of light in vacuum	c	$\equiv 2.997\,924\,58 \times 10^{10}$ cm/s

Pro and Contra

While the absence of explicit prefactors in some CGS subsystems simplifies some theoretical calculations, it has the disadvantage that sometimes the units in CGS are hard to define through experiment. Also, lack of unique unit names leads to a great confusion: thus "15 emu" may mean either 15 abvolt, or 15 emu units of electric dipole moment, or 15 emu units of magnetic susceptibility, sometimes (but not always) per gram or per mole. On the other hand, SI starts with a unit of current, the ampere, which is easier to determine through experiment, but which requires extra prefactors in the electromagnetic equations. With its system of unique named units, SI also removes any confusion in usage: 1 ampere is a fixed value of a specified quantity, and so are 1 henry and 1 ohm.

A key virtue of the Gaussian CGS system is that electric and magnetic fields have the same units, $4\pi\epsilon_0$ is replaced by 1, and the only dimensional constant appearing in the equations is c, the speed of light. The Heaviside-Lorentz system has these desirable properties as well (with ϵ_0 equaling 1), but it is a "rationalized" system (as is SI) in which the charges and fields are defined in such a way that there are many fewer factors of 4π appearing in the formulas, and it is in Heaviside–Lorentz units that the Maxwell equations take their simplest form.

In SI, and other rationalized systems (for example, Heaviside–Lorentz), the unit of current was chosen such that electromagnetic equations concerning charged spheres contain 4π, those concerning coils of current and straight wires contain 2π and those dealing with charged surfaces lack π entirely, which was the most convenient choice for electrical-engineering applications. In those fields where formulas concerning spheres dominate (for example, astronomy), it has been argued that the non-rationalized CGS system can be somewhat more convenient notationally.

In fact, in certain fields, specialized unit systems are used to simplify formulas even further than *either* SI *or* CGS, by using some system of natural units. For example, the particle physics community uses a system where every quantity is expressed by only one unit, the eV, with lengths, times, and so on all converted into eV's by inserting factors of c and $\hbar$.

This unit system is very convenient for particle-physics calculations, but would be impractical in other contexts.

MKS SYSTEM OF UNITS

The MKS system of units is a physical system of units that expresses any given measurement using fundamental units of the metre, kilogram, and/or second (MKS).

Historically the MKS system of units succeeded the cgs system of units and laid the blueprint for the International System of Units, which now serves as the international standard. Therefore the exact composition of the MKS system is a historical issue. As a matter of historical record the MKS system incorporated fundamental units other than the metre, kilogram, and second in addition to derived units. An incomplete list of the fundamental and derived units appears below. Since the MKS system of units never had a governing body to rule on a standard definition, the list of units depended on different conventions at different times.

- *Cycle*. (This dimensionless quantity became synonymous with the term "cycle per second" as an abbreviation. This circumstance confused the exact definition of the term cycle. Therefore the phrase "cycle per metre" became ill-defined. The cycle did not become an SI unit.)
- Cycle per second.
- Cycle per metre. (This measure of wavenumber became ill-defined due to the abbreviation of "cycle per second" as "cycle".)

INTERNATIONAL SYSTEM OF UNITS

The SI system (*International System of Units*) is the contemporary metric system of measurement and the dominant system of international commerce and trade. SI units are gradually replacing Imperial and USCS units.

The SI is maintained by the International Bureau of Weights and Measures (BIPM, for Bureau International des Poids et Mesures) in Paris.

The International System of Units is the modern form of

the metric system and is generally a system of units of measurement devised around seven base units and the convenience of the number ten. The older metric system included several groups of units. The SI was established in 1960, based on the metre-kilogram-second system, rather than the centimetre-gram-second system, which, in turn, had a few variants. The SI is declared as an evolving system, thus prefixes and units are created and unit definitions are modified through international agreement as the technology of measurement progresses, and as the precision of measurements improves.

SI is the world's most widely used system of measurement, which is used both in everyday commerce and in science. The system has been nearly globally adopted with the United States being the only industrialised nation that does not mainly use the metric system in its commercial and standards activities. The United Kingdom has officially partially adopted metrication, with no intention of replacing imperial units entirely. Canada has adopted it for many purposes but imperial/US units are still legally permitted and remain in common use throughout many sectors of Canadian society, particularly in the retail food, buildings trades, and railways sectors.

History

The metric system was conceived by a group of scientists (among them, Antoine-Laurent Lavoisier, who is known as the "father of modern chemistry") who had been commissioned by the *Assemblée nationale* and Louis XVI of France to create a unified and rational system of measures. On 1 August 1793, the National Convention adopted the new decimal *metre* with a provisional length as well as the other decimal units with preliminary definitions and terms. On 7 April 1795 the terms *gramme* and *kilogramme* replaced the former terms *gravet* (correctly *milligrave*) and *grave* and on 22 June 1799, after Pierre Méchain and Jean-Baptiste Delambre completed their survey, the definitive standard metre was deposited in the French National Archives. On 10 December 1799 the metric system was definitively adopted in France.

The desire for international cooperation on metrology led to the signing in 1875 of the Metre Convention, a treaty that established three international organisations to oversee the keeping of metric standards:

- General Conference on Weights and Measures – a meeting every four to six years of delegates from all member states;
- International Bureau of Weights and Measures – an international metrology centre at Sèvres in France; and
- International Committee for Weights and Measures — an administrative committee that meets annually at the BIPM.

The history of the metric system has seen a number of variations, and has spread around the world, to replace many traditional measurement systems. At the end of World War II, a number of different systems of measurement were still in use throughout the world. Some of these systems were metric-system variations, whereas others were based on customary systems. It was recognised that additional steps were needed to promote a worldwide measurement system. As a result, the 9th General Conference on Weights and Measures (CGPM), in 1948, asked the International Committee for Weights and Measures (CIPM) to conduct an international study of the measurement needs of the scientific, technical, and educational communities.

Based on the findings of this study, the 10th CGPM in 1954 decided that an international system should be derived from six base units to provide for the measurement of temperature and optical radiation in addition to mechanical and electromagnetic quantities. The six base units that were recommended are the metre, kilogram, second, ampere, degree Kelvin (later renamed kelvin), and candela. In 1960, the 11th CGPM named the system the *International System of Units*, abbreviated SI from the French name, *Le Système international d'unités*. The seventh base unit, the mole, was added in 1971 by the 14th CGPM. One of the CIPM committees, the CCU, has proposed a number of changes to the definitions of the base units used in SI. The CIPM meeting of October 2010 found that the proposal was not complete, and it is expected that the CGPM will consider the full proposal in 2015.

Units and Prefixes

The International System of Units consists of a set of units together with a set of prefixes. The units are divided into two classes—base units and derived units. There are seven base units, each representing, by convention, different kinds of physical quantities.

SI Base Units				
Unit Name	**Unit Symbol**	**Quantity Name**	**Quantity Symbol**	**Dimension Symbol**
metre	m	length	l (a lowercase L), x, r	L
kilogram [note 1]	kg	mass	m	M
second	s	time	t	T
ampere	A	electric current	I (an uppercase i)	I
kelvin	K	thermodynamic temperature	T	Θ
candela	cd	luminous intensity	I_v (an uppercase I with lowercase non-italicized v subscript)	J
mole	mol	amount of substance	n	N

Note

1. Despite the prefix "kilo-", the kilogram is the base unit of mass. The kilogram, not the gram, is used in the definitions of derived units. Nonetheless, units of mass are *named* as if the gram were the base unit.

Derived units are formed from multiplication and division of the seven base units and other derived units and are unlimited in number; for example, the SI derived unit of speed is metre per second, m/s. Some derived units have special names; for example, the unit of resistance, the ohm, symbol Ω, is uniquely defined by the relation $\Omega = m^2 \cdot kg \cdot s^{-3} \cdot A^{-2}$, which follows from the definition of the quantity electrical resistance. The radian and steradian, once given special status, are now considered dimensionless derived units.

A prefix may be added to a unit to produce a multiple of the original unit. All multiples are integer powers of ten, and beyond a hundred(th) all are integer powers of a thousand. For example, *kilo-* denotes a multiple of a thousand and *milli-* denotes a multiple of a thousandth; hence there are one thousand millimetres to the metre and one thousand metres to the kilometre. The prefixes are never combined, and multiples of the kilogram are named as if the gram was the base unit. Thus a millionth of a metre is a *micrometre,* not a millimillimetre, and a millionth of a kilogram is a *milligram,* not a microkilogram.

Table: Standard Prefixes for the SI Units of Measure

Multiples			*Fractions*		
Name	*Symbol*	*Factor* 10^0	*Name*	*Symbol*	*Factor* 10^0
deca-	da	10^1	deci-	d	10^{-1}
hecto-	h	10^2	centi-	c	10^{-2}
kilo-	k	10^3	milli-	m	10^{-3}
mega-	M	10^6	micro-	μ	10^{-6}
giga-	G	10^9	nano-	n	10^{-9}
tera-	T	10^{12}	pico-	p	10^{-12}
peta-	P	10^{15}	femto-	f	10^{-15}
exa-	E	10^{18}	atto-	a	10^{-18}
zetta-	Z	10^{21}	zepto-	z	10^{-21}
yotta-	Y	10^{24}	yocto-	y	10^{-24}

In addition to the SI units, there is also a set of non-SI units accepted for use with SI, which includes some commonly used non-coherent units such as the litre.

Writing Unit Symbols and the Values of Quantities

- The value of a quantity is written as a number

followed by a space (representing a multiplication sign) and a unit symbol; *e.g.*, '2.21 kg', '7.3×10^2 m^2', '22 K'. This rule explicitly includes the per cent sign (%). Exceptions are the symbols for plane angular degrees, minutes and seconds (°, 2 and 3), which are placed immediately after the number with no intervening space.

- Symbols for derived units formed by multiplication are joined with a centre dot (·) or a non-break space; *e.g.*, N·m or N m.
- Symbols for derived units formed by division are joined with a solidus (/), or given as a negative exponent. *E.g.*, the "metre per second" can be written m/s, m s^{-1}, m·s^{-1}, or $\frac{\text{m}}{\text{s}}$. Only one solidus should be used; *e.g.*, kg/(m·s^2) and kg·m^{-1}·s^{-2} are acceptable, but kg/m/s^2 is ambiguous and unacceptable.
- Symbols are mathematical entities, not abbreviations, and do not have an appended period/full stop (.).
- Symbols are written in upright (Roman) type (m for metres, s for seconds), so as to differentiate from the italic type used for quantities (*m* for mass, *s* for displacement). By consensus of international standards bodies, this rule is applied independent of the font used for surrounding text.
- Symbols for units are written in lower case (*e.g.*, "m", "s", "mol"), except for symbols derived from the name of a person. For example, the unit of pressure is named after Blaise Pascal, so its symbol is written "Pa", whereas the unit itself is written "pascal".
  (a) The one exception is the litre, whose original symbol "l" is unsuitably similar to the numeral "1" or the uppercase letter "i" (depending on the typeface used), at least in many English-speaking countries. The American National Institute of Standards and Technology recommends that "L" be used instead, a usage common in the US,

Canada, and Australia (but not elsewhere). This has been accepted as an alternative by the CGPM since 1979. The cursive ℓ is occasionally seen, especially in Japan and Greece, but this is not currently recommended by any standards body. The litre is not an SI unit per se and is expressed in SI terms as a cubic decimetre, *i.e.*, dm^3.

- A prefix is part of the unit, and its symbol is prepended to the unit symbol without a separator (*e.g.*, "k" in "km", "M" in "MPa", "G" in "GHz"). Compound prefixes are not allowed.
- All symbols of prefixes larger than 10^3 (kilo) are uppercase.
- Symbols of units are not pluralised; *e.g.*, "25 kg", not "25 kgs".
- The 10th resolution of CGPM in 2003 declared that "the symbol for the decimal marker shall be either the point on the line or the comma on the line." In practice, the decimal point is used in English-speaking countries and most of Asia, and the comma in most of Latin America and in continental European languages.
- Spaces may be used as a thousands separator (*1000000*) in contrast to commas or periods (*1,000,000* or *1.000.000*) in order to reduce confusion resulting from the variation between these forms in different countries. In print, the space used for this purpose is typically narrower than that between words (commonly a *thin space*).
- Any line-break inside a number, inside a compound unit, or between number and unit should be avoided, but, if necessary, the last-named option should be used.
- In Chinese, Japanese, and Korean language computing (CJK), some of the commonly used units, prefix-unit combinations, or unit-exponent combinations have been allocated predefined single characters taking up a full square. Unicode includes these in its CJK

Compatibility and Letterlike Symbols subranges for back compatibility, without necessarily recommending future usage. These are summarised in Unicode System of Units.

- When writing dimensionless quantities, the terms 'ppb' (parts per billion) and 'ppt' (parts per trillion) are recognised as language-dependent terms, since the value of billion and trillion can vary from language to language. SI, therefore, recommends avoiding these terms. However, no alternative is suggested by the International Bureau of Weights and Measures (BIPM).

Writing the Unit Names

- Names of units follow the grammatical rules associated with common nouns - in English and in French they start with a lowercase letter (*e.g.*, newton, hertz, pascal), even when the symbol for the unit begins with a capital letter. This also applies to 'degrees Celsius', since 'degree' is the unit. In German however, names of units, in common with all nouns, start with a capital letter.
- Names of units are pluralised using the normal English grammar rules; *e.g.*, "henries" is the plural of "henry". The units lux, hertz, and siemens are exceptions from this rule: they remain the same in singular and plural form. Note that this rule applies only to the full names of units, not to their symbols.
- The official US spellings for *deca, metre,* and *litre* are *deka, meter,* and *liter*, respectively.

Realisation of Units

Metrologists carefully distinguish between the definition of a unit and its realisation. The definition of each base unit of the SI is drawn up so that it is unique and provides a sound theoretical basis on which the most accurate and reproducible measurements can be made. The realisation of the definition of a unit is the procedure by which the definition may be used to establish the value and associated uncertainty of a quantity of the same kind as the unit. A description of how the definitions of some important units are realised in practice is given on the BIPM website. However, "any method consistent with the laws of physics could be used to realise any SI unit."

Related Systems

The definitions of the terms 'quantity', 'unit', 'dimension' *etc.* used in measurement, are given in the International Vocabulary of Metrology.

The quantities and equations that define the SI units are now referred to as the *International System of Quantities* (ISQ), and are set out in the ISO/IEC 80000 *Quantities and Units.*

"New SI"

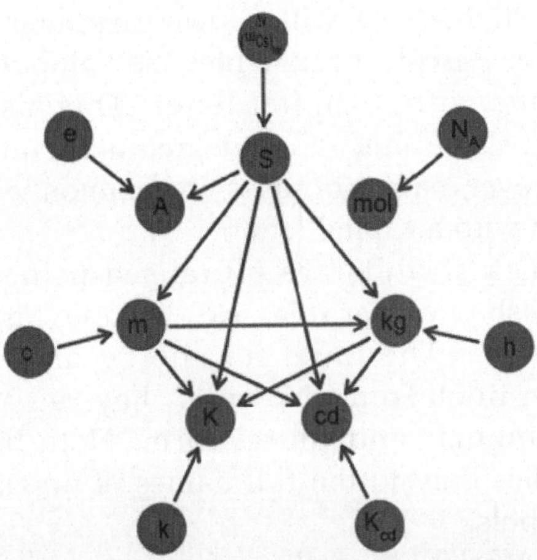

Figure 1.3 : Relations between Proposed SI Units Definitions and with Seven Fundamental Constants of Nature with Fixed Numerical Values in the Proposed System.

When the metre was redefined in 1960, the kilogram was the only SI base unit that relied on a specific artifact. Moreover, after the 1996-1998 recalibration a clear divergence between the various prototype kilograms was observed.

At its 23rd meeting (2007), The CGPM mandated the CIPM to investigate the use of natural constants as the basis for all units of measure rather than the artifacts that were then in use. At a meeting of the CCU held in Reading, United Kingdom in September 2010, a resolution and draft changes to the SI brochure that were to be presented to the next meeting of the CIPM in October 2010 were agreed to in principle. The proposals that the CCU put forward were:

- In addition to the speed of light, four constants of nature - Planck's constant, an elementary charge, Boltzmann constant and Avogadro's number be defined to have exact values.
- The international prototype kilogram be retired
- The current definitions of the kilogram, ampere, kelvin and mole be revised.
- The wording of the definitions of all the base units be tightened up.

The CIPM meeting of October 2010 found that "the conditions set by the General Conference at its 23rd meeting have not yet been fully met. For this reason the CIPM does not propose a revision of the SI at the present time". The CIPM did however sponsor a resolution at the 24th CGPM in which the changes were agreed in principal and which were expected to be finalised at the CGPM's next meeting in 2014.

Conversion Factors

The relationship between the units used in different systems is determined by convention or from the basic definition of the units. Conversion of units from one system to another is accomplished by use of a conversion factor. There are several compilations of conversion factors.

Cultural Issues

The near-worldwide adoption of the metric system as a tool of economy and everyday commerce was based to some extent on the lack of customary systems in many countries to adequately describe some concepts, or as a result of an attempt to standardise the many regional variations in the customary system. International factors also affected the adoption of the metric system, as many countries increased their trade. For use in science, the SI prefixes simplify dealing with very large and small quantities. Many units in everyday and scientific use are not SI units. In some cases these units have been designated by the BIPM as "non-SI units accepted for use with the SI". Some examples include:

- The units of time (minute, min; hour, h; day, d) in use besides the SI second, are specifically accepted for use.
- The year is specifically not included but has a recommended conversion factor.
- The Celsius temperature scale; kelvins are rarely employed in everyday use.
- Electric energy is often billed in kilowatt-hours, instead of megajoules. Similarly, battery charge is often measured as milliampere-hours (mA·h), instead of coulombs.
- The nautical mile and knot (nautical mile per hour) used to measure travel distance and speed of ships and aircraft (1 International nautical mile = 1852 m or approximately 1 minute of latitude). The Convention on International Civil Aviation permits the "temporary use" of the foot for altitude.
- Astronomical distances measured in astronomical units, parsecs, and light-years instead of, for example, petametres (a light-year is about 9.461 Pm or about 9461000000000000 m).
- Atomic scale units used in physics and chemistry, such as the ångström, electron volt, atomic mass unit and barn.
- Some physicists prefer the centimetre-gram-second (CGS) units, or systems based on physical constants, such as Planck units, atomic units, or geometric units.
- In some countries, the informal cup measurement has become 250 mL. Likewise, a 500 g metric pound is used in many countries. Liquids, especially alcoholic ones, are often sold in units whose origins are historical (for example, pints for beer and cider in glasses in the UK-although *pint* means 568 mL; Jeroboams for champagne in France).

- A metric mile of 10 km is used in Norway and Sweden. The term metric mile is also used in some countries for the 1500 m foot race.
- In the US, blood glucose measurements are recorded in milligrams per decilitre (mg/dL), which normalises to cg/L. In Canada, Australia, New Zealand, Oceania, and Europe the standard is millimole per litre (mmol/L) or mM (millimolar).
- Blood pressure is usually measured in mmHg(≈Torr).
- Atmospheric pressure in government weather reports is measured in inHg in the USA, and in the SI unit hPa in Australia, UK and most other countries.

The fine-tuning that has happened to the metric base-unit definitions over the past 200 years, as experts have tried periodically to find more precise and reproducible methods, does not affect the everyday use of metric units. Since most non-SI units in common use, such as the US customary units, are defined in SI units, any change in the definition of the SI units results in a change of the definition of the older units, as well.

DIMENSIONS AND DIMENSIONAL FORMULAE OF PHYSICAL QUANTITIES

Dimensions and Dimensional Formulae

Dimensions

Dimensions of a physical quantity are, the powers to which the fundamental units are raised to get one unit of the physical quantity.

The fundamental quantities are expressed with following symbols while writing dimensional formulas of derived physical quantities.

Mass →[M] ;
Length→[L];
Time → [T];
Electric current → [I] ;
Thermodynamic temperature → [K] ;
Intensity of light → [cd] ;
Quantity of matter → [mol].

Dimensional Formula

Dimensional formula of a derived physical quantity is the "expression showing powers to which different fundamental units are raised".

Ex : Dimensional formula of Force F → [$M^1L^1T^{-2}$]

Dimensional Equation

When the dimensional formula of a physical quantity is expressed in the form of an equation by writing the physical quantity on the left hand side and the dimensional formula on the right hand side,then the resultant equation is called Dimensional equation.

Ex: Dimensional equation of Energy is E = [$M^1L^2T^{-2}$].

Question: How can you derive Dimensional formula of a derived physical quantity.

Ans.: We can derive dimensional formula of any derived physical quantity in two ways:

- Using the formula of the physical quantity:
  Ex: let us derive dimensional formula of Force.
  Force F → ma ; substitute the dimensional formula of mass m → [M] ; acceleration → [LT^{-2}]
  we get F → [M][LT^{-2}]; F → [$M^1L^1T^{-2}$].
- Using the units of the derived physical quantity.
  Ex: let us derive the dimensional formula of momentum.
  Unit of Momentum (p) → [$kg - msec^{-1}$] ;
  kg is unit of mass → [M] ; is unit of length → [L] ; sec is the unit of time → [T]
  Substitute these dimensional formulas in above equation we get p → [$M^1L^1T^{-1}$].

Quantities having no units, can not possess dimensions: Trigonometric ratios, logarithmic functions, exponential functions, coefficient of friction, strain, poisson's ratio, specific gravity, refractive index, Relative permittivity, Relative permeability. All these quantities neither possess units nor dimensional formulas.

Quantities having units, but no dimensions : Plane angle, angular displacement, solid angle. These physical quantities possess units but they does not possess dimensional formulas.

Quantities having both units and dimensions : The following quantities are examples of such quantities.

Area, Volume, Density, Speed, Velocity, Acceleration, Force, Energy *etc.*

Physical Constants: These are two types:

- Dimension less constants (value of these constants will be same in all systems of units): Numbers, pi, exponential functions are dimension less constants.
- Dimensional constants (value of these constants will be different in different systems of units): Universal gravitational constant (G), Plank's constant (h), Boltzmann's constant (k), Universal gas constant (R), Permittivity of free space($\in_0$) , Permeability of free space (μ_0),Velocity of light (c).

Principle of Homogeneity of Dimensions

The term on both sides of a dimensional equation should have same dimensions. This is called principle of Homogeneity of dimensions. (or) Every term on both sides of a dimensional equation should have same dimensions. This is called principle of homogeneity of dimensions.

Uses of Dimensional Equations

Dimensional equations are used;

- To convert units from one system to another,
- To check the correctness of the dimensional equations;
- To derive the expressions connecting different physical quantities.

Limitations of Dimensional Method

The limitations of dimensional metthods are;

- The value of dimensionless constants can not be calculated using dimensional methods,
- We can not analyse the equations containing trigonometrical, exponential and logarithmic functions using method of dimensions.
- If a physical quantity is sum or difference of two or more than two physical quantities, such physical quantities can not be derived with dimensional methods,

- If any equation having dimensional constants like, G, R etc. can not be derived using dimensional methods,
- If any equations is involving more than three fundamental quantities in it, such expressions can not be derived using dimensional methods.

PRINCIPLE OF HOMOGENEITY

The principle of homogeneity is that the dimensions of each the terms of a dimensional equation on both sides are the same. Any equation or formula involving dimensions (like mass, length, time, temperature electricity) have the terms with same dimensions. This helps us, therefore, to convert the units in one system to another system. This also helps us to check a formula or the involvement of the dimensions in a formula.

Example: It is conjectured that time of the period of the oscillation of a pendulum is dependent on its mass, length and the acceleration due to gravity.

So time = some constant K(mass of the pendulum)^a (length l of the the pendulum)^b (acceleration due to gravity g)^c. Or

$T = Km^a l^b g^c$.

Dimensionally this is like:

$[T] = [M]^a [L]^b [LT^{-2}]^c$.

Comparing the powers of each dimensions on both sides, (K being dimensionless), we get:

T: $1 = -2c$. Therefore, $c = -1/2$

M: $0 = a$. Therefore, $a = 0$

L: $0 = b + 2c$. Therefore, $b = -2c = -1$. So the formula for the period T of the pendulum is :

$T = Km^0 L^{(1/2)} g^{(-1/2)} = K(l/g)^{(1/2)}$.

PHYSICAL HOMOGENEITY

In general, homogeneity is defined as the quality or state of being *homogeneous*. For instance, a uniform electric field (which has the same strength and the same direction at each point) would be compatible with homogeneity (all points experience the same physics). A material constructed with different constituents can be described as effectively homogeneous in the electromagnetic domain, when interacting with a directed radiation field (light, microwave frequencies, *etc.*) In physics, homogeneous usually means describing a material or system that has the same properties at every point of the space; in other words, uniform without irregularities. In physics, it also describes a substance or an object whose properties do not vary with position. For example, an object of uniform density is sometimes described as homogeneous.

Another related definition is simply a substance that is uniform in composition. Mathematically, homogeneity has the connotation of invariance, as all components of the equation have the same degree of value whether or not each of these components are scaled to different values, for example, by multiplication or addition. Cumulative distribution fits this description. "The state of having identical cumulative distribution function or values".

Context

The definition of homogeneous strongly depends on the context used. For example, a composite material is made up of different individual materials, known as "*constituents*" of the material, but may be defined as a homogeneous material when assigned a function. For example, asphalt paves our roads, but is a composite material consisting of asphalt binder and mineral aggregate, and then laid down in layers and compacted. In another context, a material is not homogeneous in so far as it composed of atoms and molecules. However, at the normal level of our everyday world, a block of wood, a pane of glass, or a sheet of metal is described as wood, glass, or stainless steel. In other words, these are each described as a homogeneous material. A few other instances of context are: *Dimensional homogeneity* is the quality of an equation having quantities of same units on both sides; *Homogeneity (in space)* implies conservation of momentum; and *homogeneity in time* implies conservation of energy.

Homogeneous Alloy

In the context of composite metals is an alloy. A blend of a metal with one or more metallic or nonmetallic materials is an alloy. The components of an alloy do not combine chemically but, rather, are very finely mixed. An alloy might be homogeneous or might contain small particles of components that can be viewed with a microscope. Brass is an example of an alloy, being a homogeneous mixture of copper and zinc. Another example is steel, which is an alloy of iron with carbon and possibly other metals. The purpose of alloying is to produce desired properties in a metal that naturally lacks them. Brass, for example, is harder than copper and has a more gold-like colour. Steel is harder than iron and can even be made rust proof (stainless steel).

Homogeneous Cosmology

Homogeneity, in another context plays a role in cosmology. From the perspective of 19th-century cosmology (and before), the universe was infinite, unchanging, homogeneous, and therefore filled with stars. In 1826, this being true according to the German astronomer Heinrich Olbers, then the entire night sky should be filled with light and as bright as daytime, but it is dark. He presented a technical paper in 1826 that attempted to answer this conundrum. The faulty premise, unknown in Olbers' time, was that the universe is not infinite, static, and homogeneous. The Big Bang cosmology replaced this model (expanding, finite, and inhomogeneous universe). However, modern astronomers supply reasonable explanations to answer this question. One of at least several explanations is that distant stars and galaxies are red shifted, which weakens their apparent light and makes the night sky dark.

Translation Invariance

By translation invariance, one means independence of (absolute) position, especially when referring to a law of physics, or to the evolution of a physical system. Fundamental laws of physics should not (explicitly) depend on position in space. That would make them quite useless. In some sense, this is also linked to the requirement that experiments should be reproducible. This principle is true for all laws of mechanics

(Newton's laws, *etc.*), electrodynamics, quantum mechanics, *etc.* In practice, this principle is usually violated, since one studies only a small subsystem of the universe, which of course "feels" the influence of rest of the universe. This situation gives rise to "external fields" (electric, magnetic, gravitational, *etc.*) which make the description of the evolution of the system depending on the position (potential wells, *etc.*). This only stems from the fact that the objects creating these external fields are not considered as (a "dynamical") part of the system.

Translational invariance as described above is equivalent to shift invariance in system analysis, although here it is most commonly used in linear systems, whereas in physics the distinction is not usually made. The notion of isotropy, for properties independent of direction, is not a consequence of homogeneity. For example, a uniform electric field (*i.e.*, which has the same strength and the same direction at each point) would be compatible with homogeneity (at each point physics will be the same), but not with isotropy, since the field singles out one "preferred" direction.

Consequences

In Lagrangian formalism, homogeneity in space implies conservation of momentum, and homogeneity in time implies conservation of energy.

Dimensional Homogeneity

As said in the introduction, *dijaat homogeneity* is the quality of an equation having quantities of same units on both sides. A valid equation in physics must be homogeneous, since equality cannot apply between quantities of different nature. This can be used to spot errors in formula or calculations. For example, if one is calculating a speed, units must always combine to [length]/[time]; if one is calculating an energy, units must always combine to [mass]•[length]²/[time]², *etc.* For example, the following formulae could be valid expressions for some energy:

$$E_k = \frac{1}{2}mv^2 ;\ E = mc^2 ;\ E = pv ;\ E = hc / \lambda$$

if m is a mass, v and c are velocities, p is a momentum, h is Planck's constant, λ a length. On the other hand, if the units of the right hand side do not combine to [mass]•[length]^2/[time]^2, it cannot be a valid expression for some energy. Being homogeneous does not necessarily mean the equation will be true, since it does not take into account numerical factors.

For example, $E = m \bullet v^2$ could be or could not be the correct formula for the energy of a particle of mass m travelling at speed v, and one cannot know if $h \bullet c/\lambda$ should be divided or multiplied by 2π. Nevertheless, this is a very powerful tool in finding characteristic units of a given problem. Theoretical physicists tend to express everything in natural units given by constants of nature, for example by taking $c = \hbar = k = 1$; once this is done, one partly loses the possibility of the above checking. The atomic number was also known as a proton number.

CONVERSION FROM ONE UNIT TO ANOTHER UNIT

UNIT CONVERSIONS

Changing between units is easy if we have a conversion equation. For example, Robert Millikan (a 20th century physicist) performed a landmark experiment with x-rays and determined the mass of an electron to be 9.1×10^{-31} kg. While this is the standard way to represent this quantity, it would also be correct to use grams (g) or milligrams (mg):

9.1×10^{-28} g = 9.1×10^{-25} mg.

How do we change between units like this? Here are two conversion equations that will help in this situation:

1 kg = 1000 g

1 g = 1000 mg

Notice that we can rearrange these equations in several ways dividing by one of the sides:

$$\frac{1\text{kg}}{1000\text{g}} = 1; \frac{1000\text{g}}{1\text{kg}} = 1; \frac{1\text{g}}{1000\text{mg}} = 1; \frac{1000\text{mg}}{1\text{m}} = 1$$

We have formed several ratios which are all equal to 1. Now we need to remember a crucial fact from arithmetic:

We can multiply any quantity by one and not change its value.

This is the key to changing units! Consider changing from kg to g. Which ratio equal to 1 should we multiply kilograms by to get grams?

Well, if we use the fraction with grams on top and kilograms on bottom, kilograms will "cancel out" when we simplify. Watch:

$$9.1\times10^{-31}\times\frac{1000\text{g}}{1\text{kg}}=\left[9.1\times10^{-31}\times1000\right]\text{g}=9.1\times10^{-28}\text{g}$$

Notice that we multiplied numbers in scientific notation. We can use the EE button on a calculator as follows:

9.1 EE -31 * EE 3

The calculator displays:

9.1 E -28

Changing from kilograms to milligrams works in the same way, except we need to convert from kg to g and then from g to mg since we aren't given a single kg-to-mg conversion equation. We *can* combine these into one step, though! Watch:

$$9.1\times10^{-31}\times\frac{1000}{1}\times\frac{1000\text{mg}}{1}$$
$$=\left[9.1\times10^{-31}\times1000\times1000\right]\text{mg}$$
$$=9.1\times10^{-25}\text{ mg}$$

We just multiplied by "one" twice, choosing the ratios that allowed us to cancel out the kg and the g units.

CONVERSION OF UNITS

Conversion of units is the conversion between different units of measurement for the same quantity, typically through multiplicative conversion factors.

TECHNIQUES

Process

The process of conversion depends on the specific situation and the intended purpose. This may be governed by regulation, contract, Technical specifications or other published standards. Engineering judgment may include such factors as:

- The precision and accuracy of measurement and the associated uncertainty of measurement.
- The statistical confidence interval or tolerance interval of the initial measurement.
- The number of significant figures of the measurement
- The intended use of the measurement including the engineering tolerances.

Some conversions from one system of units to another need to be exact, without increasing or decreasing the precision of the first measurement. This is sometimes called *soft conversion*. It does not involve changing the physical configuration of the item being measured. By contrast, a *hard conversion* or an *adaptive conversion* may not be exactly equivalent. It changes the measurement to convenient and workable numbers and units in the new system. It sometimes involves a slightly different configuration, or size substitution, of the item. Nominal values are sometimes allowed and used.

MULTIPLICATION FACTORS

Conversion between units in the metric system can be discerned by their prefixes (for example, 1 kilogram = 1000 grams, 1 milligram = 0.001 grams). Exceptions are made if the unit is commonly known by another name (for example, 1 micron = 10^{-6} metre).

TABLE ORDERING

Within each table, the units are listed alphabetically, and the SI units (base or derived) are highlighted.

Tables of Conversion Factors

The conversion factors for each of a number of physical quantities, which are listed in the index. For each physical quantity, a number of different units (some only of historical interest) are shown and expressed in terms of the corresponding SI unit.

Legend

Symbol	*Definition*
≡	exactly equal to
≈	approximately equal to
$\overline{digits}$	indicates that *digits* repeat infinitely (*e.g.* $8.294\overline{369}$ corresponds to 8.294 369 369 369 369…)
(H)	of chiefly historical interest

Density			
Name of unit	**Symbol**	**Definition**	**Relation to SI units**
gram per millilitre	g/mL	≡ g/mL	= 1,000 kg/m^3
kilogram per cubic metre (SI unit)	kg/m^3	≡ kg/m^3	= 1 kg/m^3
kilogram per litre	kg/L	≡ kg/L	= 1,000 kg/m^3
ounce (avoirdupois) per cubic foot	oz/ft^3	≡ oz/ft^3	≈ 1.001 153 961 kg/m^3
ounce (avoirdupois) per cubic inch	oz/in^3	≡ oz/in^3	≈ 1.729 994 044×10^3 kg/m^3
ounce (avoirdupois) per gallon (imperial)	oz/gal	≡ oz/gal	≈ 6.236 023 291 kg/m^3
ounce (avoirdupois) per gallon (US fluid)	oz/gal	≡ oz/gal	≈ 7.489 151 707 kg/m^3
pound (avoirdupois) per cubic foot	lb/ft^3	≡ lb/ft^3	≈ 16.01 846 337 kg/m^3

pound (avoirdupois) per cubic inch	lb/in³	≡ lb/in³	≈ 2.767 990 471×10⁴ kg/m³
pound (avoirdupois) per gallon (imperial)	lb/gal	≡ lb/gal	≈ 99.77 637 266 kg/m³
pound (avoirdupois) per gallon (US fluid)	lb/gal	≡ lb/gal	≈ 119.8 264 273 kg/m³
slug per cubic foot	slug/ft³	≡ slug/ft³	≈ 515.3 788 184 kg/m³

Speed or Velocity

Speed			
Name of Unit	**Symbol**	**Definition**	**Relation to SI Units**
foot per hour	fph	≡ 1 ft/h	≈ 8.466 667×10⁻⁵ m/s
foot per minute	fpm	≡ 1 ft/min	= 5.08×10⁻³ m/s
foot per second	fps	≡ 1 ft/s	= 3.048×10⁻¹ m/s
furlong per fortnight		≡ furlong/fortnight	≈ 1.663 095×10⁻⁴ m/s
inch per hour	iph	≡ 1 in/hr	≈ 7.05 556×10⁻⁶ m/s
inch per minute	ipm	≡ 1 in/min	≈ 4.23 333×10⁻⁴ m/s
inch per second	ips	≡ 1 in/s	= 2.54×10⁻² m/s
kilometre per hour	km/h	≡ 1 km/h	= 1/3.6 m/s ≈ 2.777 778×10⁻¹ m/s
knot	kn, kt	≡ 1 NM/h = 1.852 km/h	≈ 0.514 444 m/s
knot (Admiralty)	kn	≡ 1 NM (Adm)/h = 1.853 184 km/h	= 0.514 773 m/s
mach number	*M*	Ratio of the speed to the speed of sound in the medium. Varies especially with temperature. About 1225 km/h (761 mph) in air at sea level to about 1062 km/h (660 mph) at jet altitudes (12,200 metres (40,000 ft)).	≈ 340 to 295 m/s for aircraft

metre per second (SI unit)	m/s	≡ 1 m/s	= 1 m/s
mile per hour	mph	≡ 1 mi/h	= 0.447 04 m/s
mile per minute	mpm	≡ 1 mi/min	= 26.8224 m/s
mile per second	mps	≡ 1 mi/s	= 1 609.344 m/s
speed of light in vacuum	*c*	≡ 299 792 458 m/s	= 299 792 458 m/s
speed of sound in air	*s*	Varies especially with temperature. About 1225 km/h (761 mph) in air at sea level to about 1062 km/h (660 mph) at jet altitudes.	≈ 340 to 295 m/s at aircraft altitudes

A velocity consists of a speed combined with a direction; the speed part of the velocity takes units of speed.

Acceleration

Acceleration			
Name of unit	**Symbol**	**Definition**	**Relation to SI units**
foot per hour per second	fph/s	≡ 1 ft/(h·s)	≈ $8.466\ 667\times10^{-5}$ m/s²
foot per minute per second	fpm/s	≡ 1 ft/(min·s)	= 5.08×10^{-3} m/s^2
foot per second squared	fps^2	≡ 1 ft/s^2	= 3.048×10^{-1} m/s^2
gal; galileo	Gal	≡ 1 cm/s^2	= 10^{-2} m/s^2
inch per minute per second	ipm/s	≡ 1 in/(min·s)	≈ $4.233\ 333\times10^{-4}$ m/s^2
inch per second squared	ips^2	≡ 1 in/s^2	= 2.54×10^{-2} m/s^2
knot per second	kn/s	≡ 1 kn/s	≈ $5.144\ 444\times10^{-1}$ m/s^2
metre per second squared (SI unit)	m/s^2	≡ 1 m/s^2	= 1 m/s^2
mile per hour per second	mph/s	≡ 1 mi/(h·s)	= 4.4704×10^{-1} m/s^2
mile per minute per second	mpm/s	≡ 1 mi/(min·s)	= 26.8224 m/s^2
mile per second squared	mps^2	≡ 1 mi/s^2	= $1.609\ 344\times10^{3}$ m/s^2
standard gravity	*g*	≡ 9.806 65 m/s^2	= 9.806 65 m/s^2

Force

Force			
Name of unit	**Symbol**	**Definition**	**Relation to SI units**
atomic unit of force		$\equiv m_e \cdot \alpha^2 \cdot c^2/a_0$	≈ 8.238 722 06×10^−8^ N → $\approx 8.238\,722\,06\times10^{-8}$ N
dyne (cgs unit)	dyn	≡ g·cm/s² → $\equiv$ g·cm/s^2	= 10^{-5} N
kilogram-force; kilopond; grave-force	kgf; kp; Gf	$\equiv g \times 1$ kg	= 9.806 65 N
kip; kip-force	kip; kipf; klbf	$\equiv g \times 1\,000$ lb	= 4.448 221 615 2605×10^3 N
milligrave-force, gravet-force	mGf; gf	$\equiv g \times 1$ g	= 9.806 65 mN
newton (SI unit)	N	A force capable of giving a mass of one kg an acceleration of one metre per second, per second.	= 1 N = 1 kg·m/s^2
ounce-force	ozf	$\equiv g \times 1$ oz	= 0.278 013 850 953 7812 N
pound-force	lbf	$\equiv g \times 1$ lb	= 4.448 221 615 2605 N
poundal	pdl	≡ 1 lb·ft/s^2	= 0.138 254 954 376 N
sthene (mts unit)	sn	≡ 1 t·m/s^2	= 1×10^3 N
ton-force	tnf	$\equiv g \times 1$ sh tn	= 8.896 443 230 521×10^3 N

Chapter 2

Motion, Work, Energy and Power

CIRCULAR MOTION

In physics, circular motion is a movement of an objective along the circumference of a circle or rotation along a circular path or a circular orbit. It can be uniform, that is, with constant angular rate of rotation (and thus constant speed), or non-uniform, that is, with a changing rate of rotation. The rotation around a fixed axis of a three-dimensional body involves circular motion of its parts. The equations describing circular motion of an object do not take size or geometry into account, rather, the motion of a point mass in a plane is assumed. In practice, the centre of mass of a body can be considered to undergo circular motion.

Examples of circular motion include: an artificial satellite orbiting the Earth at constant height, a stone which is tied to a rope and is being swung in circles, a car turning through a curve in a race track, an electron moving perpendicular to a uniform magnetic field, and a gear turning inside a mechanism.

Circular motion is accelerated even if the angular rate of rotation is constant, because the object's velocity vector is constantly changing direction. Such change in direction of velocity involves acceleration of the moving object by a centripetal force, which pulls the moving object towards the centre of the circular orbit. Without this acceleration, the object would move in a straight line, according to Newton's laws of motion.

Formulas for Uniform Circular Motion

For motion in a circle of radius r, the circumference of the circle is $C = 2\pi\, r$ fig. 2.1. If the period for one rotation is T, the angular rate of rotation, also known as angular velocity, ω is:

$$\omega = \frac{2\pi}{T}$$

The speed of the object travelling the circle is:

$$v = \frac{2\pi r}{T} = \omega r$$

The angle θ swept out in a time t is:

$$\theta = 2\pi \frac{t}{T} = \omega t$$

The acceleration due to change in the direction is:

$$a = \frac{v^2}{r}$$

The vector relationships are shown in Figure. The axis of rotation is shown as a vector Ω perpendicular to the plane of the orbit and with a magnitude $\omega = d\theta/dt$. The direction of Ω is chosen using the right-hand rule. With this convention for depicting rotation, the velocity is given by a vector cross product as

$$v = \Omega \times r\,,$$

which is a vector perpendicular to both Ω and r (t), tangential to the orbit, and of magnitude $\omega\, r$. Likewise, the acceleration is given by

$$a = \Omega \times v = \Omega \times (\Omega \times r)\,,$$

which is a vector perpendicular to both Ω and v (t) of magnitude $\omega\ |v| = \omega^2\, r$ and directed exactly opposite to r (t).

Constant Speed, Mass and Radius

In the simplest case the speed, mass and radius are constant.

Consider a body of one kilogram, moving in a circle of radius one metre, with an angular velocity of one radian per second.

- The speed is one metre per second.
- The inward acceleration is one metre per square second.
- It is subject to a centripetal force of one kilogram metre per square second, which is one newton.
- The momentum of the body is one $kg \cdot m \cdot s^{-1}$.
- The moment of inertia is one $kg \cdot m^2$.
- The angular momentum is one $kg \cdot m^2 \cdot s^{-1}$.
- The kinetic energy is 1/2 joule.
- The circumference of the orbit is 2π (~6.283) metres.
- The period of the motion is 2π seconds per turn.
- The frequency is $(2\pi)^{-1}$ hertz.
- From the point of view of quantum mechanics, the system is in an excited state having quantum number $\sim 9.48 \times 10^{35}$.

Then consider a body of mass m, moving in a circle of radius r, with an angular velocity of ω.

- The speed is $v = r \cdot \omega$.
- The centripetal (inward) acceleration is $a = r \cdot \omega^2 = r^{-1} \cdot v^2$.
- The centripetal force is $F = m \cdot a = r \cdot m \cdot \omega^2 = r^{-1} \cdot m \cdot v^2$.
- The momentum of the body is $p = m \cdot v = r \cdot m \cdot \omega$.
- The moment of inertia is $I = r^2 \cdot m$.
- The angular momentum is $L = r \cdot m \cdot v = r^2 \cdot m \cdot \omega = I \cdot \omega$.
- The kinetic energy is $E = 2^{-1} \cdot m \cdot v^2 = 2^{-1} \cdot r^2 \cdot m \cdot \omega^2 = (2 \cdot m)^{-1} \cdot p^2 = 2^{-1} \cdot I \cdot \omega^2 = (2 \cdot I)^{-1} \cdot L^2$.
- The circumference of the orbit is $2 \cdot \pi \cdot r$.
- The period of the motion is $T = 2 \cdot \pi \cdot \omega^{-1}$.
- The frequency is $f = T^{-1}$. (Frequency is also often denoted by the Greek letter ν, which however is almost indistinguishable from the letter v used here for velocity).
- The quantum number is $J = 2 \cdot \pi \cdot L\ h^{-1}$

Description of Circular Motion using Polar Coordinates

During circular motion the body moves on a curve that can be described in polar coordinate system as a fixed distance *R* from the centre of the orbit taken as origin, oriented at an angle $\theta\,(t)$ from some reference direction (Fig. 2.2). The displace ment *vector* $\vec{r}$ is the radial vector from the origin to the particle location:

$$\vec{r} = R\hat{u}_R(t)\,,$$

where $\hat{u}_R(t)$ is the unit vector parallel to the radius vector at time *t* and pointing away from the origin. It is convenient to introduce the unit vector orthogonal to $\hat{u}_R$ as well, namely $\hat{u}_\theta$. It is customary to orient $\hat{u}_\theta$ to point in the direction of travel along the orbit. The velocity is the time derivative of the displacement:

$$\vec{v} = \frac{d}{dt}\vec{r}(t) = \frac{dR}{dt}\hat{u}_R + R\frac{d\hat{u}_R}{dt}\,.$$

Because the radius of the circle is constant, the radial component of the velocity is zero. The unit vector $\hat{u}_R$ has a time-invariant magnitude of unity, so as time varies its tip always lies on a circle of unit radius, with an angle θ the same as the angle of $\vec{r}(t)$. If the particle displacement rotates through an angle $d\theta$ in time *dt*, so does $\hat{u}_R$, describing an arc on the unit circle of magnitude $d\theta$. Hence:

$$\frac{d\hat{u}_R}{dt} = \frac{d\theta}{dt}\hat{u}_\theta\,,$$

where the direction of the change must be perpendicular to $\hat{u}_R$ (or, in other words, along $\hat{u}_\theta$) because any change $d\,\hat{u}_R$ in the direction of $\hat{u}_R$ would change the size of $\hat{u}_R$. The sign is positive, because an increase in $d\theta$ implies the object and have moved in the direction of $\hat{u}_\theta$. Hence the velocity becomes:

$$\vec{v} = \frac{d}{dt}\vec{r}(t) = R\frac{d\hat{u}_R}{dt} = R\frac{d\theta}{dt}\hat{u}_\theta = R\omega\hat{u}_\theta\,.$$

The acceleration of the body can also be broken into radial and tangential components. The acceleration is the time derivative of the velocity:

$$\vec{a} = \frac{d}{dt}\vec{v} = \frac{d}{dt}\left(R\,\omega\,\hat{u}_\theta\right).$$

$$= R\left(\frac{d\omega}{dt}\hat{u}_\theta + \omega\frac{d\hat{u}_\theta}{dt}\right).$$

The time derivative of $\hat{u}_\theta$ is found the same way as for $\hat{u}_R$. Again, $\hat{u}_\theta$ is a unit vector and its tip traces a unit circle with an angle that is $\pi/2 + \theta$. Hence, an increase in angle $d\theta$ by implies traces an arc of magnitude $d\theta$, and as $\hat{u}_\theta$ is orthogonal to $\hat{u}_R$, we have:

$$\frac{d\hat{u}_\theta}{dt} = -\frac{d\theta}{dt}\hat{u}_R = -\omega\hat{u}_R\,,$$

where a negative sign is necessary to keep $\hat{u}_\theta$ orthogonal to $\hat{u}_R$. (Otherwise, the angle between $\hat{u}_\theta$ and $\hat{u}_R$ would *decrease* with increase in $d\theta$.) Consequently the acceleration is:

$$\vec{a} = R\left(\frac{d\omega}{dt}\hat{u}_\theta + \omega\frac{d\hat{u}_\theta}{dt}\right)$$

$$= R\frac{d\omega}{dt}\hat{u}_\theta - \omega^2 R\,\hat{u}_R\,.$$

The centripetal acceleration is the radial component, which is directed radially inward:

$$\vec{a}_R = -\omega^2 R\hat{u}_R\,,$$

while the tangential component changes the magnitude of the velocity:

$$\vec{a}_\theta = R\frac{d\omega}{dt}\hat{u}_\theta = \frac{dR\omega}{dt}\hat{u}_\theta = \frac{d\,|\vec{v}\,|}{dt}\hat{u}_\theta\,.$$

Using Complex Numbers

Circular motion can be described using complex numbers. Let the x axis be the real axis and the y axis be the imaginary axis. The position of the body can then be given as z, a complex "vector":

$$z = x + iy = R(\cos\theta + i\sin\theta) = Re^{i\theta},$$

where i is the imaginary unit, and

$$\theta = \theta(t),$$

is the angle of the complex vector with the real axis and is a purpose of time t. Since the radius is constant:

$$\dot{R} = \ddot{R} = 0,$$

where a *dot* indicates time differentiation. With this notation the velocity becomes:

$$v = \dot{z} = \frac{d(Re^{i\theta})}{dt} = R\frac{d\theta}{dt}\frac{d(e^{i\theta})}{d\theta} = iR\dot{\theta}e^{i\theta} = i\omega \cdot Re^{i\theta} = i\omega z$$

and the acceleration becomes:

$$a = \dot{v} = i\dot{\omega}z + i\omega\dot{z} = (i\dot{\omega} - \omega^2)z$$
$$= \left(i\dot{\omega} - \omega^2\right)Re^{i\theta}$$
$$= -\omega^2 Re^{i\theta} + \dot{\omega}e^{i\frac{\pi}{2}}Re^{i\theta}.$$

The first term is opposite in direction to the displacement vector and the second is perpendicular to it, just like the earlier results shown before.

SPEED AND VELOCITY

Every moving object can be described using the kinematic concepts. The motion of a moving object can be explained using either Newton's Laws and vector principles or by means of the Work-Energy Theorem. The same concepts and principles used to describe and explain the motion of an object can be used to describe and explain the parabolic motion of a projectile. In this unit, we will see that these same concepts and principles can also be used to describe and explain the motion of objects that either move in circles or can be approximated to be moving in circles. Kinematic concepts and motion principles will be applied to the motion of objects in circles and then extended to analyse the motion of such objects as roller coaster cars, a football player making a *circular* turn, and a planet orbiting the sun. The beauty and power of physics lies in the fact that a few simple concepts and principles can be used to explain the mechanics of the entire universe. The development of kinematic and dynamic ideas that can be used to describe and explain the motion of objects in circles.

Expect that you were driving a car with the steering wheel turned in such a manner that your car followed the path of a perfect circle with a constant radius. And suppose that as you drove, your speedometer maintained a constant reading of 10 mi/hr. In such a situation as this, the motion of your car could be described as experiencing uniform circular motion. Uniform circular motion is the motion of an object in a circle with a constant or uniform speed.

Calculation of the Average Speed

Uniform circular motion - circular motion at a steady speed - is one of many forms of circular motion. An object moving in uniform circular motion would cover the same linear distance in each second of time. When moving in a circle, an object traverses a distance around the perimeter of the circle. So if your car were to move in a circle with a constant speed of 5 m/s, then the car would travel 5 metres along the perimeter of the circle in each second of time. The distance of one complete cycle around the perimeter of a circle is known as the circumference.

With a uniform speed of 5 m/s, a car could make a complete cycle around a circle that had a circumference of 5 meters. At this uniform speed of 5 m/s, each cycle around the 5-m circumference circle would require 1 second. At 5 m/s, a circle with a circumference of 20 meters could be made in 4 seconds; and at this uniform speed, every cycle around the 20-m circumference of the circle would take the same time period of 4 seconds.

This relationship between the circumference of a circle, the time to complete one cycle around the circle, and the speed of the object is merely an extension of the average speed equation.

$$\text{Average Speed} = \frac{\text{Distance}}{\text{Time}} = \frac{\text{Circumference}}{\text{Time}}$$

The circumference of any circle can be computed using from the radius according to the equation

$$\text{Circumference} = 2\pi R$$

Combining these two equations above will lead to a new equation relating the speed of an object moving in uniform circular motion to the radius of the circle and the time to make one cycle around the circle (period).

$$\text{Average Speed} = \frac{2 \times \pi \times R}{T}$$

where R represents the radius of the circle and T represents the period. This equation, like all equations, can be used as an algebraic recipe for problem solving. It also can be used to guide our thinking about the variables in the equation relate to each other. For instance, the equation suggests that for objects moving around circles of different radius in the same period, the object traversing the circle of larger radius must be travelling with the greatest speed. In fact, the average speed and the radius of the circle are directly proportional. A twofold increase in radius corresponds to a twofold increase in speed; a three-fold increase in radius corresponds to a three-fold increase in speed; and so on. To illustrate, consider a strand of four LED lights positioned at various locations along the strand. The strand is held at one end and spun rapidly in a circle. Each LED light traverses a circle of different radius. Yet since they are connected to the same wire, their period of rotation is the same. Subsequently, the LEDs that are further from the centre of the circle are travelling faster in order to sweep out the circumference of the larger circle in the same amount of time. If the room lights are turned off, the LEDs created an arc that could be perceived to be longer for those LEDs that were travelling faster - the LEDs with the greatest radius. This is illustrated in the diagram at the right.

The Way of the Velocity Vector

Objects moving in uniform circular motion will have a constant speed. But does this denote that they will have a constant velocity? Speed is a scalar quantity and velocity is a vector quantity. Velocity, being a vector, has both a magnitude and a direction. The magnitude of the velocity vector is the instantaneous speed of the object.

The direction of the velocity vector is directed in the same direction that the object moves. Since an object is moving in a circle, its direction is continuously changing. At one moment, the object is moving northward such that the velocity vector is directed northward. One quarter of a cycle later, the object would be moving eastward such that the velocity vector is directed eastward.

As the object *rounds* the circle, the direction of the velocity vector is different than it was the instant before. So while the magnitude of the velocity vector may be constant, the direction of the velocity vector is changing. The best word that can be used to describe the direction of the velocity vector is the word tangential. The direction of the velocity vector at any instant is in the direction of a tangent line drawn to the circle at the object's location. (A tangent line is a line that touches a circle at one point but does not intersect it.) The diagram at the right shows the direction of the velocity vector at four different points for an object moving in a clockwise direction around a circle. While the actual direction of the object (and thus, of the velocity vector) is changing, its direction is always tangent to the circle.

To summarize, an object moving in uniform circular motion is moving around the perimeter of the circle with a constant speed. While the speed of the object is constant, its velocity is changing. Velocity, being a vector, has a constant magnitude but a changing direction. The direction is always directed tangent to the circle and as the object turns the circle, the tangent line is always pointing in a new direction.

Acceleration

An object moving in uniform circular motion is moving in a circle with a uniform or constant speed. The velocity vector is constant in magnitude but changing in direction. Because the speed is constant for such a motion, many students have the misconception that there is no acceleration. "After all," they might say, "if I were driving a car in a circle at a constant speed of 20 m/hr, then the speed is neither decreasing nor increasing; therefore there must not be an acceleration." At the centre of this common student misconception is the wrong belief that acceleration has to do with speed and not with velocity. But the fact is that an accelerating object is an object that is changing its velocity. And since velocity is a vector that has both magnitude and direction, a change in either the magnitude or the direction constitutes a change in the velocity. For this reason, it can be safely concluded that an object moving in a circle at constant speed is indeed accelerating. It is accelerating because the direction of the velocity vector is changing.

To understand this at a deeper level, we will have to combine the definition of acceleration with a review of some basic vector principles. As such, it is calculated using the following equation:

$$\text{Average acceleration} = \frac{\Delta\,\text{velocity}}{\text{time}} = \frac{\nabla_f - \nabla_i}{t}$$

where v_i represents the initial velocity and v_f represents the final velocity after some time of t. The numerator of the equation is found by subtracting one vector (v_i) from a second vector (v_f). But the addition and subtraction of vectors from each other is done in a manner much different than the addition and subtraction of scalar quantities. In a time of t seconds, the object has moved from point A to point B. In this time, the velocity has changed from v_i to v_f. The process of subtracting v_i from v_f is shown in the vector diagram; this process yields the change in velocity.

Direction of the Acceleration Vector

Note in the diagram above that there is a velocity change for an object moving in a circle with a constant speed. A careful inspection of the velocity change vector in the above diagram shows that it points down and to the left. At the midpoint along the arc connecting points A and B, the velocity change is directed towards point C - the centre of the circle. The acceleration of the object is dependent upon this velocity change and is in the same direction as this velocity change. The acceleration of the object is in the same direction as the velocity change vector; the acceleration is directed towards point C as well - the centre of the circle. Objects moving in circles at a constant speed accelerate towards the centre of the circle.

The acceleration of an object is often measured using a device known as an accelerometer. A simple accelerometer consists of an object immersed in a fluid such as water. Consider a sealed jar that is filled with water. A cork attached to the lid by a string can serve as an accelerometer. To test the direction of acceleration for an object moving in a circle, the jar can be inverted and attached to the end of a short section of a wooden 2 × 4. A second accelerometer constructed in the same manner can be attached to the opposite end of the 2 × 4. If the 2 × 4 and accelerometers are clamped to a rotating platform and spun in a circle, the direction of the acceleration can be clearly seen by the direction of lean of the corks. As the cork-water combination spins in a circle, the cork leans towards the centre of the circle. The least massive of the two objects always leans in the direction of the acceleration. In the case of the cork and the water, the cork is less massive (on a per mL basis) and thus it experiences the greater acceleration. Having less inertia (owing to its smaller mass on a per mL basis), the cork resists the acceleration the least and thus *leans* to the inside of the jar towards the centre of the circle. This is observable evidence that an object moving in circular motion at constant speed experiences an acceleration that is directed towards the centre of the circle.

Another effortless homemade accelerometer involves a lit candle centred vertically in the middle of an open-air glass. If the glass is held level and at rest (such that there is no acceleration), then the candle flame extends in an upward direction. However, if you hold the glass-candle system with an outstretched arm and spin in a circle at a constant rate (such that the flame experiences an acceleration), then the candle flame will no longer extend vertically upwards. Instead the flame deflects from its upright position. This signifies that there is an acceleration when the flame moves in a circular path at constant speed.

The deflection of the flame will be in the direction of the acceleration. This can be explained by asserting that the hot gases of the flame are less massive (on a per mL basis) and thus have less inertia than the cooler gases that surround it. Subsequently, the hotter and lighter gases of the flame experience the greater acceleration and will lean in the direction of the acceleration. A careful examination of the flame reveals that the flame will point towards the centre of the circle, thus indicating that not only is there an acceleration; but that there is an inward acceleration. This is one more piece of observable evidence that indicates that objects moving in a circle at a constant speed experience an acceleration that is directed towards the centre of the circle.

ROTATION MOTION

Up to now, we have only analysed the dynamics of *point masses* (*i.e.*, objects whose spatial extent is either negligible or plays no role in their motion). Let us now broaden our approach in order to take *extended objects* into account. Now, the only type of motion which a point mass object can exhibit is *translational motion*: *i.e.*, motion by which the object moves from one point in space to another. However, an extended object can exhibit another, quite distinct, type of motion by which it remains located (more or less) at the same spatial position, but constantly changes its orientation with respect to other fixed points in space. This new type of motion is called *rotation*. Let us investigate rotational motion.

Rigid Body Rotation

Consider a rigid body executing pure rotational motion (*i.e.*, rotational motion which has no translational component). It is possible to define an *axis of rotation* (which, for the sake of simplicity, is assumed to pass through the body)—this axis corresponds to the straight-line which is the locus of all points inside the body which remain stationary as the body rotates. A general point located inside the body executes *circular motion* which is centred on the rotation axis, and orientated in the plane perpendicular to this axis.

Fig. 2.8 shows a typical rigidly rotating body. The axis of rotation is the line *AB*. A general point lying within the body executes a circular orbit, centred on *AB*, in the plane perpendicular to *AB*. Let the line *QP* be a radius of this orbit which links the axis of rotation to the instantaneous position of *P* at time *t*. Obviously, this implies that *QP* is normal to *AB*. Suppose that at time $t + \delta t$ point *P* has moved to *P′* and the radius *QP* has rotated through an angle $\delta\phi$. The instantaneous *angular velocity* of the body *w(t)* is defined

$$\omega = \lim_{\delta t \to 0} \frac{\delta\phi}{\delta t} = \frac{d\phi}{dt}.$$

Note that if the body is indeed rotating rigidly, then the calculated value of w should be the same for all possible points *P* lying within the body (except for those points lying exactly on the axis of rotation, for which w is ill-defined). The rotation speed v of point *P* is related to the angular velocity w of the body via

$$v = \sigma\omega$$

where σ is the *perpendicular distance* from the axis of rotation to point *P*. Thus, in a rigidly rotating body, the rotation speed increases *linearly* with (perpendicular) distance from the axis of rotation.

It is helpful to introduce the *angular acceleration* $\alpha(t)$ of a rigidly rotating body: this quantity is defined as the time derivative of the angular velocity. Thus,

$$\alpha = \frac{d\omega}{dt} = \frac{d^2\phi}{dt^2},$$

where ϕ is the angular coordinate of some arbitrarily chosen point reference within the body, measured with respect to the rotation axis. Note that angular velocities are conventionally measured in radians per second, whereas angular accelerations are measured in radians per second squared.

For a body rotating with constant angular velocity, ω, the angular acceleration is zero, and the rotation angle increases linearly with time:

$$\phi(t) = \phi_0 + \omega t,$$

Where $\phi_0 = \phi(t=0)$. Likewise, for a body rotating with constant angular acceleration, the angular velocity increases linearly with time, so that

$$\omega(t) = \omega_0 + \alpha t,$$

and the rotation angle satisfies

$$\phi(t) = \phi_0 + \omega_0 t + \frac{1}{2}\alpha t^2.$$

Here, $\omega_0 = \omega(t=0)$.

Note that there is a clear analogy between the above equations, and the equations of rectilinear motion at constant acceleration introduced rotation angle plays the role of displacement, angular velocity plays the role of (regular) velocity, and angular acceleration plays the role of (regular) acceleration.

The Vector Product

The possible to combine two vectors multiplicatively, by means of a *scalar product*, to form a scalar. Recall that the scalar product of two vectors $a = (a_x, a_y, a_z)$ and $b = (b_x, b_y, b_z)$ is defined

$$a \cdot b = a_x b_x + a_y b_y + a_z b_z = |a|\,|b| \cos\theta,$$

where is the angle subtended between the directions of *a* and *b*.

Is it also possible to combine two vector multiplicatively to form a third (non-coplanar) vector? It turns out that this goal can be achieved via the use of the so-called *vector product*. By definition, the vector product, *a* × *b*, of two vectors $a=(a_x,a_y,a_z)$ and $b=(b_x,b_y,b_z)$ is of magnitude

$$|a \times b| = |a|\,|b| \sin\theta.$$

The direction of *a* × *b* is *mutually perpendicular* to *a* and *b*, in the sense given by the right-hand grip rule when vector a is rotated onto vector b (the direction of rotation being such that the angle of rotation is less than 180°). In coordinate form,

$$a \times b = (a_y b_z - a_z b_y, a_z b_x - a_x b_z, a_x b_y - a_y b_x).$$

There are a number of fairly obvious consequences of the above definition. Firstly, if vector b is parallel to vector a, so that we can write $b = \lambda a$, then the vector product *a* × *b* has *zero magnitude*. The easiest way of seeing this is to note that if a and b are parallel then the angle θ subtended between them is zero, hence the magnitude of the vector product, $|a|\,|b| \sin\theta$, must also be zero (since). Secondly, the order of multiplication matters. Thus, b×a is *not* equivalent to *a* × *b*.

$$b \times a = -a \times b.$$

In other words, *b* × *a* has the same magnitude as a×b, but points in diagrammatically the opposite direction.

Now that we have defined the vector product of two vectors, let us find a use for this concept. A rigid body rotating with angular velocity ω. For the sake of simplicity, the axis of rotation, which runs parallel to ω, is assumed to pass through the origin *O* of our coordinate system. Point *P*, whose position vector is r, represents a general point inside the body. What is the velocity of rotation v at point *P*? Well, the magnitude of this velocity is simply

$$v = \sigma\omega = \omega r \sin\theta$$

where σ is the perpendicular distance of point P from the axis of rotation, and θ is the angle subtended between the directions of ω and r. The direction of the velocity is *into* the page. Another way of saying this, is that the direction of the velocity is mutually perpendicular to the directions of ω and r, in the sense indicated by the right-hand grip rule when ω is rotated onto r (through an angle less than 180°). It follows that we can write

$$v = \omega \times r$$

Note, incidentally, that the direction of the angular velocity vector ω indicates the compass reading of the axis of rotation—however, nothing actually moves in this direction; in fact, all of the motion is *perpendicular* to the direction of ω.

Rotational Motion of a Rigid Body

Rotational motion is additional complicated than linear motion, and only the motion of rigid bodies will be considered here. A rigid body is an object with a mass that holds a rigid shape, such as a phonograph turntable, in contrast to the sun, which is a ball of gas. Many of the equations for the mechanics of rotating objects are similar to the motion equations for linear motion.

Angular Velocity and Angular Acceleration

The angular displacement of a rotating wheel is the angle between the radius at the beginning and the end of a given time interval. The SI units are radians. The average angular velocity (ω, Greek letter omega), measured in radians per second, is

$$\omega = \frac{\text{angular displacement}}{\text{elapsed time}} = \frac{\theta}{t}$$

The angular acceleration (α, Greek letter alpha) has the same form as the linear quantity

$$\alpha = \frac{\text{change in angular velocity}}{\text{elapsed time}} = \frac{\omega_f - \omega_e}{t}$$

and is measured in radians/second/second or rad/s^2.

The kinematics equations for rotational motion at constant angular acceleration are

$\omega_f = \omega_0 \alpha t$ Angular velocity as a function of time

$\theta = \frac{1}{2}(\omega_e + \omega_f)t$ Angular displacement as a function of velocity and time

$\theta = \omega_e t + \frac{1}{2}\alpha t^2$ Angular displacement as a function of time

$\omega_f^{\ 2} = \omega_0^{\ 2} + 2\alpha\theta$ Angular velocity as a function of displacement

Think a wheel rolling without slipping in a straight line. The forward displacement of the wheel is equal to the linear displacement of a point fixed on the rim.

In this case, the average forward speed of the wheel is $v = d/t = (r\theta)/t = r\omega$, where r is the distance from the centre of rotation to the point of the calculated velocity. The direction of the velocity is tangent to the path of the point of rotation.

The average forward acceleration of the wheel is $a_T = r(\omega f - \omega o)/t = r\alpha$. This component of the acceleration is tangential to the point of rotation and represents the changing speed of the object. The direction is the same as the velocity vector. The radial component of the linear acceleration is $a_r = v^2/r = \omega^2 r$.

Torque

It is easier to open a door by pushing on the edge farthest from the hinges than by pushing in the middle. It is intuitive that the magnitude of the force applied and the distance from the point of application to the hinge affect the tendency of the door to rotate. This physical quantity, torque, is t = r × F sin θ, where F is the force applied, r is the distance from the point of application to the centre of the rotation, and θ is the angle from r to F.

Moment of Inertia

Substitute Newton's second law into the definition for

torque with θ of 90 degrees (a right angle between *F* and *r*) and use the relationship between linear acceleration and tangential angular acceleration to obtain $t = r\ F = rma = mr^2\ (a/r) = mr^2\alpha$. The quantity mr^2 is defined as moment of inertia of a point mass about the centre of rotation.

Imagine two objects of the same mass with different distribution of that mass. The first object might be a heavy ring supported by struts on an axle like a flywheel. The second object could have its mass close to the central axis. Even though the masses of the two objects are equal, it is intuitive that the flywheel will be more difficult to push to a high number of revolutions per second because not only the amount of mass but also the distribution of the mass affects the ease in initiating rotation for a rigid body. The general definition of moment of inertia, also called rotational inertia, for a rigid body is $I = \Sigma\ m_i\ r_i^2$ and is measured in SI units of kilogram-meters^2.

ANGULAR MOMENTUM

Angular momentum is rotational momentum that is conserved in the similar way that linear momentum is conserved. For a rigid body, the angular momentum *(L)* is the product of the moment of inertia and the angular velocity: $L = I\omega$. For a point of mass, angular momentum can be expressed as the product of linear momentum and the radius (*r*): $L = mvr$. *L* is measured in units of kilograms-meters^2 per second or more commonly joule-seconds. The law of conservation of angular momentum can be stated that the angular momentum of a system of objects is conserved if there is not external net torque acting on the system.

Analogous to Newton's law [$F = \Delta(mv)/\Delta\ t$] there is a rotational counterpart for rotational motion: $t = \Delta\ L/\Delta\ t$, or torque is the rate of change of angular momentum.

Consider the example of a child who runs tangential to the edge of a playground merry-go-round with a velocity v_o and jumps on while the merry-go-round is at rest. The only external forces are that of gravity and the contact forces provided by the support bearings, neither of which causes a torque because they are not applied to cause a horizontal rotation. Treat the child's mass as a point of mass and the merry-go-round as a disc with a radius R and mass M. From the conservation law, the total angular momentum of the child before the interaction is equal to the total angular momentum of the child and merry-go-round after the collision: $mrv_0 = mrv2 + I\omega$, where r is the radial distance from the centre of the merry-go-round to the place where the child hits. If the child jumps on the edge, $(r = R)$ and the angular velocity for the child after the collision can be substituted for the linear velocity, $mRv_0 = mR(R\omega)+(1/2)\,MR^2$. If the values for the masses and the initial velocity of the child are given, the final velocity of the child and merry-go-round can be calculated.

A single object may have a change in angular velocity due to the conservation of angular momentum if the distribution of the mass of the rigid body is altered. For example, when a figure skater pulls in her extended arms, her moment of inertia will decrease, causing an increase in angular velocity. According to the conservation of angular momentum, $I_0(\omega_0) = I_f(\omega_f)$ where I_0 is the moment of inertia of the skater with arms extended, I_f is her moment of inertia with her arms close to her body, ω_0 is her original angular velocity, and ω_f is her final angular velocity.

Rotational kinetic energy, work, and power. Kinetic energy, work, and power are defined in rotational terms as $K.E = (1/2)\,I\omega^2$, $W = t\theta$, $P = t\omega$.

EQUATION OF MOTION (CONSTANT ACCELERATION)

In earlier units you have been introduced to the concepts of displacement, velocity, and acceleration. Some of these quantities are defined in terms of others. We can employ mathematical equations based on how an object is currently moving to predict its future motion. Mathematical models of the behaviour of moving objects, such as stars and planets, allow predictions to be made about their position and speed at certain times. The motion of the Earth around the sun is governed by the laws of circular motion but the positions and speeds of objects moving in a straight line can also be modelled mathematically.

Modelling, based on mathematical descriptions of motion and forces, is used extensively to test the viability of engineering structures before construction.

Movement, like that in a roller coaster, usually involves both curved and straight sections. This unit will introduce the mathematical equations governing uniform accelerations or decelerations for objects moving in a straight line.

KINEMATIC EQUATIONS FOR ONE PARTICLE

Position Vector

In any differential equations of motion, the position vector is the most sought-after quantity because this function defines the motion of the particle - its location relative to a given coordinate system at some time t. In three dimensions, it is a function of any set of spatial coordinates, such as Cartesian, spherical polar and cylindrical polar coordinates, and time, which can also be a parameter (common variable) of all the coordinate;

$$\begin{aligned} \mathbf{r} &\equiv \mathbf{r}(x,y,z,t) \equiv x(t)\hat{\mathbf{e}}_x + y(t)\hat{\mathbf{e}}_y + z(t)\hat{\mathbf{e}}_z \\ &\equiv \mathbf{r}(r,\theta,\phi,t) \equiv r(t)\hat{\mathbf{e}}_r(\theta(t),\phi(t)) \\ &\equiv \mathbf{r}(r,\theta,z,t) \equiv r(t)\hat{\mathbf{e}}_r(\theta(t)) + z(t)\hat{\mathbf{e}}_z \\ &\ldots \end{aligned}$$

These are dissimilar *representations* for the position vector. Any set of three dimensional coordinates and their corresponding unit vectors can be used to define the motion - whichever is the simplest may be used. Each coordinate can be parameterized using time; since each successive value of time corresponds to a sequence of successive spatial locations given by the coordinates, so the continuum limit of many successive locations is the path the particle traces.

The Cartesian coordinates are the magnitudes of the vector components, which are scalar-multiplied by corresponding unit vectors, then these are vector-added to obatain the full vector. Coordinates and vectors are *not* exactly the same thing, but are closely related. In the above representations, x, y, z are coordinates, and $\hat{e}_x, \hat{e}_y, \hat{e}_z$ are unit vectors in the directions of the matching coordinate axes respectively. In the case of one dimension, the position has only one component, so it effectively degenerates to a scalar coordinate. It could be, say, a vector in the x-direction, or the radial direction. Frequently s is used for an arbitrary one-dimensional displacement vector. Explicitly;

$$x \equiv x \equiv x(t), \quad r \equiv r(t), \quad s \equiv s(t) \cdots$$

Kinematic Quantities

From the instantaneous position r = r (t) (instantaneous meaning at an instant value of time t), the instantaneous velocity v = v (t) and acceleration a = a (t) have the general, coordinate-independent definitions;

$$v = \frac{dr}{dt}, \quad a = \frac{dv}{dt} = \frac{d^2r}{dt^2}$$

The rotational analogues are the angular position (angle the particle rotates about some axis) $\theta = \theta(t)$, angular velocity $\omega = \omega(t)$, and angular acceleration $a = a(t)$:

$$\omega = \hat{n}\frac{d\theta}{dt}, \quad \alpha = \frac{d\omega}{dt} = \hat{n}\frac{d^2\theta}{dt^2}$$

where

$$\hat{n} = \hat{e}_r \times \hat{e}_\theta$$

is a unit axial vector, pointing parallel to the axis of rotation, $\hat{e}_r$ = unit vector in direction of r, $\hat{e}_\theta$ = unit vector tangential to the angle.

NB: In these rotational definitions, the angle can be any angle about the specified axis of rotation. It is customary to use θ, but this does not have to be the polar angle used in polar coordinate systems. For a rotating rigid body, the following relations useful for describing the motion hold:

$$v = \omega \times r$$

$$a = \alpha \times r + \omega \times v$$

where r is a radial position.

Uniform Acceleration

Constant Linear Acceleration

These equations be relevant to a particle moving linearly, in three dimensions in a straight line, with constant acceleration. Since the vectors are collinear (parallel, and lie on the same line) - only the magnitudes of the vectors are necessary, hence non-bold letters are used for magnitudes, and because the motion is along a straight line, the problem effectively reduces from three dimensions to one.

Derivation

$$v = at + v_0$$

$$r = \frac{at^2}{2} + v_0 t + r_0$$

$$r = r_0 + \left(\frac{v + v_0}{2}\right)t$$

$$v^2 = v_0^2 + 2a(r - r_0)$$

$$r = r_0 + vt - \frac{at^2}{2}$$

where r_0 and v_0 are the particle's initial position and velocity, r, v, a are the final position (displacement), velocity and acceleration of the particle after the time interval.

Here a is *constant* acceleration, or in the case of bodies moving under the influence of gravity, the standard gravity g is used. Note that each of the equations contains four of the five variables, so in this situation it is sufficient to know three out of the five variables to calculate the remaining two.

SUVAT Equations

In elementary physics the above formulae are frequently written:

$$v = at + u$$

$$s = ut + \frac{at^2}{2}$$

$$s = \left(\frac{v+u}{2}\right)t$$

$$v^2 = u^2 + 2as$$

$$s = vt - \frac{at^2}{2}$$

where u has replaced v_0, s replaces r, and $s_0 = 0$. They are often referred to as the "SUVAT" equations, eponymous from to the variables: s = displacement (s_0 = initial displacement), u = initial velocity, v = final velocity, a = acceleration, t = time.

Applications

Elementary and frequent examples in kinematics involve projectiles, for example a ball thrown upwards into the air. Given initial speed u, one can calculate how high the ball will travel before it begins to fall. The acceleration is local acceleration of gravity g. At this point one must remember that while these quantities appear to be scalars, the direction of displacement, speed and acceleration is important. They could in fact be considered as uni-directional vectors. Choosing s to measure up from the ground, the acceleration a must be in fact $-g$, since the force of gravity acts downwards and therefore also the acceleration on the ball due to it. At the highest point, the ball will be at rest: therefore $v = 0$. Using equation in the set above, we have:

$$s = \frac{v^2 - u^2}{-2g}.$$

Substituting and cancelling minus signs gives:

$$s = \frac{u^2}{2g}.$$

Steady Circular Acceleration

The analogues of the above equations can be written for rotation. Again these axial vectors must all be parallel (to the axis of rotation), so only the magnitudes of the vectors are necessary:

$$\omega = \omega_0 + \alpha t$$

$$\theta = \theta_0 + \omega_0 t + \frac{1}{2}\alpha t^2$$

$$\theta = \theta_0 + \frac{1}{2}(\omega_0 + \omega)t$$

$$\omega^2 = \omega_0^2 + 2\alpha(\theta - \theta_0)$$

$$\theta = \theta_0 + \omega t - \frac{1}{2}\alpha t^2$$

where α is the constant angular acceleration, ω is the angular velocity, ω_0 is the initial angular velocity, θ is the angle turned through (angular displacement), θ_0 is the initial angle, and t is the time taken to rotate from the initial state to the final state.

General Planar Motion

These are the kinematic equations for a particle traversing a path in a plane, described by position r = r(t). They are actually no more than the time derivatives of the position vector in plane polar coordinates in the context of physical quantities (like angular velocity ω). The position, velocity and acceleration of the particle are respectively:

$$r = r(r,\theta,t) = r\hat{e}_r$$

$$v = \hat{e}_r \frac{dr}{dt} + r\omega\hat{e}_\theta$$

$$a = \left(\frac{d^2r}{dt^2} - r\omega^2\right)\hat{e}_r + \left(r\alpha + 2\omega\frac{dr}{dt}\right)\hat{e}_\theta$$

where $\hat{e}_r, \hat{e}_\theta$, are the polar unit vectors. Notice for a the components ($-r\omega^2$) and $2\omega dr/dt$ are the centripetal and Coriolis accelerations respectively. Special cases of motion described be these equations are summarized qualitatively in the table below. In the cases that either the radial components or the angular components are zero, and the non-zero component of motion describes uniform acceleration.

State of motion	**Constant *r***	**Linear *r***	**Quadratic *r***	**Non-linear *r***
Constant *θ*	Stationary	Uniform translation (constant translational velocity)	Uniform translational acceleration	Non-uniform translation
Linear *θ*	Uniform angular motion in a circle (constant angular velocity)	Uniform angular motion in a spiral, constant radial velocity	Angular motion in a spiral, constant radial acceleration	Angular motion in a spiral, varying radial acceleration
Quadratic *θ*	Uniform angular acceleration in a circle	Uniform angular acceleration in a spiral, constant radial velocity	Uniform angular acceleration in a spiral, constant radial acceleration	Uniform angular acceleration in a spiral, varying radial acceleration
Non-linear *θ*	Non-uniform angular acceleration in a circle	Non-uniform angular acceleration in a spiral, constant radial velocity	Non-uniform angular acceleration in a spiral, constant radial acceleration	Non-uniform angular acceleration in a spiral, varying radial acceleration

General 3d Motion

It is certainly possible to derive analogue equations for motion in 3D space, but the equations become more complicated and unwieldy. Using the spherical coordinates (r, θ, ϕ) with corresponding unit vectors $\hat{e}_r, \hat{e}_\theta, \hat{e}_\phi$.

The position, velocity, and acceleration are respectively:

$$r = r(t) = r\hat{e}_r$$

$$v = v\hat{e}_r + r\frac{d\theta}{dt}\hat{e}_\theta + r\frac{d\phi}{dt}\sin\theta\hat{e}_\phi$$

$$a = \left(a - r\left(\frac{d\theta}{dt}\right)^2 - r\left(\frac{d\phi}{dt}\right)^2 \sin^2\theta\right)\hat{e}_r$$

$$+\left(r\frac{d^2\theta}{dt^2} + 2v\frac{d\theta}{dt} - r\left(\frac{d\phi}{dt}\right)^2 \sin\theta\cos\theta\right)\hat{e}_\theta$$

$$+\left(r\frac{d^2\phi}{dt^2}\sin\theta + 2v\frac{d\phi}{dt}\sin\theta + 2r\frac{d\theta}{dt}\frac{d\phi}{dt}\cos\theta\right)\hat{e}_\phi$$

In the case of a constant ϕ this reduces to the planar equations above.

Harmonic Motion of one Particle

Translation

The kinematic equation of motion for a simple harmonic oscillator (SHO), oscillating in one dimension (the $\pm x$ direction) in a straight line is:

$$\frac{d^2x}{dt} = \omega^2 x$$

where ω is the angular frequency of the oscillatory motion, related to the general frequency f and the time period T (time taken for one cycle of oscillation):

$$\omega = 2\pi f = 2\pi / T$$

Many systems approximately execute simple harmonic motion (SHM). The complex harmonic oscillator is a superposition of simple harmonic oscillators:

$$\frac{d^2x}{dt} = \sum_n \omega_n^2 x$$

It is possible for simple harmonic motions to occur in any direction:

$$\frac{d^2r}{dt} = \sum_n \omega_n^2 r_n$$

known as a multidimensional harmonic oscillator. In cartesian coordinates, each component of the position will be a superposition of sinusiodal SHM.

Rotation Analogue

The rotational analogue of SHM in a straight line is angular oscillation about a pivot:

$$\frac{d^2\theta}{dt} = \omega^2\theta$$

where ω is still the angular frequency of the oscillatory motion-though *not* the angular velocity which is the rate of change of θ. This form can be identified (at least approximately) as libration. The complex analogue is again a superposition of simple harmonic oscillators:

$$\frac{d^2\theta}{dt} = \sum_n \omega_n^2\theta$$

DYNAMIC EQUATIONS OF MOTION

Important Dynamic Quantities

Some important dynamic quantities needed to describe forces are momentum p, angular momentum L and moment of inertia *I* are as follows:

$$p = mv, \quad L = r \times p, \quad I = \sum_i m_i r_i^2$$

Another quantity, which is useful for simplification of forces but not essential, is the instantaneous mass moment:

$$m = mR\hat{e}_R$$

where $R = R\,(t)$ = instantaneous radius of curvature at r on the curve, and $\hat{e}_R$ = unit vector directed to centre of circle of curvature.

Some useful relations for describing the motion of rotating rigid bodies, analogous to the above, are:

$$p = \omega \times m$$

$$L = I \cdot \omega$$

Newtonian Mechanics

It may be simple to write down the equations of motion in vector form using Newton's laws of motion, but the components may vary in complicated ways with spatial coordinates and time, and solving them is not easy. Often there is an excess of variables to solve for the problem completely, so Newton's laws are not the most efficient method for generally finding and solving for the motion of a particle. In simple cases of rectangular geometry, the use of Cartesian coordinates works fine, but other coordinate systems can become dramatically complex.

Newton's 2nd law for translation

The first developed and most famous is Newton's 2nd law of motion:

$$\mathbf{F} = \frac{d\mathbf{p}}{dt}$$

where $\mathbf{p} = \mathbf{p}(t)$ is the momentum of the particle and $\mathbf{F} = \mathbf{F}(t)$ is the resultant external force acting on the particle (not any force the particle exerts) - in each case at time t. This is a differential equation of momentum, so solving this equation obtains the momentum vector as a function of time. This version of the formula is actually not much use, since the momentum is simply

$$\mathbf{p} = m\mathbf{v} = m\frac{d\mathbf{r}}{dt}$$

for a particle at position $\mathbf{r} = \mathbf{r}(t)$, velocity $\mathbf{v} = \mathbf{v}(t)$, and of mass $m = m(t)$, again each at time t. In general mass can vary with time, if the system gains or loses mass in some way. Velocity $\mathbf{v}$ is usually known as a 'function of time'.

Hence in usual application, Newton's second law is a differential equation of position and time, rather than momentum and time, using the product rule for differentiation:

$$\begin{aligned}\mathbf{F} &= m\frac{d\mathbf{v}}{dt} + \mathbf{v}\frac{dm}{dt} \\ &= m\frac{d^2\mathbf{r}}{dt^2} + \frac{d\mathbf{r}}{dt}\frac{dm}{dt}\end{aligned}$$

where $\mathbf{a}$ = acceleration of particle. This is a differential equation in terms of position **r**. The solution is **r** as a function of the spatial coordinates and time (in general), for example in cartesian coordinates **r** = (x, y, z, t), or in spherical polar coordinates r = (r, θ, ϕ, t). Time is usually a parameter of the spatial coordinates, so explicitly **r** = $(x(t), y(t), z(t), t)$.

For a number of particles, the equation of motion for one particle i is:

$$\frac{d\mathbf{p}_i}{dt} = \mathbf{F}_E + \sum_{i \neq j} \mathbf{F}_{ij}$$

where $\mathbf{p}_i$ = momentum of particle i, $\mathbf{F}_{ij}$ = force **on** particle i **by** particle j, $\mathbf{F}_{ij}$ = force **on** body j **by** particle i, and $\mathbf{F}_E$ = resultant external force (due to any agent not part of system). Particle i does not exert a force on itself.

Newton's Second Law for Rotation

The analogue for rotation is:

$$\boldsymbol{\tau} = \frac{d\mathbf{L}}{dt}$$

where τ denotes the torque acting on the body. Again this form isn't much use, so re-writing it:

$$\boldsymbol{\tau} = \frac{d\mathbf{r}}{dt} \times \mathbf{p} + \mathbf{r} \times \frac{d\mathbf{p}}{dt}$$

that is, the resultant torque acting on the system is the moment of the resultant force:

$$\boldsymbol{\tau} = \mathbf{r} \times \mathbf{F}$$

since momentum and velocity are always parallel by definition:

$$\mathbf{v} \times \mathbf{p} = 0$$

For rigid bodies, Newton's 2nd law for rotation takes the same form as for translation:

$$\mathbf{L} = I\boldsymbol{\omega}$$

again by the product rule:

$$\boldsymbol{\tau} = I\frac{d\omega}{dt} + \omega\frac{dI}{dt}$$

$$= \hat{\mathbf{n}}\left(I\frac{d^2\theta}{dt^2} + \frac{d\theta}{dt}\frac{dI}{dt}\right)$$

Likewise, for a number of particles, the equation of motion for one particle i is:

$$\frac{d\mathbf{L}_i}{dt} = \boldsymbol{\tau}_E + \sum_{i \neq j} \boldsymbol{\tau}_{ij}$$

where $\mathbf{L}_i$ = angular momentum of particle i, $\boldsymbol{\tau}_{ij}$ = torque ON particle i BY particle j, $\boldsymbol{\tau}_{ji}$ = torque ON body j BY particle i, and $\boldsymbol{\tau}_E$ = resultant external torque (due to any agent not part of system).

Particle i does not exert a torque on itself.

Applications

Some examples of Newton's law include describing the motion of a pendulum:

$$mg\sin\theta = m\frac{d^2(\ell\theta)}{dt^2} + 0 \Rightarrow g\sin\theta = \ell\frac{d^2\theta}{dt^2}$$

a damped, driven harmonic oscillator:

$$F_0 \sin\omega_0 t = m\frac{d^2x}{d^2t} + bm\frac{dx}{dt} + \omega^2 x$$

or a ball thrown in the air, in air currents (such as wind) described by a vector field of resistive forces R = R(x, y, z, t):

$$-\frac{GmM}{|r|^2}\hat{e}_r + R = m\frac{d^2r}{dt^2} + 0 \Rightarrow -\frac{GM}{|r|^2}\hat{e}_r + A = \frac{d^2r}{dt^2}$$

where G = gravitational constant, M = mass of the earth and A is the acceleration of the projectile due to the air currents at position r and time t. Newton's law of gravity has been used. The mass m of the ball cancels.

Euler's Equations for Rigid Body Dynamics

Euler also worked out analogous laws of motion to those of Newton. These extend the scope of Newton's laws to rigid bodies, but are essentially the same as above. A new equation Euler formulated is:

$$I\cdot\alpha + \omega \times (I\cdot\omega) = \tau$$

where I is the moment of inertia tensor.

General Planar Motion

The previous equations for planar motion can be used here: corollaries of momentum, angular momentum, *etc.* can immediately follow by applying the above definitions. For any object moving in any path in a plane,

$$r = r(t) = r\hat{e}_r$$

the following are general dynamic results.

The momentum and angular momenta are:

$$p = m\left(\hat{e}_r \frac{d^2 r}{dt^2} + r\omega\hat{e}_\theta\right)$$

$$L = mr \times \left(\hat{e}_r \frac{d^2 r}{dt^2} + r\omega\hat{e}_\theta\right)$$

The centripetal force is

$$F_\perp = -m\omega^2 R\hat{e}_r = -\omega^2 m$$

where again m is the mass moment, and the coriolis force is

$$F_C = 2\omega \frac{dr}{dt}\hat{e}_\theta = 2\omega v\hat{e}_\theta$$

Lagrangian and Hamiltonian Mechanics

More powerful equations of motion are the Euler-Lagrange equations and Hamilton's equations.

Generalized Coordinates

In Newtonian mechanics, it is customary to use fully all three Cartesian coordinates (or other 3d coordinate systems) to define the position of a particle. In a mechanical situation - there are normally constraints of motion, so using a full set of Cartesian coordinates is often unnecessary: they will be related to each other by equations corresponding to the constraint. For example a particle may be confined to move on a curved surface - the equation of the curve relates the coordinates into a constraint equation: the particle must have a position on the curve and not any other (no position off the curve).

The Eulerian-Lagrangian and Hamiltonian formalisms, the constraints of the situation are incorporated into the geometry of the motion, and in doing so the number of coordinates is reduced to only the minimum number needed to define the motion. There are almost always multiple choices of this - it makes no difference which is chosen. These are known as *generalized coordinates,* denoted q_i (for $i = 1, 2, 3...$) and are governed *only by convenience.*

For a one-particle system, the generalized coordinates define the position of the particle. For many particle systems, each particle has its own subset of the full set of generalized coordinates.

Each generalized coordinate is not for each particle in a many-particle system, the set of all generalized coordinates uniquely defines the configuration of the system: two may be needed for one particle, three may be needed for another, only one for another, and so on.

The number of generalized coordinates N equals the number of spatial dimensions minus the number of constraint equations.

Corresponding to generalized coordinates are their time derivatives: *generalized velocities*. There are also *generalized momenta,* denoted p_i, and their time derivatives: *generalized forces,* often denoted by Q_i.

There are two functions of energy: the Lagrangian and Hamiltonian functions, in terms of generalized coordinates, and velocities or momenta, and time. The Lagrangian or Hamiltonian function is set up from the system using these coordinates, then these are inserted into the Euler-Lagrange or Hamilton's equations to obtain differential equations of the system. These are solved for the function of the coordinates (inserted to begin with).

Euler-Lagrange Equations

The Euler-Lagrange equations are:

$$\frac{d}{dt}\left(\frac{\partial L}{\partial \dot{q}_i}\right)=\frac{\partial L}{\partial q_i}$$

where L is the Lagrangian function (function of generalized coordinates and momenta), which generally has the form:

$$L=\left[q(t),\dot{q}(t),t\right]$$

in which:

$$q(t)=[q_1(t),q_2(t)\ldots q_N(t)],\quad \dot{q}(t)=[\dot{q}_1(t),\dot{q}_2(t)\cdots\dot{q}_N(t)]$$

are vectors whose components are generalized coordinates and velocities respectively; wherein the generalized velocities are:

$$\dot{q}_i=\frac{dq_i}{dt}$$

After substituting for the Lagrangian, evaluating the partial derivatives, and simplifying, a 2nd order ODE in q_i is obtained (as in the introduction above).

Hamilton's Equations

Alternatively Hamilton's equations can be used:

$$\dot{p}_i=-\frac{\partial H}{\partial q_i}\quad \dot{q}_i=+\frac{\partial H}{\partial p_i}$$

where p and q are as above, and H is the Hamiltonian function

(function of generalized coordinates and momenta) - which generally has the form

$$H = \left[q(t), p(t), t\right]$$

where

$$p(t) = [p_1(t), p_2(t) \cdots p_N(t)], \quad \dot{p}(t) = [\dot{p}_1(t), \dot{p}_2(t) \cdots \dot{p}_N(t)]$$

are vectors whose components are generalized momenta and forces respectively, and

$$p_i(t) = \frac{\partial L}{\partial \dot{q}_i}$$

are the generalized momenta. Notice the equations are symmetric (remain in the same form) by making these interchanges *simaltaneously*:

$$p_i \to q_i, H \to -H.$$

After substituting the Hamiltonian, evaluating the partial derivatives, and simplifying, two 1st order ODEs in q_i and p_i are obtained (as in the introduction above).

Hamilton-Jacobi Equation

Hamilton's formalism can be generalized further:

$$H = -\frac{\partial S}{\partial t}$$

where

$$H = H\left(q_1, q_2 \cdots q_N, \frac{\partial S}{\partial q_1}, \frac{\partial S}{\partial q_2} \cdots \frac{\partial S}{\partial q_N}, t\right)$$

is the Hamiltonian and

$$S = S(q_1, q_2 \ldots q_N, t)$$

is Hamilton's principal function, it is also the classical action. Although the equation has a simple form, its actually a *non-*

linear partial differential equation, first order in $N + 1$ variables, rather than $2N$ such equations. Due to the action S, it can be used to identify conserved quantities for mechanical systems, even when the mechanical problem itself cannot be solved fully, because any differentiable symmetry of the action of a physical system has a corresponding conservation law, a theorem due to Emmy Noether. Also action forms part of a powerful variation principle: the principle of least action, from which the system's behaviour can be determined.

Electrodynamics Force

In electrodynamics, the force on a charged particle of charge q is the Lorentz force:

$$F = q(E + v \times B)$$

Combining with Newton's 2nd law gives a first order differential equation of motion, in terms of position of the particle:

$$m\frac{d^2r}{dt^2} = q\left(E + \frac{dr}{dt} \times B\right)$$

or its momentum:

$$\frac{dp}{dt} = q\left(E + \frac{p \times B}{m}\right)$$

The same equation can be obtained using the Lagrangian (and applying Lagrange's equations above) for a charged particle of mass m and charge q:

$$L = \frac{m}{2}\dot{r}\cdot\dot{r} + qA\cdot\dot{r} - q\phi$$

where A and ϕ are the electromagnetic scalar and vector potential fields, or the Hamiltonian (and substituting into the equations):.

$$H = \frac{(P - qA)^2}{2m} - q\phi$$

All equations above state the motion of a chargd particle is fundamentally determined by the charge of the particle and the electromagnetic field.

The Lagrangian and Hamiltonian expressions indicate an additional detail: the momentum of a charged particle is not only due to its mass and velocity (*m*v), but there is an extra momentum contribution from the charge of the particle and the field itself (given by *q*A). The Lagrangian expression was first used to derive the force equation.

Non-relativistic Physics - Wave Equations

Mechanical Waves

The analogue of an equation of motion for waves is a *wave equation*. From Newton's law the classical mechanical wave equation can be derived, the solutions to the wave equation describe wave motion for some prescribed wave, for both travelling and standing waves. There are other wave equations for very specific applications (aside from quantum mechanics).

Quantum Mechanics

In quantum mechanics, the analogue of the equation of motion is the Schrödinger equation:

$$\hat{H}\Psi = i\hbar \frac{\partial \Psi}{\partial t}$$

where $\hat{H}$ is the Hamiltonian operator (rather than a function as above), ψ is the wavefunction and $\hbar$ is the Reduced Planck constant. Setting up the Hamiltonian and inserting it into the equation results in a differential equation, the solution is the wavefunction as a function of space and time.

LAWS OF MOTION

Newton's laws of motion are three physical laws that form

the basis for classical mechanics. They describe the relationship between the forces acting on a body and its motion due to those forces. They have been expressed in several different ways over nearly three centuries, and can be summarized as follows:

- First law: The velocity of a body remains constant unless the body is acted upon by an external force.
- Second law: The acceleration a of a body is parallel and directly proportional to the net force F and inversely proportional to the mass *m*, *i.e.*, F = *m*a.
- Third law: The mutual forces of action and reaction between two bodies are equal, opposite and collinear.

The three laws of motion were first compiled by Sir Isaac Newton in his work *Philosophiæ Naturalis Principia Mathematica*, first published in 1687.

Newton used them to explain and investigate the motion of many physical objects and systems. For example, in the third volume of the text, Newton showed that these laws of motion, combined with his law of universal gravitation, explained Kepler's laws of planetary motion.

Overview of Laws

Newton's laws are applied to bodies (objects) which are considered or idealized as a particle, in the sense that the extent of the body is neglected in the evaluation of its motion, *i.e.*, the object is small compared to the distances involved in the analysis, or the deformation and rotation of the body is of no importance in the analysis. Therefore, a planet can be idealized as a particle for analysis of its orbital motion around a star.

In their original form, Newton's laws of motion are not adequate to characterize the motion of rigid bodies and deformable bodies. Leonard Euler in 1750 introduced a generalization of Newton's laws of motion for rigid bodies called the Euler's laws of motion, later applied as well for deformable bodies assumed as a continuum. If a body is represented as an assemblage of discrete particles, each governed by Newton's laws of motion, then Euler's laws can be derived from Newton's laws. Euler's laws can, however, be taken as axioms describing the laws of motion for extended bodies, independently of any particle structure.

Newton's laws hold only with respect to a certain set of frames of reference called Newtonian or inertial reference frames. Some authors interpret the first law as defining what an inertial reference frame is; from this point of view, the second law only holds when the observation is made from an inertial reference frame, and therefore the first law cannot be proved as a special case of the second. Other authors do treat the first law as a corollary of the second. The explicit concept of an inertial frame of reference was not developed until long after Newton's death.

In the given interpretation mass, acceleration, momentum, and (most importantly) force are assumed to be externally defined quantities. This is the most common, but not the only interpretation: one can consider the laws to be a definition of these quantities.

Newtonian mechanics has been superseded by special relativity, but it is still useful as an approximation when the speeds involved are much slower than the speed of light.

Newton's First Law

Law I: Every body persists in its state of being at rest or of moving uniformly straight forward, except insofar as it is compelled to change its state by force impressed.

This law states that if the net force (the vector sum of all forces acting on an object) is zero, then the velocity of the object is constant. Mathematically stated:

$$\sum F = 0 \Rightarrow \frac{dv}{dt} = 0.$$

Consequently:

- An object that is at rest will stay at rest unless an unbalanced force acts upon it.
- An object that is in motion will not change its velocity unless an unbalanced force acts upon it.

Newton placed the first law of motion to establish frames

of reference for which the other laws are applicable. The first law of motion postulates the existence of at least one frame of reference called a Newtonian or inertial reference frame, relative to which the motion of a particle not subject to forces is a straight line at a constant speed. Newton's first law is often referred to as the *law of inertia*. Thus, a condition necessary for the uniform motion of a particle relative to an inertial reference frame is that the total net force acting on it is zero. In this sense, the first law can be restated as:

In every material universe, the motion of a particle in a preferential reference frame Φ is determined by the action of forces whose total vanished for all times when and only when the velocity of the particle is constant in Φ. That is, a particle initially at rest or in uniform motion in the preferential frame Φ continues in that state unless compelled by forces to change it.

Newton's laws are valid only in an inertial reference frame. Any reference frame that is in uniform motion with respect to an inertial frame is also an inertial frame, *i.e.* Galilean invariance or the principle of Newtonian relativity. Newton's first law is a restatement of the law of inertia which Galileo had already described and Newton gave credit to Galileo. Aristotle had the view that all objects have a natural place in the universe: that heavy objects like rocks wanted to be at rest on the Earth and that light objects like smoke wanted to be at rest in the sky and the stars wanted to remain in the heavens. He thought that a body was in its natural state when it was at rest, and for the body to move in a straight line at a constant speed an external agent was needed to continually propel it, otherwise it would stop moving. Galileo, however, realised that a force is necessary to change the velocity of a body, *i.e.*, acceleration, but no force is needed to maintain its velocity. This insight leads to Newton's First Law —no force means no acceleration, and hence the body will maintain its velocity.

The law of inertia apparently occurred to several different natural philosophers and scientists independently, including Thomas Hobbes in his *Leviathan*. The 17th century philosopher René Descartes also formulated the law, although he did not perform any experiments to confirm it.

Newton's Second Law

The second law states that the net force on a particle is equal to the time rate of change of its linear momentum p in an inertial reference frame:

$$F = \frac{dp}{dt} = \frac{d(mv)}{dt},$$

where, since the law is valid only for constant-mass systems, the mass can be taken outside the differentiation operator by the constant factor rule in differentiation. Thus,

$$F = m\frac{dv}{dt} = ma,$$

where F is the net force applied, m is the mass of the body, and a is the body's acceleration. Thus, the net force applied to a body produces a proportional acceleration. In other words, if a body is accelerating, then there is a force on it.

Any mass that is gained or lost by the system will cause a change in momentum that is not the result of an external force. A different equation is necessary for variable-mass systems.

Consistent with the first law, the time derivative of the momentum is non-zero when the momentum changes direction, even if there is no change in its magnitude; such is the case with uniform circular motion. The relationship also implies the conservation of momentum: when the net force on the body is zero, the momentum of the body is constant. Any net force is equal to the rate of change of the momentum.

Newton's second law requires modification if the effects of special relativity are to be taken into account, because at high speeds the approximation that momentum is the product of rest mass and velocity is not accurate.

Impulse

An impulse J occurs when a force F acts over an interval of time Δt, and it is given by

$$J = \int_{\Delta t} F\,dt.$$

Since force is the time derivative of momentum, it follows that

$$J = \Delta p = m\Delta v.$$

This relation between impulse and momentum is closer to Newton's wording of the second law.

Impulse is a concept frequently used in the analysis of collisions and impacts.

Variable-mass Systems

Variable-mass systems, like a rocket burning fuel and ejecting spent gases, are not closed and cannot be directly treated by making mass a function of time in the second law. The reasoning, given in *An Introduction to Mechanics* by Kleppner and Kolenkow and other modern texts, is that Newton's second law applies fundamentally to particles. In classical mechanics, particles by definition have constant mass. In case of a well-defined system of particles, Newton's law can be extended by summing over all the particles in the system:

$$F_{\text{net}} = Ma_{\text{cm}}$$

where F_{net} is the total external force on the system, M is the total mass of the system, and a_{cm} is the acceleration of the centre of mass of the system.

Variable-mass systems like a rocket or a leaking bucket cannot usually be treated as a system of particles, and thus Newton's second law cannot be applied directly. Instead, the general equation of motion for a body whose mass m varies with time by either ejecting or accreting mass is obtained by rearranging the second law and adding a term to account for the momentum carried by mass entering or leaving the system:

$$F + u\frac{dm}{dt} = m\frac{dv}{dt}$$

where u is the relative velocity of the escaping or incoming mass with respect to the centre of mass of the body. Under some conventions, the quantity ($u\,dm/dt$) on the left-hand side, known as the thrust, is defined as a force (the force exerted on the body by the changing mass, such as rocket exhaust) and is included in the quantity F. Then, by substituting the definition of acceleration, the equation becomes

$$F = ma.$$

History of Laws

Law II: *The alteration of motion is ever proportional to the motive force impress'd; and is made in the direction of the right line in which that force is impress'd.*

According to modern ideas of how Newton was using his terminology, this is understood, in modern terms, as an equivalent of:

The change of momentum of a body is proportional to the impulse impressed on the body, and happens along the straight line on which that impulse is impressed.

If a force generates a motion, a double force will generate double the motion, a triple force triple the motion, whether that force be impressed altogether and at once, or gradually and successively. And this motion (being always directed the same way with the generating force), if the body moved before, is added to or subtracted from the former motion, according as they directly conspire with or are directly contrary to each other; or obliquely joined, when they are oblique, so as to produce a new motion compounded from the determination of both.

The sense or senses in which Newton used his terminology, and how he understood the second law and intended it to be understood, have been extensively discussed by historians of science, along with the relations between Newton's formulation and modern formulations.

Newton's Third Law

Law III: To every action there is always opposed an equal reaction: or the mutual actions of two bodies upon each other are always equal, and directed to contrary parts. Whatever draws or presses another is as much drawn or pressed by that other. If you press a stone with your finger, the finger is also pressed by the stone. If a horse draws a stone tied to a rope, the horse (if I may so say) will be equally drawn back towards the stone: for the distended rope, by the same endeavour to relax or unbend itself, will draw the horse as much towards the stone, as it does the stone towards the horse, and will obstruct the progress of the one as much as it advances that of the other. If a body impinges upon another, and by its force changes the motion of the other, that body also (because of the equality of the mutual pressure) will undergo an equal change, in its own motion, towards the contrary part. The changes made by these actions are equal, not in the velocities but in the motions of the bodies; that is to say, if the bodies are not hindered by any other impediments. For, as the motions are equally changed, the changes of the velocities made towards contrary parts are reciprocally proportional to the bodies. This law takes place also in attractions, as will be proved in the next scholium.

In the above, as usual, *motion* is Newton's name for momentum, hence his careful distinction between motion and velocity.

The Third Law means that all forces are *interactions* between different bodies, and thus that there is no such thing as a unidirectional force or a force that acts on only one body. Whenever a first body exerts a force **F** on a second body, the second body exerts a force –**F** on the first body. **F** and –**F** are equal in magnitude and opposite in direction. This law is sometimes referred to as the *action-reaction law,* with F called the "action" and –**F** the "reaction". The action and the reaction are simultaneous.

As shown in the diagram opposite, the skaters' forces on each other are equal in magnitude, but act in opposite directions. Although the forces are equal, the accelerations are not: the less massive skater will have a greater acceleration due to Newton's second law. The two forces in Newton's third law are of the same type (*e.g.*, if the road exerts a forward frictional force on an accelerating car's tires, then it is also a frictional force that Newton's third law predicts for the tires pushing backward on the road).

Put very simply: a force acts between a pair of objects, and not on a single object. So each and every force has two ends. Each of the two ends is the same except for being opposite in direction. The ends of a force are mirror images of each other, one might say. From a mathematical point of view, Newton's third law is a one-dimensional vector equation, which can be stated as follows. Given two objects A and B, each exerting a force on the other,

$$\sum \mathbf{F}_{a,b} = -\sum \mathbf{F}_{b,a}$$

where;

$\mathbf{F}_{a,b}$ are the forces from B acting on A, and

$\mathbf{F}_{b,a}$ are the forces from A acting on B.

Newton used the third law to derive the law of *conservation of momentum*; however from a deeper perspective, conservation of momentum is the more fundamental idea (derived via Noether's theorem from Galilean invariance), and holds in cases where Newton's third law appears to fail, for instance when force fields as well as particles carry momentum, and in quantum mechanics.

Importance and Range of Validity

Newton's laws were verified by experiment and observation for over 200 years, and they are excellent approximations at the scales and speeds of everyday life. Newton's laws of motion, together with his law of *universal gravitation* and the mathematical techniques of calculus, provided for the first time a unified quantitative explanation for a wide range of physical phenomena.

These three laws hold to a good approximation for macroscopic objects under everyday conditions. However, Newton's laws (combined with universal gravitation and classical electrodynamics) are inappropriate for use in certain circumstances, most notably at very small scales, very high speeds (in special relativity, the Lorentz factor must be included in the expression for momentum along with rest mass and velocity) or very strong gravitational fields. Therefore, the laws cannot be used to explain phenomena such as conduction of electricity in a semiconductor, optical properties of substances, errors in non-relativistically corrected GPS systems and superconductivity.

Explanation of these phenomena requires more sophisticated physical theories, including general relativity and quantum field theory. In quantum mechanics concepts such as force, momentum, and position are defined by linear operators that operate on the quantum state; at speeds that are much lower than the speed of light, Newton's laws are just as exact for these operators as they are for classical objects. At speeds comparable to the speed of light, the second law holds in the original form $\mathbf{F} = d\mathbf{p}/\boxed{dt}$.

Relationship to the Conservation Laws

In modern physics, the laws of conservation of momentum, energy, and angular momentum are of more general validity than Newton's laws, since they apply to both light and matter, and to both classical and non-classical physics.

This can be stated simply, "Momentum, energy and angular momentum cannot be created or destroyed."

Because force is the time derivative of momentum, the concept of force is redundant and subordinate to the conservation of momentum, and is not used in fundamental theories (*e.g.*, quantum mechanics, quantum electrodynamics, general relativity, *etc.*). The standard model explains in detail how the three fundamental forces known as gauge forces originate out of exchange by virtual particles. Other forces such as gravity and fermionic degeneracy pressure also arise from the momentum conservation. Indeed, the conservation of 4-momentum in inertial motion via curved space-time results in what we call gravitational force in general relativity theory. Application of space derivative (which is a momentum operator in quantum mechanics) to overlapping wave functions of pair of fermions (particles with half-integer spin) results in shifts of maxima of compound wavefunction away from each other, which is observable as "repulsion" of fermions.

Newton stated the third law within a world-view that assumed instantaneous action at a distance between material particles. However, he was prepared for philosophical criticism of this action at a distance, and it was in this context that he stated the famous phrase "I feign no hypotheses". In modern physics, action at a distance has been completely eliminated, except for subtle effects involving quantum entanglement. However in modern engineering in all practical applications involving the motion of vehicles and satellites, the concept of action at a distance is used extensively.

Conservation of energy was discovered nearly two centuries after Newton's lifetime, the long delay occurring because of the difficulty in understanding the role of microscopic and invisible forms of energy such as heat and infra-red light.

Energy

In physics, energy is an indirectly observed quantity. It is often understood as the ability a physical system has to do work on other physical systems. Since work is defined as a force acting through a distance (a length of space), energy is always equivalent to the ability to exert pulls or pushes against the basic forces of nature, along a path of a certain length.

The total energy contained in an object is identified with its mass, and energy (like mass), cannot be created or destroyed. When matter (ordinary material particles) is changed into energy (such as energy of motion, or into radiation), the mass of the system does not change through the transformation process. However, there may be mechanistic limits as to how much of the matter in an object may be changed into other types of energy and thus into work, on other systems.

Energy, like mass, is a scalar physical quantity. In the International System of Units (SI), energy is measured in joules, but in many fields other units, such as kilowatt-hours and kilocalories, are customary. All of these units translate to units of work, which is always defined in terms of forces and the distances that the forces act through.

A system can transfer energy to another system by simply transferring matter to it (since matter is equivalent to energy, in accordance with its mass). However, when energy is transferred by means other than matter-transfer, the transfer produces changes in the second system, as a result of work done on it. This work manifests itself as the effect of force(s) applied through distances within the target system. For example, a system can emit energy to another by transferring (radiating) electromagnetic energy, but this creates forces upon the particles that absorb the radiation. Similarly, a system may transfer energy to another by physically impacting it, but in that case the energy of motion in an object, called kinetic energy, results in forces acting over distances (new energy) to appear in another object that is struck. Transfer of thermal energy by heat occurs by both of these mechanisms: heat can be transferred by electromagnetic radiation, or by physical contact in which direct particle-particle impacts transfer kinetic energy.

Energy may be stored in systems without being present as matter, or as kinetic or electromagnetic energy. Stored energy is created whenever a particle has been moved through a field it interacts with (requiring a force to do so), but the energy to accomplish this is stored as a new position of the particles in the field—a configuration that must be "held" or fixed by a different type of force (otherwise, the new configuration would resolve itself by the field pushing or pulling the particle back towards its previous position). This type of energy "stored" by force-fields and particles that have been forced into a new physical configuration in the field by doing work on them by another system, is referred to as potential energy.

A simple example of potential energy is the work needed to lift an object in a gravity field, up to a support. Each of the basic forces of nature is associated with a different type of potential energy, and all types of potential energy (like all other types of energy) appears as system mass, whenever present. For example, a compressed spring will be slightly more massive than before it was compressed. Likewise, whenever energy is transferred between systems by any mechanism, an associated mass is transferred with it. Any form of energy may be transformed into another form. For example, all types of potential energy are converted into kinetic energy when the objects are given freedom to move to different position (as for example, when an object falls off a support). When energy is in a form other than thermal energy, it may be transformed with good or even perfect efficiency, to any other type of energy, including electricity or production of new particles of matter. With thermal energy, however, there are often limits to the efficiency of the conversion to other forms of energy, as described by the second law of thermodynamics.

In all such energy transformation processes, the total energy remains the same, and a transfer of energy from one system to another, results in a loss to compensate for any gain. This principle, the conservation of energy, was first postulated in the early 19th century, and applies to any isolated system. According to Noether's theorem, the conservation of energy is a consequence of the fact that the laws of physics do not change over time.

Although the total energy of a system does not change with time, its value may depend on the frame of reference. For example, a seated passenger in a moving airplane has zero kinetic energy relative to the airplane, but non-zero kinetic energy (and higher total energy) relative to the Earth.

Applications of the Perception of Energy

Energy is subject to a strict global conservation law; that is, whenever one measures (or calculates) the total energy of a system of particles whose interactions do not depend explicitly on time, it is found that the total energy of the system always remains constant.

- The total energy of a system can be subdivided and classified in various ways. For example, it is sometimes convenient to distinguish potential energy (which is a function of coordinates only) from kinetic energy (which is a function of coordinate time derivatives only). It may also be convenient to distinguish gravitational energy, electric energy, thermal energy, and other forms. These classifications overlap; for instance, thermal energy usually consists partly of kinetic and partly of potential energy.

- The *transfer* of energy can take various forms; familiar examples include work, heat flow, and advection.
- The word "energy" is also used outside of physics in many ways, which can lead to ambiguity and inconsistency. The vernacular terminology is not consistent with technical terminology. For example, while energy is always conserved (in the sense that the total energy does not change despite energy transformations), energy can be converted into a form, *e.g.*, thermal energy, that cannot be utilized to perform work. When one talks about "conserving energy by driving less," one talks about conserving fossil fuels and preventing useful energy from being lost as heat. This usage of "conserve" differs from that of the law of conservation of energy.

In classical physics energy is considered a scalar quantity, the canonical conjugate to time. In special relativity energy is also a scalar (although not a Lorentz scalar but a time component of the energy-momentum 4-vector). In other words, energy is invariant with respect to rotations of space, but not invariant with respect to rotations of space-time (= boosts).

Energy Transfer

Because energy is strictly conserved and is also locally conserved (wherever it can be defined), it is important to remember that by the definition of energy the transfer of energy between the "system" and adjacent regions is work. A familiar example is *mechanical work*. In simple cases this is written as the following equation:

$$\Delta E = W$$

if there are no other energy-transfer processes involved. Here E is the amount of energy transferred, and W represents the work done on the system.

More generally, the energy transfer can be split into two categories:

$$\Delta E = W + Q$$

Where Q represents the heat flow into the system.

There are other ways in which an open system can gain or lose energy. In chemical systems, energy can be added to a system by means of adding substances with different chemical potentials, which potentials are then extracted (both of these process are illustrated by fueling an auto, a system which gains in energy thereby, without addition of either work or heat). Winding a clock would be adding energy to a mechanical system.

These terms may be added to the above equation, or they can generally be subsumed into a quantity called "energy addition term E" which refers to *any* type of energy carried over the surface of a control volume or system volume. Examples may be seen above, and many others can be imagined (for example, the kinetic energy of a stream of particles entering a system, or energy from a laser beam adds to system energy, without either being either work-done or heat-added, in the classic senses).

$$\Delta E = W + Q + E$$

Where E in this general equation represents other additional advected energy terms not covered by work done on a system, or heat added to it.

Energy is also transferred from potential energy (E_p) to kinetic energy (E_k) and then back to potential energy constantly.

This is referred to as conservation of energy. In this closed system, energy cannot be created or destroyed; therefore, the initial energy and the final energy will be equal to each other. This can be demonstrated by the following:

$$E_{pi} + E_{ki} = E_{pF} + E_{kF}$$

The equation can then be simplified further since $E_p = mgh$ (mass times acceleration due to gravity times the height) and $E_k = \frac{1}{2}mv^2$ (half mass times velocity squared). Then the total amount of energy can be found by adding $E_p + E_k = E_{total}$.

Conservation of Energy

Energy is subject to the law of conservation of energy. According to this law, energy can neither be created (produced) nor destroyed by itself. It can only be transformed.

Most kinds of energy (with gravitational energy being a notable exception) are subject to strict local conservation laws as well.

In this case, energy can only be exchanged between adjacent regions of space, and all observers agree as to the volumetric density of energy in any given space. There is also a global law of conservation of energy, stating that the total energy of the universe cannot change; this is a corollary of the local law, but not vice versa. Conservation of energy is the mathematical consequence of translational symmetry of time (that is, the indistinguishability of time intervals taken at different time).

According to Conservation of energy the total inflow of energy into a system must equal the total outflow of energy from the system, plus the change in the energy contained within the system.

This law is a fundamental principle of physics. It follows from the translational symmetry of time, a property of most phenomena below the cosmic scale that makes them independent of their locations on the time coordinate. Put differently, yesterday, today, and tomorrow are physically indistinguishable.

This is because energy is the quantity which is canonical conjugate to time. This mathematical entanglement of energy and time also results in the uncertainty principle - it is impossible to define the exact amount of energy during any definite time interval. The uncertainty principle should not be confused with energy conservation - rather it provides mathematical limits to which energy can in principle be defined and measured.

In quantum mechanics energy is expressed using the Hamiltonian operator. On any time scales, the uncertainty in the energy is by

$$\Delta E \Delta t \geq \frac{\hbar}{2}$$

which is similar in form to the Heisenberg uncertainty principle (but not really mathematically equivalent thereto, since H and t are not dynamically conjugate variables, neither in classical nor in quantum mechanics).

In particle physics, this inequality permits a qualitative understanding of virtual particles which carry momentum, exchange by which and with real particles, is responsible for the creation of all known fundamental forces (more accurately known as fundamental interactions). Virtual photons (which are simply lowest quantum mechanical energy state of photons) are also responsible for electrostatic interaction between electric charges (which results in Coulomb law), for spontaneous radiative decay of exited atomic and nuclear states, for the Casimir force, for van der Waals bond forces and some other observable phenomena.

Energy and the Laws of Motion

In classical mechanics, energy is a conceptually and mathematically useful property, as it is a conserved quantity. Several formulations of mechanics have been developed using energy as a core concept.

The Hamiltonian

The total energy of a system is sometimes called the Hamiltonian, after William Rowan Hamilton. The classical equations of motion can be written in terms of the Hamiltonian, even for highly complex or abstract systems. These classical equations have remarkably direct analogs in nonrelativistic quantum mechanics.

The Lagrangian

Another energy-related concept is called the Lagrangian, after Joseph Louis Lagrange. This is even more fundamental than the Hamiltonian, and can be used to derive the equations of motion. It was invented in the context of classical mechanics, but is generally useful in modern physics. The Lagrangian is defined as the kinetic energy *minus* the potential energy. Usually, the Lagrange formalism is mathematically more convenient than the Hamiltonian for non-conservative systems (such as systems with friction).

Noether's Theorem

Noether's (first) theorem (1918) states that any differentiable symmetry of the action of a physical system has a corresponding conservation law. Noether's theorem has become a fundamental tool of modern theoretical physics and the calculus of variations. A generalization of the seminal formulations on constants of motion in Lagrangian and Hamiltonian mechanics (1788 and 1833, respectively), it does not apply to systems that cannot be modelled with a Lagrangian; for example, dissipative systems with continuous symmetries need not have a corresponding conservation law.

Energy and Thermodynamics

Internal Energy

Internal energy is the sum of all microscopic forms of energy of a system. It is the energy needed to create the system. It is related to the potential energy, *e.g.*, molecular structure, crystal structure, and other geometric aspects, as well as the motion of the particles, in form of kinetic energy. Thermodynamics is chiefly concerned with changes in internal energy and not its absolute value, which is impossible to determine with thermodynamics alone.

The First Law of Thermodynamics

The first law of thermodynamics asserts that energy is conserved and that heat flow is a form of energy transfer. For homogeneous systems, with a well-defined temperature and pressure, a commonly used corollary of the first law is that, for a system subject only to pressure forces and heat transfer (*e.g.*, a cylinder-full of gas), the differential change in the internal energy of the system (with a *gain* in energy signified by a positive quantity) is given as

$$dE = TdS - PdV,$$

where the first term on the right is the heat transfered into the system, expressed in terms of temperature T and entropy S (in which entropy increases and the change dS is positive when the system is heated), and the last term on the right hand side is identified as work done on the system, where pressure is P and volume V (the negative sign results since compression of the system requires work to be done on it and so the volume change, dV, is negative when work is done on the system).

This equation is highly specific, ignoring all chemical, electrical, nuclear, and gravitational forces, effects such as advection of any form of energy other than heat and pV-work. The general formulation of the first law (*i.e.*, conservation of energy) is valid even in situations in which the system is not homogeneous. For these cases the change in internal energy of a *closed* system is expressed in a general form by

$$dE = \delta Q + \delta W$$

where δQ is the heat supplied to the system and is the work applied to the system.

Equipartition of Energy

The energy of a mechanical harmonic oscillator (a mass on a spring) is alternatively kinetic and potential. At two points in the oscillation cycle it is entirely kinetic, and alternatively at two other points it is entirely potential. Over the whole cycle, or over many cycles, net energy is thus equally split between kinetic and potential. This is called equipartition principle; total energy of a system with many degrees of freedom is equally split among all available degrees of freedom.

This principle is vitally important to understanding the behaviour of a quantity closely related to energy, called entropy. Entropy is a measure of evenness of a distribution of energy between parts of a system. When an isolated system is given more degrees of freedom (*i.e.*, given new available energy states that are the same as existing states), then total energy spreads over all available degrees equally without distinction between "new" and "old" degrees. This mathematical result is called the second law of thermodynamics.

Oscillators, Phonons and Photons

In an ensemble (connected collection) of unsynchronized oscillators, the average energy is spread equally between kinetic and potential types. In a solid, thermal energy (often referred to loosely as heat content) can be accurately described by an ensemble of thermal phonons that act as mechanical oscillators. In this model, thermal energy is equally kinetic and potential.

In an ideal gas, the interaction potential between particles is essentially the delta function which stores no energy: thus, all of the thermal energy is kinetic.

Because an electric oscillator (LC circuit) is analogous to a mechanical oscillator, its energy must be, on average, equally kinetic and potential. It is entirely arbitrary whether the magnetic energy is considered kinetic and whether the electric energy is considered potential, or vice versa. That is, either the inductor is analogous to the mass while the capacitor is analogous to the spring, or vice versa.

- By extension of the previous line of thought, in free space the electromagnetic field can be considered an ensemble of oscillators, meaning that radiation energy can be considered equally potential and kinetic. This model is useful, for example, when the electromagnetic Lagrangian is of primary interest and is interpreted in terms of potential and kinetic energy.

- On the other hand, in the key equation $m^2c^4 = E^2 - p^2c^2$, the contribution mc^2 is called the rest energy, and all other contributions to the energy are called kinetic energy. For a particle that has mass, this implies that the kinetic energy is 0.5 p^2/m at speeds much smaller than c, as can be proved by writing

  $$E = mc^2\sqrt{(1+p^2m^{-2}c^{-2})}$$

  and expanding the square root to lowest order. By this line of reasoning, the energy of a photon is entirely kinetic, because the photon is massless and has no rest energy. This expression is useful, for example, when the energy-versus-momentum relationship is of primary interest.

The two analyses are entirely consistent. The electric and magnetic degrees of freedom in item 1 are *transverse* to the direction of motion, while the speed in item 2 is *along* the direction of motion. For non-relativistic particles these two notions of potential versus kinetic energy are numerically equal, so the ambiguity is harmless, but not so for relativistic particles.

Work and Virtual Work

Work, a form of energy, is force times distance.

$$W = \int_C F \cdot ds$$

This says that the work (W) is equal to the line integral of the force F along a path C.

Work and thus energy is frame dependent. For example, consider a ball being hit by a bat. In the centre-of-mass reference frame, the bat does no work on the ball. But, in the reference frame of the person swinging the bat, considerable work is done on the ball.

Quantum Mechanics

In quantum mechanics energy is defined in terms of the energy operator as a time derivative of the wave function. The Schrödinger equation equates the energy operator to the full energy of a particle or a system. In results can be considered as a definition of measurement of energy in quantum mechanics. The Schrödinger equation describes the space- and time-dependence of slow changing (non-relativistic) wave function of quantum systems.

The solution of this equation for bound system is discrete (a set of permitted states, each characterized by an energy level) which results in the concept of quanta. In the solution of the Schrödinger equation for any oscillator (vibrator) and for electromagnetic waves in a vacuum, the resulting energy states are related to the frequency by the Planck equation $E = h\nu$ (where h is the Planck's constant and the frequency). In the case of electromagnetic wave these energy states are called quanta of light or photons.

Relativity

When calculating kinetic energy (work to accelerate a mass from zero speed to some finite speed) relativistically - using Lorentz transformations instead of Newtonian mechanics, Einstein discovered an unexpected by-product of these calculations to be an energy term which does not vanish at zero speed. He called it rest mass energy - energy which every mass must possess even when being at rest. The amount of energy is directly proportional to the mass of body:

$$E = mc^2,$$

where;

m is the mass,

c is the speed of light in vacuum,

E is the rest mass energy.

For example, consider electron-positron annihilation, in which the rest mass of individual particles is destroyed, but the inertia equivalent of the system of the two particles (its invariant mass) remains (since all energy is associated with mass), and this inertia and invariant mass is carried off by photons which individually are massless, but as a system retain their mass. This is a reversible process - the inverse process is called pair creation - in which the rest mass of particles is created from energy of two (or more) annihilating photons. In this system the matter (electrons and positrons) is destroyed and changed to non-matter energy (the photons). However, the total system mass and energy do not change during this interaction.

In general relativity, the stress-energy tensor serves as the source term for the gravitational field, in rough analogy to the way mass serves as the source term in the non-relativistic Newtonian approximation.

It is not uncommon to hear that energy is "equivalent" to mass. It would be more accurate to state that every energy has an inertia and gravity equivalent, and because mass is a form of energy, then mass too has inertia and gravity associated with it.

Energy and Life

Any living organism relies on an external source of energy-radiation from the Sun in the case of green plants; chemical energy in some form in the case of animals—to be able to grow and reproduce. The daily 1500–2000 Calories (6-8 MJ) recommended for a human adult are taken as a combination of oxygen and food molecules, the latter mostly carbohydrates and fats, of which glucose ($C_6H_{12}O_6$) and stearin ($C_{57}H_{110}O_6$) are convenient examples. The food molecules are oxidised to carbon dioxide and water in the mitochondria

$$C_6H_{12}O_6 + 6O_2 \rightarrow 6CO_2 + 6H_2O$$

$$C_{57}H_{110}O_6 + 81.5O_2 \rightarrow 57CO_2 + 55H_2O$$

and some of the energy is used to convert ADP into ATP

$$ADP + HPO_4^{2-} \rightarrow ATP + H_2O$$

The rest of the chemical energy in the carbohydrate or fat is converted into heat: the ATP is used as a sort of "energy currency", and some of the chemical energy it contains when split and reacted with water, is used for other metabolism (at each stage of a metabolic pathway, some chemical energy is converted into heat). Only a tiny fraction of the original chemical energy is used for work:

- Gain in kinetic energy of a sprinter during a 100 m race: 4 kJ
- Gain in gravitational potential energy of a 150 kg weight lifted through 2 metres: 3kJ
- Daily food intake of a normal adult: 6–8 MJ.

It would appear that living organisms are remarkably inefficient (in the physical sense) in their use of the energy they receive (chemical energy or radiation), and it is true that most real machines manage higher efficiencies. In growing organisms the energy that is converted to heat serves a vital purpose, as it allows the organism tissue to be highly ordered with regard to the molecules it is built from. The second law of thermodynamics states that energy (and matter) tends to become more evenly spread out across the universe: to concentrate energy (or matter) in one specific place, it is necessary to spread out a greater amount of energy (as heat) across the remainder of the universe ("the surroundings"). Simpler organisms can achieve higher energy efficiencies than more complex ones, but the complex organisms can occupy ecological niches that are not available to their simpler brethren. The conversion of a portion of the chemical energy to heat at each step in a metabolic pathway is the physical reason behind the pyramid of biomass observed in ecology: to take just the first step in the food chain, of the estimated 124.7 Pg/a of carbon that is fixed by photosynthesis, 64.3 Pg/a (52%) are used for the metabolism of green plants, *i.e.* reconverted into carbon dioxide and heat.

PHYSICAL MECHANICAL WORK

In physics, mechanical work is a scalar quantity that can be described as the product of a force times the distance through which it acts, and it is called *the work of the force*. Only the component of a force in the direction of the movement of its point of application does work. The term *work* was first coined in 1826 by the French mathematician Gaspard-Gustave Coriolis.

If a constant force of magnitude F acts on a point that moves d in the direction of the force, then the work W done by this force is calculated $W = Fd$. For example, if a force of 10 newtons (F = 10 N) acts along a path of 2 metres (d = 2 m), it will do work W equal to W = (10 N)(2 m) = 20 Nm = 20 J, where joule (J) is the SI unit for work (defined as the product Nm, so that a joule is a newton-metre).

For moving objects, the quantity of work/time enters calculations as distance/time, or velocity. Thus, at any instant, the rate of the work done by a force (measured in joules/second, or watts) is the scalar product of the force (a vector) with the velocity vector of the point of application. This scalar product of force and velocity is called instantaneous power. Just as velocities may be integrated over time to obtain a total distance, by the fundamental theorem of calculus, the total work along a path is similarly the time-integral of instantaneous power applied along the trajectory of the point of application.

The first law of thermodynamics states that when work is done to a system (and no other energy is subtracted in other ways), the system's energy state changes by the same amount of the work input. This equates work and energy. In the case of rigid bodies, Newton's laws can be used to derive a similar relationship called the work-energy theorem.

Work and Kinetic Energy

According to the work-energy theorem, if one or more external forces act upon a rigid object, causing its kinetic energy to change from E_{k1} to E_{k2}, then the work (W) done by the net force is equal to the change in kinetic energy. For translational motion, the theorem can be specified as:

$$W = \Delta E_k = E_{k2} - E_{k1} = \frac{1}{2}m(v_2^2 - v_1^2)$$

where m is the mass of the object and v is the object's velocity.

The theorem is particularly simple to prove for a constant force acting in the direction of motion along a straight line. For more complex cases, however, *e.g.*, a curvilinear path or a variable force (or both), we can use integration to get the same result. In rigid body dynamics, a formula equating work and the change in kinetic energy of the system is obtained as a first integral of Newton's second law of motion.

To see this, consider a particle P that follows the trajectory X(t) with a force F acting on it. Newton's second law provides a relationship between the force and the acceleration of the particle as

$$\mathrm{F} = m\ddot{\mathrm{X}},$$

where m is the mass of the particle.

The scalar product of each side of Newton's law with the velocity vector yields

$$\mathrm{F}\cdot\dot{\mathrm{X}} = m\ddot{\mathrm{X}}\cdot\dot{\mathrm{X}},$$

which is integrated from the point $X(t_1)$ to the point $X(t_2)$ to obtain

$$\int_{t_1}^{t_2} \mathrm{F}\cdot\dot{\mathrm{X}}\,dt = m\int_{t_1}^{t_2} \ddot{\mathrm{X}}\cdot\dot{\mathrm{X}}\,dt.$$

The left side of this equation is the work of the force as it acts on the particle along the trajectory from time t_1 to time t_2. This can also be written as

$$W = \int_{t_1}^{t_2} \mathrm{F}\cdot\dot{\mathrm{X}}\,dt = \int_{X(t_1)}^{X(t_2)} \ddot{\mathrm{F}}\cdot d\mathbf{X}.$$

This integral is computed along the trajectory X(t) of the particle and is therefore path dependent.

The right side of the first integral of Newton's equations can be simplified using the following identity

$$\frac{1}{2}\frac{d}{dt}(\dot{\mathrm{X}}\cdot\dot{\mathrm{X}}) = \ddot{\mathrm{X}}\cdot\dot{\mathrm{X}},$$

which is obtained using the product rule and which can be integrated explicitly to obtain the change in kinetic energy,

$$\Delta K = m\int_{t_1}^{t_2} \ddot{X}\cdot\dot{X}\,dt = \frac{m}{2}\int_{t_1}^{t_2} \frac{d}{dt}(\dot{X}\cdot\dot{X})dt = \frac{m}{2}\dot{X}\cdot\dot{X}(t_2) - \frac{m}{2}\dot{X}\cdot\dot{X}(t_1),$$

where the kinetic energy of the particle is defined by the scalar quantity,

$$K = \frac{m}{2}\dot{X}\cdot\dot{X}.$$

The result is the work-energy principle for rigid body dynamics,

$$W = \Delta K.$$

This derivation can be generalized to arbitrary rigid body systems.

TORQUE: MOMENT OF FORCE

Torque, moment or moment of force, is the tendency of a force to rotate an object about an axis, fulcrum, or pivot. Just as a force is a push or a pull, a torque can be thought of as a twist to an object.

Loosely speaking, torque is a measure of the turning force on an object such as a bolt or a flywheel. For example, pushing or pulling the handle of a wrench connected to a nut or bolt produces a torque (turning force) that loosens or tightens the nut or bolt. The symbol for torque is typically τ, the Greek letter *tau*. When it is called moment, it is commonly denoted *M*.

The magnitude of torque depends on three quantities: the force applied, the length of the *lever arm* connecting the axis to the point of force application, and the angle between the force vector and the lever arm. In symbols:

$$\tau = \mathbf{r} \times \mathbf{F}$$

$$\tau = rF\sin\theta$$

where

- τ is the torque vector and τ is the magnitude of the torque,
- r is the displacement vector (a vector from the point from which torque is measured to the point where

force is applied), and *r* is the length (or magnitude) of the lever arm vector,

F is the force vector, and *F* is the magnitude of the force,

× denotes the cross product,

θ is the angle between the force vector and the lever arm vector.

The length of the lever arm is particularly important; choosing this length appropriately lies behind the operation of levers, pulleys, gears, and most other simple machines involving a mechanical advantage.

PHYSICAL POWER

Power is the rate at which energy is transferred, used, or transformed. For example, the rate at which a light bulb transforms electrical energy into heat and light is measured in watts-the more wattage, the more power, or equivalently the more electrical energy is used per unit time.

Energy transfer can be used to do work, so power is also the rate at which this work is performed. The output power of an electric motor is the product of the torque the motor generates and the angular velocity of its output shaft. The power expended to move a vehicle is the product of the traction force of the wheels and the velocity of the vehicle. The integral of power over time defines the work done. Because this integral depends on the trajectory of the point of application of the force and torque, this calculation of work is said to be "path dependent".

Average Power

As a simple example, burning a kilogram of coal releases much more energy than does detonating a kilogram of TNT, but because the TNT reaction releases energy much more quickly, it delivers far more power than the coal. If ΔW is the amount of work performed during a period of time of duration Δt, the average power P_{avg} over that period is given by the formula

$$P_{avg} = \frac{\Delta W}{\Delta t}.$$

It is the average amount of work done or energy converted per unit of time. The average power is often simply called "power" when the context makes it clear.

The instantaneous power is then the limiting value of the average power as the time interval Δt approaches zero.

$$P = \lim_{\Delta t \to 0} P_{avg} = \lim_{\Delta t \to 0} \frac{\Delta W}{\Delta t} = \frac{dW}{dt}.$$

In the case of constant power P, the amount of work performed during a period of duration T is given by:

$$W = PT.$$

In the context of energy conversion it is more customary to use the symbol E rather than W.

Mechanical Power

Power in mechanical systems is the combination of forces and movement. In particular, power is the product of a force on an object and the object's velocity, or the product of a torque on a shaft and the shaft's angular velocity. Mechanical power is also described as the time derivative of work. In mechanics, the work done by a force F on an object that travels along a curve C is given by the line integral:

$$W_C = \int_C F \cdot dx = \int_C F \cdot v dt,$$

where x defines the path C and v is the velocity along this path. The time derivative of the equation for work yields the instantaneous power,

$$P(t) = F \cdot v.$$

In rotational systems, power is the product of the torque τ and angular velocity ω,

$$P(t) = \tau\omega,$$

where ω measured in radians per second.

In fluid power systems such as hydraulic actuators, power is given by

$$P(t) = pQ,$$

where p is pressure in pascals, or N/m^2 and Q is volumetric flow rate in m^3/s in SI units.

Mechanical Advantage

If a mechanical system has no losses then the input power must equivalent the output power. This provides a simple formula for the mechanical advantage of the system. Let the input power to a device be a force F_A acting on a point that moves with velocity v_A and the output power be a force F_B acts on a point that moves with velocity v_B. If there are no losses in the system, then

$$P = F_A v_A = F_B v_B,$$

and the mechanical advantage of the system is given by

$$MA = \frac{F_B}{F_A} = \frac{v_A}{v_B}.$$

A similar relationship is obtained for rotating systems, where T_A and ω_A are the torque and angular velocity of the input and T_B and ω_B are the torque and angular velocity of the output. If there are no losses in the system, then

$$P = T_A \omega_A = T_B \omega_B,$$

which yields the mechanical advantage

$$MA = \frac{T_B}{T_A} = \frac{\omega_A}{\omega_B}.$$

These relations are important because they define the maximum performance of a device in terms of velocity ratios determined by its physical dimensions.

Electrical Power

The instantaneous electrical power P delivered to a component is given by

$$P(t) = I(t) \cdot V(t)$$

where;

$P(t)$ is the instantaneous power, measured in watts (joules per second)

$V(t)$ is the potential difference (or voltage drop) across the component, measured in volts

$I(t)$ is the current through it, measured in amperes

If the component is a resistor with time-invariant voltage to current ratio, then:

$$P = I \cdot V = I^2 \cdot R = \frac{V^2}{R}$$

where

$$R = V / I$$

is the resistance, measured in ohms.

Peak Power and Duty Cycle

In the case of a periodic signal $s(t)$ of period T, like a train of identical pulses, the instantaneous power $p(t) = |s(t)|^2$ is also a periodic function of period T. The *peak power* is simply defined by:

$$P_0 = \max[p(t)].$$

The peak power is not always readily measurable, however, and the measurement of the average power P_{avg} is more commonly performed by an instrument. If one defines the energy per pulse as:

$$\epsilon_{pulse} = \int_0^T p(t)dt$$

then the average power is:

$$P_{avg} = \frac{1}{T}\int_0^T p(t)dt = \frac{\epsilon_{pulse}}{T}.$$

One may define the pulse length τ such that $P_0\tau = \epsilon_{pulse}$ so that the ratios

$$\frac{P_{avg}}{P_0} = \frac{\tau}{T}$$

are equal. These ratios are called the *duty cycle* of the pulse train.

Chapter 3

Principles of Quantum Mechanics

QUANTUM MECHANICS

Quantum Mechanics (QM) is a relatively new ground of physics that was developed at the beginning of the last century as the common effort of different scientists. Up to that time, it was possible to describe all known physical phenomena with the laws of classical physics as either *particles* (classical mechanics, kinematics) or *waves* (optics, classical electromagnetism). The detection of new phenomena such as *e.g.* the *photoelectric effect* has lead to the development of a new physics that has revolutionized the way we look at the world around us. Many insights from quantum mechanics are at primary sight counterintuitive (*i.e.* they differ substantially from what we would expect in a classical picture!) which makes this field one of the most fascinating areas of modern physics. Quantum mechanics is a branch of physics dealing with physical phenomena where the action is on the arrange of the Planck constant. Quantum mechanics departs from classical mechanics primarily at the *quantum realm* of atomic and subatomic length scales. QM provides a mathematical description of much of the dual *particle-like* and *wave-like* behaviour and interactions of energy and matter.

In advanced topics of quantum mechanics, some of these behaviours are macroscopic and only emerge at extreme (*i.e.,* very low or very high) energies or temperatures. The name *quantum mechanics* derives from the observation that some physical quantities can change only in *discrete* amounts (Latin *quanta*), and not in a continuous (*cf.* analog) way. For example, the angular momentum of an electron bound to an atom or molecule is quantized. In the context of quantum mechanics, the wave-particle duality of energy and matter and the uncertainty principle provide a unified view of the behaviour of photons, electrons, and other atomic-scale objects.

The mathematical formulations of quantum mechanics are abstract. A mathematical purpose called the wavefunction provides information about the probability amplitude of position, momentum, and other physical properties of a particle. Mathematical manipulations of the wavefunction usually involve the braket notation, which requires an understanding of complex numbers and linear functionals. The wavefunction treats the object as a quantum harmonic oscillator, and the mathematics is akin to that describing acoustic resonance. Many of the results of quantum mechanics are not easily visualized in terms of classical mechanics - for instance, the ground state in a quantum mechanical model is a non-zero energy state that is the lowest permitted energy state of a system, as opposed a more "traditional" system that is thought of as simply being at rest, with zero kinetic energy. Instead of a traditional static, unchanging zero state, quantum mechanics allows for far more dynamic, chaotic possibilities, according to John Wheeler.

The earliest versions of quantum mechanics were formulated in the first decade of the 20th century. At around the same time, the atomic theory and the corpuscular theory of light (as updated by Einstein) first came to be widely accepted as scientific fact; these latter theories can be viewed as quantum theories of matter and electromagnetic radiation, respectively. Early quantum theory was significantly reformulated in the mid-1920s by Werner Heisenberg, Max Born, Wolfgang Pauli and their collaborators, and the Copenhagen interpretation of Niels Bohr became widely accepted. By 1930, quantum mechanics had been further unified and formalized by the work of Paul Dirac and John von Neumann, with a greater emphasis placed on measurement in quantum mechanics, the statistical nature of our knowledge of reality, and philosophical speculation about the role of the observer.

Quantum mechanics has since branched out into almost every aspect of 20th century physics and other disciplines, such as quantum chemistry, quantum electronics, quantum optics, and quantum information science. Much 19th century physics has been re-evaluated as the "classical limit" of quantum mechanics, and its more advanced developments in terms of quantum field theory, string theory, and speculative quantum gravity theories.

Particles and Waves

All phenomena in classical physics can be described either as a particle or a wave.

Wave-functions and Operators

The theory of quantum mechanics is built upon the fundamental concepts of *wave-functions* and *operators*. The wave-function is a single-valued square-integrable function of the system parameters and time which provides a complete description of the system. Linear Hermitian operators act on the wave-function and correspond to the physical *observables*, those dynamical variables which can be measured, *e.g.* position, momentum and energy.

For systems of atomic nuclei and electrons, which are the subject of this dissertation, the system parameters might be taken to be a set of position variables of the constituent particles *i.e.*, $\{(\mathrm{r}_i),(\mathrm{r}_\alpha)\}$ their momenta $\{(\mathrm{p}_i)$, (p_α) or even a mixture of the two *e.g.* $\{(\mathrm{r}_i),(\mathrm{p}_\alpha)\}$. In contrast to a Newtonian system which is completely described by the positions *and* momenta of its constituents, the quantum-mechanical wave-function is a function of only one of these parameters per particle. The wave-function for the system is thus typically denoted by $\psi\{(\mathrm{r}_i),(\mathrm{r}_\alpha),t\}$.

A notation due to Dirac is often employed, which reflects the fact that this wave-function is simply one of many representations of a single *state-vector* in a Hilbert space, which is written as $|\Psi\rangle$, known as a *ket*.

There also exists a *dual space* containing a set of *bra* vectors, denoted $|\Psi\rangle$, defined by their scalar products and in one-to-one correspondence with the kets.

The scalar product is written as a *braket* and is anti-linear in the first argument and linear in the second: thus $|\Psi | \Phi\rangle = (\langle\Psi | \Phi\rangle)^*$.

It is worth noting here that state-vectors which differ only by a multiplicative non-zero complex constant describe the same state: we can thus restrict our interest to the set of *normalised* vectors defined such that the scalar product of the vector with its own conjugate equals unity:

$$\langle\Psi | \Psi\rangle = \int \prod_j dr_\beta \, \Psi^* \left(\{r_i\},\{r_a\},t\right) = 1.$$

The operator corresponding to some observable O is often written $\hat{O}$, and in general when this operator acts on some state-vector $|\Psi\rangle$, a different (not necessarily normalised) state-vector $|\Phi\rangle$ results:

$$\hat{O} | \Psi\rangle = | \Phi\rangle.$$

However, for each operator there exists a set of normalised *eigenstates*, say $\{|\chi_n\rangle\}$, which remain unchanged by the action of the operator *i.e.*

$$\hat{O} | \chi_n\rangle = \lambda_n | \chi_n\rangle$$

in which the constant λ_n (always real for Hermitian operators) is the *eigenvalue*.

The postulates of quantum mechanics state that for a system in state $|\Psi\rangle$:

- the outcome of a measurement of a dynamical variable is always one of the eigenvalues λ_n of the corresponding operator,

- immediately following a measurement, the state-vector collapses to the eigenstate $|\chi_n\rangle$ corresponding to the measured eigenvalue,
- the probability of such a measurement is

$P(\lambda_n) = |\langle\chi_n|\Psi\rangle|^2$.

Wave Phenomena

Not all phenomena of classical physics are describable in a particle picture. A second large class of physical events can be described as *waves*. A *wave* is a disturbance that propagates through space or space and time, often transferring energy.

From every day live, you are already familiar with many wave phenomena, such as for instance water waves or sound waves (periodical compressions of air that travel through space and can be detected by a mechanosensitive device in your inner ear).

Water waves and sound waves are examples for mechanical waves that exist in a medium (which on deformation is capable of producing elastic restoring forces).

Wave Phenomena: Interference and Diffraction

Waves can exhibit phenomena that cannot be explain in a classical particle pictures. Typical such wave phenomena are interference and diffraction. Two or more waves can superimpose and form a new wave, this effect is called interference. When two sinusoidal waves place over, the resulting waveform depends on the frequency, the amplitude and in particular on the relative difference in phase (the *phase shift*) of the two waves.

If the two waves have the same amplitude A and wavelength the resultant waveform will have an amplitude between 0 and $2A$ depending on whether the two waves are *in phase* (*i.e.* both waves have their minima and maxima at exactly the same time) or *out of phase* (*i.e.* one wave has a maximum when the other one has a minimum). Consider two waves that are in phase, with amplitudes A_1 and A_2. Their troughs and peaks line up and the resultant wave will have an amplitude $A = A_1 + A_2$. This is known as *constructive interference*.

If the two waves are π radians, or 180°, out of phase, then one wave's crests will coincide with another wave's troughs and so will tend to cancel out. The resultant amplitude is A = | A1 - A2 |. If A1 = A2, the resultant amplitude will be zero. This is known as *destructive interference*.

DE BROGLIE HYPOTHESIS

After Albert Einstein's photon theory became accepted, the query became whether this was true only for light or whether material objects also exhibited wave-like behaviour. In quantum mechanics (QM) particles and waves have identity crises because one can act as a particle or a wave; and when not a particle, its "matter-wave" has a frequency proportional to its kinetic and relativistic energy.

Motivated by this, and a number of similarities between QM and time-frequency analysis (TFA), comes the idea that signals can be represented and synthesized by an dynamic system of particles construed as waves. Vice versa, a sound might be "materialized" into its corresponding system of particles, and modifications made in that domain to synthesize variants. Essentially what is developed here is a technique of sound work of art using classical many-body mechanics with the most natural mapping of parameters. Such a direct mapping of both multi-dimensional fields not only allows an interchange of concepts to enrich both, for instance sonifying particle collisions for musical purposes, but also enables an additional level of comprehension of the underlying physical concepts—an important goal of sonification. Consequently, when using this technique for composition and synthesis, the composer must also possess skill in physics to do an effective job. Interestingly, it has been observed that, when composing with these techniques, the compositional and scientific concerns merge into the "composerscientist"—a state of thought where physics and music become identical.

It has also been found that the audience need not be versed

in physics to appreciate or enjoy what they hear; however, more compositions need to be developed to explore this experience.

Separately from these concepts, some problematic issues currently exist in the system and its execution. The computational complexity required for physical subdivision simulations can be enormous, and when compounded with requirements for audio, there is a large latency period between execution and resultant signal. If precaution is not taken, one is at risk of spending several hours for a sound that could have more easily been produced, albeit without a "physical" correspondence. It can be said that even if a simple sound were created, one would hear it differently because of what it represents. Thus there exists a programmatic issue, whereby a composition developed through this technique might only be interesting within this context. In addition to these, psychoacoustic principles have yet to be integrated to facilitate a more perceivable and precise audification of the system. These issues, and more, will obviously be addressed in future work.

De Broglie's Thesis

In his 1923 (or 1924, depending on the source) doctoral dissertation, the French physicist Louis de Broglie made a bold assertion. Considering Einstein's relationship of wavelength *lambda* (λ) to momentum p, de Broglie proposed that this relationship would determine the wavelength of any matter, in the relationship:

$$\lambda = h/p$$

recall that h is Planck's constant.

This wavelength is called the *de Broglie wavelength*. The reason he chose the momentum equation over the energy equation is that it was unclear, with matter, whether E should be total energy, kinetic energy, or total relativistic energy. For photons they are all the same, but not so for matter.

Assuming the momentum relationship, however, allowed the derivation of a similar de Broglie relationship for frequency f using the kinetic energy E_k:

$f = E_k/h$

Alternate Formulations

De Broglie's relationships are sometimes expressed in terms of Dirac's constant, $\hbar = h/(2\pi)$, and the angular frequency w and wavenumber k:

$$p = \hbar k$$

$$E_k = \hbar w.$$

Experimental Confirmation

In 1927, physicists Clinton Davisson and Lester Germer, of Bell Labs, performed an experiment where they passionate electrons at a crystalline nickel target.

The resulting diffraction pattern matched the predictions of the de Broglie wavelength.

De Broglie received the 1929 Nobel Prize for his theory (the first time it was ever awarded for a Ph.D. thesis) and Davisson/Germer jointly won it in 1937 for the experimental discovery of electron diffraction (and thus the proving of de Broglie's hypothesis).

Further experiments have held de Broglie's hypothesis to be true, including the quantum variants of the double slit experiment.

Diffraction experiments in 1999 confirmed the de Broglie wavelength for the behaviour of molecules as large as buckeyballs (complex molecules made up of 60 or more carbon atoms).

Significance of the de Broglie Hypothesis

The de Broglie hypothesis showed that wave particle duality was not merely an aberrant behaviour of light, but rather was a fundamental principle exhibited by both radiation and matter. As such, it becomes possible to use wave equations to describe material behaviour, so long as one properly applies the de Broglie wavelength. This would prove crucial to the development of quantum mechanics.

Macroscopic Objects and Wavelength

Though de Broglie's hypothesis predicts wavelengths for matter of any size, there are realistic limits on when it's helpful. A baseball thrown at a pitcher has a de Broglie wavelength that is smaller than than the diameter of a proton... by about 20 orders of magnitude. The wave aspects of a macroscopic object are so tiny as to be unobservable in any useful sense.

Photoelectric Effect

Though at first observed in 1839, the photoelectric effect was documented by Heinrich Hertz in 1887 in a paper to the *Annalen der Physik*. It was originally called the Hertz effect, in fact, though this name fell out of use. When a light source (or, more generally, electromagnetic radiation) is incident upon a metallic surface, the surface can emit electrons. Electrons emitted in this fashion are called *photoelectrons* (although they are still just electrons).

Setting Up the Photoelectric Effect

To observe the photoelectric result, you create a vacuum chamber with the photoconductive metal at one end and a collector at the other. When a light shines on the metal, the electrons are released and move through the vacuum towards the collector.

By administering a negative voltage potential (the black box in the picture) to the collector, it takes more energy for the electrons to complete the journey and initiate the current. The point at which no electrons make it to the collector is called the stopping potential V_s, and can be used to determine the maximum kinetic energy K_{max} of the electrons (which have electronic charge e) by using the following equation:

$$K_{max} = eV_s$$

It is significant to note that not all of the electrons will have this energy, but will be emitted with a range of energies based upon the properties of the metal being used. The above equation allows us to calculate the maximum kinetic energy or, in other words, the energy of the particles knocked free of the metal surface with the greatest speed, which will be the trait that is most useful in the rest of this analysis.

The Classical Wave Explanation

In classical wave theory, the energy of electromagnetic radiation is carried within the wave itself. As the electromagnetic wave (of intensity *I*) collides with the surface, the electron absorbs the energy from the wave until it exceeds the binding energy, releasing the electron from the metal. The minimum energy needed to remove the electron is the *work function phi* (ϕ) of the material. (ϕ is in the range of a few electron-volts for most common photoelectric materials.) Three main predictions come from this classical explanation:

- The intensity of the radiation should have a proportional relationship with the resulting maximum kinetic energy.
- The photoelectric effect should occur for any light, regardless of frequency or wavelength.
- There should be a delay on the order of seconds between the radiation's contact with the metal and the initial release of photoelectrons.

The Experimental Consequence

By 1902, the properties of the photoelectric consequence were well documented. Experiment showed that:

- The intensity of the light source had no effect on the maximum kinetic energy of the photoelectrons.
- Below a certain frequency, the photoelectric effect does not occur at all.
- There is no significant delay (less than 10^{-9} s) between the light source activation and the emission of the first photoelectrons.

As you can tell, these three results are the exact opposite of the wave theory predictions. Not only that, but they are all three completely counter-intuitive. Why would low-frequency light not trigger the photoelectric effect, since it still carries energy? How do the photoelectrons release so quickly? And, perhaps most curiously, why does adding more intensity not result in more energetic electron releases? Why does the wave theory fail so utterly in this case, when it works so well in so many other situation

Einstein's Wonderful Time

In 1905, Albert Einstein published four papers in the *Annalen der Physik* journal, each of which was significant enough to warrant a Nobel Prize in its own right. The first paper (and the only one to actually be recognized with a Nobel) was his explanation of the photoelectric effect.

Building on Max Planck's blackbody radiation theory, Einstein proposed that radiation energy is not continuously distributed over the wavefront, but is instead localized in small bundles (later called photons). The photon's energy would be associated with its frequency (ν), through a proportionality constant known as *Planck's constant* (h), or alternately, using the wavelength (*lambda*) and the speed of light (c):

$$E = h\nu = hc/\lambda$$

or the momentum equation: $p = h/\lambda$

In Einstein's theory, a photoelectron releases as a effect of an interaction with a single photon, rather than an interaction with the wave as a whole. The energy from that photon transfers instantaneously to a single electron, knocking it free from the metal if the energy (which is, recall, proportional to the frequency ν) is high enough to overcome the work function (ϕ) of the metal. If the energy (or frequency) is too low, no electrons are knocked free.

If, however, there is excess energy, beyond ϕ, in the photon, the excess energy is converted into the kinetic energy of the electron:

$$K_{max} = h\nu - \phi.$$

Therefore, Einstein's theory predicts that the maximum kinetic energy is completely independent of the intensity of the light (because it doesn't show up in the equation anywhere). Shining twice as much light results in twice as many photons, and more electrons releasing, but the maximum kinetic energy of those individual electrons won't change unless the energy, not the intensity, of the light changes.

The maximum kinetic energy results when the least-tightly-bound electrons break free, but what about the most-tightly-bound ones; The ones in which there is *just* enough energy in the photon to knock it loose, but the kinetic energy that results in zero? Setting K_{max} equal to zero for this *cutoff frequency* (ν_c), we get:

$$\nu_c = \phi/h$$

or the cutoff wavelength: $\lambda_c = hc/\phi$

These equations indicate why a low-frequency light source would be unable to free electrons from the metal, and thus would produce no photoelectrons.

After Einstein

Experimentation in the photoelectric result was carried out extensively by Robert Millikan in 1915, and his work confirmed Einstein's theory. Einstein won a Nobel Prize for his photon theory (as applied to the photoelectric effect) in 1921, and Millikan won a Nobel in 1923 (in part due to his photoelectric experiments).

Most significantly, the photoelectric effect, and the photon theory it inspired, crushed the classical wave theory of light. Though no one could deny that light behaved as a wave, after Einstein's first paper, it was undeniable that it was also a particle.

Matter Waves

We have seen that in certain experiments electrons produce patterns attributed to waves. From this observation, we concluded that electrons have wave-like properties. We also concluded that as the energy of electrons increases their wavelength decreases.

Electrons are a form of matter, so these waves are called 'matter waves'. In this tutorial we will relate quantitative features of matter waves with familiar, measurable physical quantities such as energy, mass, and momentum. We will apply these relationships to forms of matter other than electrons, and see how these results can be applied to the electron microscope.

Historical Context

At the end of the 19th century, light was thought to consist of waves of electromagnetic fields which propagated according to Maxwell's equations, while matter was thought to consist of localized particles. This division was challenged when, in his 1905 paper on the photoelectric effect, Albert Einstein postulated that light was emitted and absorbed as localized packets, or "quanta" (now called photons). These quanta would have an energy

$$E = h\nu$$

where ν is the incidence of the light and h is Planck's constant.

Einstein's postulate was confirmed experimentally by Robert Millikan and Arthur Compton over the next two decades. Thus it became apparent that light has both wave-like and particle-like properties. De Broglie, in his 1924 PhD thesis, sought to expand this wave-particle duality to all particles:

> "When I conceived the first basic ideas of wave mechanics in 1923-24, I was guided by the aim to perform a real physical synthesis, valid for all particles, of the coexistence of the wave and of the corpuscular aspects that Einstein had introduced for photons in his theory of light quanta in 1905."

Experimental Confirmation

Elementary Particles

In 1927 at Bell Labs, Clinton Davisson and Lester Germer fired slow-moving electrons at a crystalline nickel target. The angular dependence of the reflected electron intensity was measured, and was determined to have the same diffraction pattern as those predicted by Bragg for x-rays.

Before the acceptance of the de Broglie hypothesis,

diffraction was a property that was thought to be only exhibited by waves. Therefore, the presence of any diffraction effects by matter demonstrated the wave-like nature of matter. When the de Broglie wavelength was inserted into the Bragg condition, the observed diffraction pattern was predicted, thereby experimentally confirming the de Broglie hypothesis for electrons.

This was a pivotal result in the development of quantum mechanics. Just as the photoelectric effect demonstrated the particle nature of light, the Davisson-Germer experiment showed the wave-nature of matter, and completed the theory of wave-particle duality. For physicists this idea was important because it means that not only can any particle exhibit wave characteristics, but that one can use wave equations to describe phenomena in matter if one uses the de Broglie wavelength.

Since the original Davisson-Germer experiment for electrons, the de Broglie hypothesis has been confirmed for other elementary particles. The wavelength of a thermalized electron in a non-metal at room temperature is about 8 nm.

Neutral Atoms

Experiments with Fresnel diffraction and specular reflection of neutral atoms confirm the application of the de Broglie hypothesis to atoms, *i.e.* the existence of atomic waves which undergo diffraction, interference and allow quantum reflection by the tails of the attractive potential. Advances in laser cooling have allowed cooling of neutral atoms down to nanokelvin temperatures. At these temperatures, the thermal de Broglie wavelengths come into the micrometre range. Using Bragg diffraction of atoms and a Ramsey interferometry technique, the de Broglie wavelength of cold sodium atoms was explicitly measured and found to be consistent with the temperature measured by a different method.

This effect has been used to demonstrate atomic holography, and it may allow the construction of an atom probe imaging system with nanometer resolution. The description of these phenomena is based on the wave properties of neutral atoms, confirming the de Broglie hypothesis.

Waves of Molecules

Recent experiments even corroborate the relations for molecules and even macromolecules, which are normally considered too large to undergo quantum mechanical effects. In 1999, a research team in Vienna demonstrated diffraction for molecules as large as fullerenes. The researchers calculated a De Broglie wavelength of the most probable C_{60} velocity as 2.5 pm. More recent experiments prove the quantum nature of molecules with a mass up to 6910 amu. In general, the De Broglie hypothesis is expected to apply to any well isolated object.

Davisson and Germer Experiment

The Davisson-Germer experiment demonstrated the wave nature of the electron, confirming the earlier hypothesis of deBroglie. Putting wave-particle duality on a firm experimental footing, it represented a major step forward in the development of quantum mechanics. The Bragg law for diffraction had been applied to x-ray diffraction, but this was the first application to particle waves.

Davisson and Germer intended and built a vacuum apparatus for the purpose of measuring the energies of electrons scattered from a metal surface. Electrons from a heated filament were accelerated by a voltage and allowed to strike the surface of nickel metal. The electron beam was directed at the nickel target, which could be rotated to observe angular dependence of the scattered electrons. Their electron detector (called a Faraday box) was mounted on an arc so that it could be rotated to observe electrons at different angles. It was a great surprise to them to find that at certain angles there was a peak in the intensity of the scattered electron beam. This peak indicated wave behaviour for the electrons, and could be interpreted by the Bragg law to give values for the lattice spacing in the nickel crystal.

The experimental data above, reproduced above Davisson's article, shows repeated peaks of scattered electron intensity with increasing accelerating voltage. This data was collected at a fixed scattering angle. Using the Bragg law, the de Broglie wavelength expression, and the kinetic energy of the accelerated electrons gives the relationship.

$$\underbrace{\frac{1}{\lambda}}_{\text{Electron wavelength}} = \underbrace{\frac{n}{2d\sin\theta}}_{\text{Bragg law}} = \underbrace{\frac{p}{h}}_{\text{deBroglie relationship}} = \frac{\sqrt{2mE}}{h} = \underbrace{\frac{\sqrt{2meV}}{h}}_{\text{Acceleration through voltage } V}$$

In the historical data, an accelerating voltage of 54 volts gave a definite peak at a scattering angle of 50°. The angle theta in the Bragg law corresponding to that scattering angle is 65°, and for that angle the calculated lattice spacing is 0.092 nm. For that lattice spacing and scattering angle, the relationship for wavelength as a function of voltage is empirically.

$$\frac{1}{\lambda(nm)} = \frac{n}{2d\sin\theta} = 0.815\sqrt{V}$$

Trying this relationship for n = 1, 2, 3 gives values for the square root of voltage 7.36, 14.7 and 22, which appear to agree with the first, third and fifth peaks above. Then what gives the second, fourth and sixth peaks? Perhaps they originate from a different set of planes in the crystal. Those peaks satisfy a sequence 2, 3, 4, suggesting that the first peak of that series would have been at 5.85. That corresponds to an electron wavelength of 0.21 nm and a lattice spacing of 0.116 nm.

History and Overview

According to Maxwell's equations in the late 19th century, light was thought to consist of waves of electromagnetic fields and matter consist of localized particles. However this was challenged in Albert Einstein's 1905 paper on the photoelectric effect, which described light as discrete and localized quanta of energy (now called photons), and won him the Nobel Prize in Physics in 1921. In 1927 Louis de Broglie presented his thesis concerning the wave-particle duality theory, which proposed the idea that all matter displays the wave-particle duality of photons. According to de Broglie for all matter and for radiation alike, the energy E of the particle was related to the frequency of its associated wave ν by the Planck relation:

$$E = h\nu$$

And that the momentum of the particle p was related to its wavelength by what is now known as the de Broglie relation:

$$p = \frac{h}{\lambda},$$

where h is Planck's constant.

An important contribution to the Davisson–Germer experiment was made by Walter M. Elsasser in Göttingen in the 1920s, who remarked that the wave-like nature of matter might be investigated by electron scattering experiments on crystalline solids, just as the wave-like nature of X-rays had been confirmed through X-ray scattering experiments on crystalline solids.

This suggestion of Elsasser was then communicated by his senior colleague (and later Nobel Prize recipient) Max Born to physicists in England. When the Davisson and Germer experiment was performed, the results of the experiment were explained by Elsasser's proposition. However the initial intention of the Davisson and Germer experiment was not to confirm the de Broglie hypothesis, but rather to study the surface of nickel.

In 1927 at Bell Labs, Clinton Davisson and Lester Germer fired slow moving electrons at a crystalline nickel target. The angular dependence of the reflected electron intensity was measured and was determined to have the same diffraction pattern as those predicted by Bragg for X-rays. This experiment was independently replicated by George Paget Thomson, and Davisson and Thomson shared the Nobel Prize in Physics in 1937. The Davisson -Germer experiment confirmed the de Broglie hypothesis that matter has wave-like behaviour. This, in combination with the Compton effect discovered by Arthur Compton (who won the Nobel Prize for Physics in 1927), established the wave–particle duality hypothesis which was a fundamental step in quantum theory.

Experiment

Davisson and Germer's actual objective was to study the surface of a piece of nickel by directing a beam of electrons at the surface and observing how many electrons bounced off at various angles. They expected that for electrons even the smoothest crystal surface would be too rough and so the electron beam would experience diffuse reflection.

The experiment consisted of firing an electron beam from an electron gun directed to a piece of nickel crystal at normal incidence (*i.e.* perpendicular to the surface of the crystal). The experiment included an electron gun consisting of a heated filament that released thermally excited electrons, which were then accelerated through a potential difference giving them a certain amount of kinetic energy towards the nickel crystal. To avoid collisions of the electrons with other molecules on their way towards the surface, the experiment was conducted in a vacuum chamber. To measure the number of electrons that were scattered at different angles, an electron detector that could be moved on an arc path about the crystal was used. The detector was designed to accept only elastically scattered electrons.

During the experiment an accident occurred and air entered the chamber, producing an oxide film on the nickel surface. To remove the oxide, Davisson and Germer heated the specimen in a high temperature oven, not knowing that this affected the formerly polycrystalline structure of the nickel to form large single crystal areas with crystal planes continuous over the width of the electron beam.

When they started the experiment again and the electrons hit the surface, they were scattered by atoms which originated from crystal planes inside the nickel crystal. As Max von Laue proved in 1912 the crystal structure serves as a type of three dimensional diffraction grating. The angles of maximum reflection are given by Bragg's condition for constructive interference from an array, Bragg's law

$$n\lambda = 2d\sin\left(90^\circ - \frac{\theta}{2}\right),$$

for $n = 1$, $\theta = 50°$, and for the spacing of the crystalline planes of nickel ($d = 0.091$ nm) obtained from previous X-ray scattering experiments on crystalline nickel.

By varying the applied voltage to the electron gun, the maximum intensity of electrons diffracted by the atomic surface was found at different angles. The highest intensity was observed at an angle $\theta = 50°$ with a voltage of 54 V, giving the electrons a kinetic energy of 54 eV.

According to the de Broglie relation and Bragg's law, a beam of 54 eV had a wavelength of 0.165 nm. The experimental outcome was 0.167 nm, which closely matched the predictions.

Davisson and Germer's accidental discovery of the diffraction of electrons was the first direct evidence confirming de Broglie's hypothesis that particles can have wave properties as well.

HEISENBERG UNCERTAINTY PRINCIPLE

THE UNCERTAINTY PRINCIPLE

The position and momentum of a particle cannot be simultaneously measured with arbitrarily high precision. There is a minimum for the product of the uncertainties of these two measurements. There is likewise a minimum for the product of the uncertainties of the energy and time.

$$\Delta \times \Delta p > \frac{\hbar}{2}$$

$$\Delta E \Delta t > \frac{\hbar}{2}$$

This is not a declaration about the inaccuracy of measurement instruments, nor a reflection on the quality of experimental methods; it arises from the wave properties inherent in the quantum mechanical description of nature.

Even with perfect instruments and technique, the uncertainty is inherent in the nature of things.

Matter Wave Interpretation

According to the de Broglie hypothesis, every object in our Universe is a wave, a situation which gives rise to this phenomenon. Consider the measurement of the position of a particle. The particle's wave packet has non-zero amplitude, meaning that the position is uncertain – it could be almost anywhere along the wave packet. To obtain an accurate reading of position, this wave packet must be 'compressed' as much as possible, meaning it must be made up of increasing numbers of sine waves added together. The momentum of the particle is proportional to the wavenumber of one of these waves, but it *could be* any of them. So a more precise position measurement-by adding together more waves–means that the momentum measurement becomes less precise (and *vice versa*).

The only kind of wave with a definite position is concentrated at one point, and such a wave has an indefinite wavelength (and therefore an indefinite momentum). Conversely, the only kind of wave with a definite wavelength is an infinite regular periodic oscillation over all space, which has no definite position. So in quantum mechanics, there can be no states that describe a particle with both a definite position and a definite momentum. The more precise the position, the less precise the momentum.

A mathematical statement of the principle is that every quantum state has the property that the root mean square (RMS) deviation of the position from its mean (the standard deviation of the x-distribution):

$$\sigma_x = \sqrt{\langle (x - \langle x \rangle)^2 \rangle}$$

times the RMS deviation of the momentum from its mean (the standard deviation of p):

$$\sigma_p = \sqrt{\langle (p - \langle p \rangle)^2 \rangle}$$

can never be smaller than a fixed fraction of Planck's constant:

$$\sigma_x \sigma_p \geq \hbar / 2.$$

The uncertainty principle can be restated in terms of other measurement processes, which involves collapse of the wavefunction. When the position is initially localized by preparation, the wavefunction collapses to a narrow bump in an interval $\Delta x > 0$, and the momentum wavefunction becomes spread out (cf. wave packet). The particle's momentum is left uncertain by an amount inversely proportional to the accuracy of the position measurement:

$$\sigma_p \geq \pi\hbar / \Delta x.$$

If the initial preparation in Δx is understood as an observation or disturbance of the particles then this means that the uncertainty principle is related to the observer effect. However, this is not true in the case of the measurement process corresponding to the former inequality but only for the latter inequality.

Robertson-Schrödinger Uncertainty Relations

The most common general form of the doubt principle is the *Robertson uncertainty relation*. For an arbitrary Hermitian operator $\hat{O}$, we can associate a standard deviation

$$\sigma_O = \sqrt{\langle \hat{O}^2 \rangle - \langle \hat{O} \rangle^2},$$

where the brackets $\langle O \rangle$ indicate an expectation value. For a pair of operators $\hat{A}$ and $\hat{B}$, we may define their *commutator* as

$$[\hat{A}, \hat{B}] = \hat{A}\hat{B} - \hat{B}\hat{A},$$

In this notation, the Robertson uncertainty relation is given by

$$\sigma_A \sigma_B \geq \left| \frac{1}{2i} \langle [\hat{A}, \hat{B}] \rangle \right|.$$

The Robertson uncertainty relation immediately follows from a slightly stronger inequality, the *Schrödinger uncertainty relation,*

$$\sigma_A^2\sigma_B^2 \geq \left(\frac{1}{2}\langle\{\hat{A},\hat{B}\}\rangle - \langle\hat{A}\rangle\langle\hat{B}\rangle\right)^2 + \left(\frac{1}{2i}\langle[\hat{A},\hat{B}]\rangle\right)^2,$$

where we have introduced the *anticommutator*,

$$\{\hat{A},\hat{B}\} = \hat{A}\hat{B} + \hat{B}\hat{A}.$$

Proof of the Schrödinger Uncertainty Relation

Since the Robertson and Schrödinger relations are for general operators, the relations can be applied to any two observables to obtain specific uncertainty relations. A few of the most common relations found in the literature are given below.

- For position and linear momentum, the canonical commutation relation $[\hat{x},\hat{p}] = i\hbar$ implies the Kennard inequality from above:

$$\sigma_x\sigma_p \geq \frac{\hbar}{2}$$

- For two orthogonal components of the total angular momentum operator of an object:

$$\sigma_{J_i}\sigma_{J_j} \geq \frac{\hbar}{2}\left|\langle J_k\rangle\right|,$$

where i, j, k are distinct and J_i denotes angular momentum along the x_i axis.

This relation implies that only a single component of a system's angular momentum can be defined with arbitrary precision, normally the component parallel to an external (magnetic or electric) field. Moreover, for $[J_x, J_y] = i\hbar\epsilon_{xyz}J_z$, a choice $\hat{A} = J_x$, $\hat{B} = J_y$, in angular momen-tum multiplets, $\psi = |j, m\rangle$, bounds the Casimir invariant (angular momentum squared, $\langle J_x^2 + J_y^2 + J_z^2\rangle$) from below and thus yields useful constraints such as $j(j+1) \geq m(m+1)$, and hence $j \geq m$, among others.

- For the number of electrons in a superconductor and the phase of its Ginzburg-Landau order parameter $\Delta N\Delta\phi \geq 1$.

History

Werner Heisenberg formulated the Uncertainty Principle at Niels Bohr's institute in Copenhagen, while working on the mathematical foundations of quantum mechanics. In 1925, following pioneering work with Hendrik Kramers, Heisenberg developed matrix mechanics, which replaced the ad-hoc old quantum theory with modern quantum mechanics. The central assumption was that the classical concept of motion does not fit at the quantum level, and that electrons in an atom do not travel on sharply defined orbits. Rather, the motion is smeared out in a strange way: the Fourier transform of time only involve those frequencies that could be seen in quantum jumps.

Heisenberg's paper did not admit any unobservable quantities like the exact position of the electron in an orbit at any time; he only allowed the theorist to talk about the Fourier components of the motion. Since the Fourier components were not defined at the classical frequencies, they could not be used to construct an exact trajectory, so that the formalism could not answer certain overly precise questions about where the electron was or how fast it was going.

The most striking property of Heisenberg's infinite matrices for position and momentum is that they do not commute. Heisenberg's canonical commutation relation indicates by how much:

$$[X,P] = XP - PX = i\hbar$$

and this result did not have a clear physical interpretation in the beginning.

In March 1926, working in Bohr's institute, Heisenberg realised that the non-commutativity implies the uncertainty principle. This implication provided a clear physical interpretation for the non-commutativity, and it laid the foundation for what became known as the Copenhagen interpretation of quantum mechanics. Heisenberg showed that the commutation relation implies an uncertainty, or in Bohr's language a complementarity. Any two variables that do not commute cannot be measured simultaneously — the more precisely one is known, the less precisely the other can be known. Heisenberg wrote: It can be expressed in its simplest form as follows: One can never know with perfect accuracy both of those two important factors which determine the movement of one of the smallest particles—its position and its velocity. It is impossible to determine accurately *both* the position and the direction and speed of a particle *at the same instant.*

One way to understand the complementarity between position and momentum is by wave-particle duality. If a particle described by a plane wave passes through a narrow slit in a wall like a water-wave passing through a narrow channel, the particle diffracts and its wave comes out in a range of angles.

The narrower the slit, the wider the diffracted wave and the greater the uncertainty in momentum afterward. The laws of diffraction require that the spread in angle $\Delta\theta$ is about λ / d, where d is the slit width and λ is the wavelength. Reasoning based on the de Broglie relation shows that the size of the slit and the range in momentum of the diffracted wave are related by Heisenberg's rule:

$$\Delta x \Delta p \approx h.$$

In his celebrated 1927 paper, "*Über den anschaulichen Inhalt der quantentheoretischen Kinematik und Mechanik*" ("On the Perceptual Content of Quantum Theoretical Kinematics and Mechanics"), Heisenberg established this expression as the minimum amount of unavoidable momentum disturbance caused by any position measurement, but he did not give a precise definition for the uncertainties Δx and Δp.

Instead, he gave some plausible estimates in each case separately. In his Chicago lecture he refined his principle:

$$\Delta x \Delta p \gtrsim h$$

Kennard in 1927 first proved the modern inequality:

$$\sigma_x \sigma_p \geq \frac{\hbar}{2}$$

where $\hbar = h/2\pi$, and σ_x, σ_p are the standard deviations of position and momentum. Heisenberg himself only proved relation for the special case of Gaussian states.

Heisenberg's Microscope

The principle is quite counter-intuitive, so the early students of quantum theory had to be reassured that naive measurements to violate it were bound to be always unworkable. One way in which Heisenberg originally illustrated the intrinsic impossibility of violating the uncertainty principle is by using an imaginary microscope as a measuring device. He imagines an experimenter trying to calculate the position and momentum of an electron by shooting a photon at it.

Problem 1 : If the photon has a short wavelength, and therefore a large momentum, the position can be measured accurately. But the photon scatters in a random direction, transferring a large and uncertain amount of momentum to the electron. If the photon has a long wavelength and low momentum, the collision does not disturb the electron's momentum very much, but the scattering will reveal its position only vaguely.

Problem 2 : If a large aperture is used for the microscope, the electron's location can be well resolved ; but by the principle of conservation of momentum, the transverse momentum of the incoming photon and hence the new momentum of the electron resolves poorly. If a small aperture is used, the accuracy of both resolutions is the other way around.

The combination of these trade-offs imply that no matter what photon wavelength and aperture size are used, the product of the uncertainty in measured position and measured momentum is greater than or equal to a lower limit, which is (up to a small numerical factor) equal to Planck's constant. Heisenberg did not care to formulate the uncertainty principle as an exact limit, and preferred to use it instead as a heuristic quantitative statement, correct up to small numerical factors, which makes the radically new noncommutativity of quantum mechanics inevitable.

Critical Reactions

The Copenhagen interpretation of quantum mechanics and Heisenberg's Uncertainty Principle were in fact seen as twin targets by detractors who believed in an underlying determinism and realism. According to the Copenhagen interpretation of quantum mechanics, there is no fundamental reality that the quantum state describes, just a prescription for calculating experimental results. There is no way to say what the state of a system fundamentally is, only what the result of observations might be.

Albert Einstein believed that randomness is a reflection of our ignorance of some fundamental property of reality, while Niels Bohr believed that the probability distributions are fundamental and irreducible, and depend on which measurements we choose to perform. Einstein and Bohr debated the uncertainty principle for many years.

Einstein's Slit

The first of Einstein's thought experiments challenging the uncertainty principle went as follows:

Consider a particle passing through a slit of width d. The slit introduces an uncertainty in momentum of approximately h/d because the particle passes through the wall. But let us determine the momentum of the particle by measuring the recoil of the wall. In doing so, we find the momentum of the particle to arbitrary accuracy by conservation of momentum.

Bohr's response was that the wall is quantum mechanical as well, and that to measure the recoil to accuracy Δp the momentum of the wall must be known to this accuracy before the particle passes through. This introduces an uncertainty in the position of the wall and therefore the position of the slit equal to $h / \Delta p$, and if the wall's momentum is known precisely enough to measure the recoil, the slit's position is uncertain enough to disallow a position measurement.

A similar analysis with particles diffracting through multiple slits is given by Richard Feynman.

Einstein's Box

Bohr was present when Einstein future the thought experiment which has become known as Einstein's box. Einstein argued that "Heisenberg's uncertainty equation implied that the uncertainty in time was related to the uncertainty in energy, the product of the two being related to Planck's constant." Consider, he said, an ideal box, lined with mirrors so that it can contain light indefinitely. The box could be weighed before a clockwork mechanism opened an ideal shutter at a chosen instant to allow one single photon to escape. "We now know, explained Einstein, precisely the time at which the photon left the box." "Now, weigh the box again. The change of mass tells the energy of the emitted light. In this manner, said Einstein, one could measure the energy emitted and the time it was released with any desired precision, in contradiction to the uncertainty principle."

Bohr spent a sleepless night considering this argument, and eventually realised that it was flawed. He pointed out that if the box were to be weighed, say by a spring and a pointer on a scale, "since the box must move vertically with a change in its weight, there will be uncertainty in its vertical velocity and therefore an uncertainty in its height above the table.... Furthermore, the uncertainty about the elevation above the earth's surface will result in an uncertainty in the rate of the clock," because of Einstein's own theory of gravity's effect on time. "Through this chain of uncertainties, Bohr showed that Einstein's light box experiment could not simultaneously measure exactly both the energy of the photon and the time of its escape."

EPR Paradox for Tangled Particles

Bohr was compelled to modify his understanding of the uncertainty principle after another thought experiment by Einstein. In 1935, Einstein, Podolsky and Rosen published an analysis of widely separated entangled particles. Measuring one particle, Einstein realised, would alter the probability distribution of the other, yet here the other particle could not possibly be disturbed. This example led Bohr to revise his understanding of the principle, concluding that the uncertainty was not caused by a direct interaction.

But Einstein came to much more far-reaching conclusions from the same thought experiment. He believed the "natural basic assumption" that a complete description of reality would have to predict the results of experiments from "locally changing deterministic quantities", and therefore would have to include more information than the maximum possible allowed by the uncertainty principle.

In 1964 John Bell showed that this assumption can be falsified, since it would imply a certain inequality between the probabilities of different experiments. Experimental results confirm the predictions of quantum mechanics, ruling out Einstein's basic assumption that led him to the suggestion of his *hidden variables*.

While it is possible to assume that quantum mechanical predictions are due to *nonlocal* hidden variables, and in fact David Bohm invented such a formulation, this resolution is not satisfactory to the vast majority of physicists. The question of whether a random outcome is predetermined by a nonlocal theory can be philosophical, and it can be potentially intractable. If the hidden variables are not constrained, they could just be a list of random digits that are used to produce the measurement outcomes. To make it sensible, the assumption of nonlocal hidden variables is sometimes augmented by a second assumption — that the size of the observable universe puts a limit on the computations that these variables can do. A nonlocal theory of this sort predicts that a quantum computer encounters fundamental obstacles when it tries to factor numbers of approximately 10,000 digits or more; an achievable task in quantum mechanics.

Popper's Criticism

Karl Popper approached the difficulty of indeterminacy as a logician and metaphysical realist. He disagreed with the application of the uncertainty relations to individual particles rather than to ensembles of identically prepared particles, referring to them as "statistical scatter relations". In this statistical interpretation, a *particular* measurement may be made to arbitrary precision without invalidating the quantum theory. This directly contrasts the Copenhagen interpretation of quantum mechanics, which is non-deterministic but lacks local hidden variables. In 1934 Popper published *Zur Kritik der Ungenauigkeitsrelationen* (*Critique of the Uncertainty Relations*) in *Naturwissenschaften,* and in the same year *Logik der Forschung* (translated and updated by the author as *The Logic of Scientific Discovery* in 1959), outlining his arguments for the statistical interpretation. In 1982, he further developed his theory in *Quantum theory and the schism in Physics,* writing:

> [Heisenberg's] formulae are, beyond all doubt, derivable *statistical formulae* of the quantum theory. But they have been *habitually misinterpreted* by those quantum theorists who said that these formulae can be interpreted as determining some upper limit to the *precision of our measurements*. Popper proposed an experiment to falsify the uncertainty relations, though he later withdrew his initial version after discussions with Weizsäcker, Heisenberg, and Einstein; this experiment may have influenced the formulation of the EPR experiment.

Many-worlds Uncertainty

The many-worlds interpretation originally outlined by Hugh Everett III in 1957 is partly meant to reconcile the differences between the Einstein and Bohr's views by replacing Bohr's wave function collapse with an ensemble of deterministic and independent universes whose *distribution* is governed by wave functions and the Schrödinger equation. Thus, uncertainty in the many-worlds interpretation follows from each observer within any universe having no knowledge of what goes on in the other universes.

Chapter 4

Electron Theory of Metals

ELECTRON THEORY

Electricity is the movement of electrons from side to side a conductor. Electrons are attracted to protons. Since we have excess electrons on the other end of the conductor, we have many electrons being attracted to the protons. This attraction sort of pushes the electrons towards the protons. This push is normally called electrical pressure. The amount of electrical pressure is determined by the number of electrons that are attracted to protons. The electrical force or electromotive force (EMF) attempts to push an electron out of its orbit and towards the excess protons. If an electron is freed from its orbit, the atom acquires a positive charge because it now has one more proton than it has electrons. The unbalanced atom or ion attempts to return to its balanced state so it will attract electrons from the orbit of other balanced atoms. This starts a chain reaction as one atom captures an electron and another releases an electron. As this action continues to occur, electrons will flow through the conductor. A stream of free electrons forms and an electrical current is started.

This does not denote a single electron travels the length of the insulator, it means the overall effect is electrons moving in one direction. All this happens at the speed of light. The strength of the electron flow is dependant on the potential difference or voltage. The three elements of electricity are voltage, current, and resistance. How these three elements interrelate governs the behaviour of electricity. Once the you comprehend the laws that govern electricity, understanding the function and operation of the various automotive electrical systems is an easier task.

So far we have described present as the movement of electrons through a conductor. Electrons are negatively charged particles that move towards something that is positively charged. Electrons move because of this potential difference. This describes one of the common theories about current flow. The electron theory states that since electrons are negatively charged, current flows from the most negative to the most positive point within an electrical circuit. In other words, current flows from negative to positive. This theory is widely accepted by the electronic industry.

Another current flow theory is called the conventional theory. This states that current flows from positive to negative. The basic idea behind this theory is simply that although electrons move towards the protons, the energy or force that is released as the electrons move begins at the point where the first electron moved to the most positive charge. As electrons continue to move in one direction, the released energy moves in the opposite direction. This theory is the oldest theory and serves as the basis for most electrical diagrams.

Trying to make sense of it all may be difficult for you. It is also difficult for scientists and engineers. In fact, another theory has been developed to explain the mysteries of current flow. This theory is called the hole-flow theory and is actually based on both electron theory and the conventional theory.

CLASSICAL FREE ELECTRON THEORY OF METALS

This theory was developed by Drude and Lorentz and hence is also known as Drude-Lorentz theory. According to this theory, a metal consists of electrons which are free to move about in the crystal like molecules of a gas in a container. Mutual repulsion between electrons is ignored and hence potential energy is taken as zero. Therefore the total energy of the electron is equal to its kinetic energy. All metal atoms consist of valence electrons which are responsible for electrical conduction. Valence electrons are loosely bound to the nucleus. When a large number of atoms join to form a metal, the boundaries of the neighbouring atoms overlap, and thus, valence electrons can move easily throughout the body of the metal. These electrons are called free electrons or conduction electrons which account for properties such as electrical conductivity, thermal conductivity, opacity, surface luster *etc.*

Classical Free Electron Theory

This theory was developed by Drude and Lorentz and hence is also known as Drude-Lorentz theory. According to this theory, a metal consists of electrons which are free to move about in the body of the metal like molecules of a gas in a container.

Drift Velocity

If no electric field is applied on a conductor, the free electrons move in random directions. They collide with each other and also with the positive ions. Since the motion is completely random, average velocity in any direction is zero. If a constant electric field is established inside a conductor, the electrons experience a force $F = -eE$ due to which they move in the direction opposite to direction of the field. These electrons undergo frequent collisions with positive ions. In each such collision, direction of motion of electrons undergoes random changes. As a result, in addition to the random motion, the electrons are subjected to a very slow directional motion. This motion is called drift and the average velocity of this motion is called drift velocity.

FREE-ELECTRON THEORY OF METALS

The treatment of a metal as containing a gas of electrons completely free to move within it. The theory was originally proposed in 1900 to describe and correlate the electrical and thermal properties of metals. Later, quantum mechanics became the basis for the theory of most of the general properties of simple metals such as sodium, with one free electron per atom, magnesium with two, and aluminum with three. Transition metals, such as iron, have partially filled electronic *d* states and are not treated by the free-electron model.

Three years after J. J. Thomson's 1897 discovery of the electron, P. Drude suggested that the transport properties of metals might be understood by assuming that their electrons are free and in thermal equilibrium with their atoms. This theory was made more quantitative by H. A. Lorentz. Assuming that the mean free path of electrons was limited by collisions, he was able to derive Ohm's law for the electrical conductivity and obtain the ratio of thermal to electrical conductivity in excellent agreement with experiment. This ratio, divided by the absolute temperature, is called the Wiedemann-Franz ratio and had been observed to be universal 50 years earlier.

The theory, however, had two main shortcomings. First, it predicted a large component of the specific heat of a metal, not present in insulators, which was not observed. Second, comparison of the theory with experiment indicated that the mean free path of the electrons became extremely large at low temperatures; the model offered no justification.

In 1928 A. Sommerfeld revised Lorentz's treatment by using quantum statistics, which removed the difficulty of the specific heat without losing the successful description of transport properties. The resulting theory remains the basis for the understanding of most transport properties of metals and semiconductors. At about the same time, W. V. Houston and F. Bloch solved the quantum-mechanical wave equation for electrons in a regular periodic structure, finding that they could indeed have arbitrarily large mean free paths if there were no defects in the periodicity, thereby putting the free-electron theory on a firm basis.

Even in the context of a free-electron gas, there are strong Coulomb interactions between electrons which are frequently neglected in the free-electron theory of metals. This neglect was justified in the late 1950s by L. D. Landau, who asserted that, even with strong electron–electron interactions, there is a one-to-one correspondence between the excited states, called quasiparticle states, of the real system and the one-electron excitations from the ground state of the noninteracting electron gas. Thus, the formulations for free-electron theory still follow, but perhaps with modifications of parameters such as mass. Subsequent theory indicates that indeed these modification due to the electron-electron interaction are extremely small for the low-energy excitations present in thermal equilibrium, and so again the simplest theory succeeds for many properties, although substantial modifications are required for the higher-energy excitations caused by light. There are additional corrections, which are much larger than those from the electron-electron interaction, arising from the interaction between electrons and phonons, the quantum-mechanical term for lattice vibrations. In many metals these vibrations reduce the electron velocities by factors of as much as 2, increasing the electronic specific heat although they turn out not to modify the conductivity itself.

Another feature of the electron–phonon interaction is a resulting interaction among electrons, which is attractive and tends to cancel or exceed the repulsive electron-electron interaction.

At low temperatures the net attraction binds electrons in pairs in a superconducting state. The theory of J. Bardeen, J.R. Schrieffer, and L.N. Cooper (the BCS theory of superconductivity), which first explained this phenomenon, is also a free-electron theory, but assumes that the free electrons have such a net attractive interaction. In contrast, it is generally believed that the high-temperature superconductors discovered in 1986 are very far from free-electron in character, and most workers do not believe that phonons are primarily responsible for the attractive interaction.

FREE ELECTRON MODEL

In solid-state physics, the free electron model is a simple model for the behaviour of valence electrons in a crystal structure of a metallic solid. It was developed principally by

Arnold Sommerfeld who combined the classical Drude model with quantum mechanical Fermi-Dirac statistics and hence it is also known as the Drude–Sommerfeld model. The free electron Empty Lattice Approximation forms the basis of the band structure model known as nearly-free electron model. Given its simplicity, it is surprisingly successful in explaining many experimental phenomena mentioned below:

- the Wiedemann-Franz law which relates electrical conductivity and thermal conductivity;
- the temperature dependence of the heat capacity;
- the shape of the electronic density of states;
- the range of binding energy values;
- electrical conductivities;
- thermal electron emission and field electron emission from bulk metals.

Ideas and Assumptions

As in the Drude model, valence electrons are assumed to be completely detached from their ions (forming an electron gas). As in an ideal gas, electron-electron interactions are completely neglected. The electrostatic fields in metals are weak because of the screening effect.

The crystal lattice is not explicitly taken into account. A quantum-mechanical justification is given by Bloch's Theorem:

> an unbound electron moves in a periodic potential as a free electron in vacuum, except for the electron mass m becoming an effective mass m^* which may deviate considerably from m (one can even use negative effective mass to describe conduction by electron holes). Effective masses can be derived from band structure computations. While the static lattice does not hinder the motion of the electrons, electrons can be scattered by impurities and by phonons; these two interactions determine electrical and thermal conductivity (superconduc-tivity requires a more refined theory than the free electron model).

According to the Pauli exclusion principle, each phase space element $(\Delta k)^3(\Delta x)^3$ can be occupied only by two electrons (one per spin quantum number). This restriction of available electron states is taken into account by Fermi-Dirac statistics. Main predictions of the free-electron model are derived by the Sommerfeld expansion of the Fermi-Dirac occupancy for energies around the Fermi level.

Energy and Wave Function of a Free Electron

For a free particle the potential is $V(\mathbf{r})=0$. The Schrödinger equation for such a particle, like the free electron, is

$$-\frac{\hbar^2}{2m}\nabla^2\Psi(\mathbf{r},t)=i\hbar\frac{\partial}{\partial t}\Psi(\mathbf{r},t)$$

The wave function $\Psi(\mathbf{r},t)$ can be split into a solution of a time dependent and a solution of a time independent equation. The solution of the time dependent equation is

$$\Psi(\mathbf{r},t)=\psi(\mathbf{r})e^{-i\omega t}$$

with energy

$$E=\hbar\omega$$

The solution of the time independent equation is

$$\psi_{\mathbf{k}}(\mathbf{r})=\frac{1}{\sqrt{\Omega_r}}e^{i\mathbf{k}\cdot\mathbf{r}}$$

with a wave vector k. Ω_r is the volume of space where the electron can be found. The electron has a kinetic energy

$$E=\frac{\hbar^2k^2}{2m}$$

The plane wave solution of this Schrödinger equation is

$$\Psi(\mathbf{r},t)=\frac{1}{\sqrt{\Omega_r}}e^{i\mathbf{k}\cdot\mathbf{r}-i\omega t}$$

For solid state and condensed matter physics the time independent solution $\psi_{\mathbf{k}}(\mathbf{r})$ is of major interest. It is the basis of electronic band structure models that are widely used in solid-state physics for model Hamiltonians like the nearly-free electron model and the Tight binding model and different models that use a Muffin-tin approximation. The eigenfunctions of these Hamiltonians are Bloch waves which are modulated plane waves.

QUANTUM FREE ELECTRON THEORY

Classical free electron theory could not give details many physical properties. In 1928, Sommerfeld developed a new theory applying quantum mechanical concepts and Fermi-Dirac statistics to the free electrons in the metal. This theory is called quantum free electron theory.

Classical free electron theory permits all electrons to gain energy. But quantum free electron theory permits only a fraction of electrons to gain energy. In order to determine the actual number of electrons in a given energy range (dE), it is necessary to know the number of states (dNs) which have energy in that range.

The number of states per unit energy range is called the density of states g(E).

Therefore, g(E) = dNs/dE

According to Fermi-Dirac statistics, the probability that a particular energy statewith energy E is occupied by an electron is given by,

f(E) = 1/[1 + e(E – EF/KT)]

where EF is called Fermi level. Fermi level is the highest filled energy level at 0 K. Energy corresponding to Fermi level is known as Fermi energy. Now the actual number of electrons present in the energy range dE,

dN = f(E) g(E)dE

Need of Quantum Theory

Classical (Newtonian) mechanics works completely in explaining the world around us, and is accurate enough for even charting the trajectory of probes sent to Jupiter and beyond. So why are we not content with classical physics? Where does the need for quantum theory arise? Quantum theory unveils a new level of reality, the world of intrinsic uncertainty, a world of possibilities, which is totally absent in classical physics. And this bizarre world of quantum physics not only offers us the most compelling explanation of physical phenomena presently known, but is also one of the most prolific source of modern technologies, providing society with a cornucopia of devices and instruments.

Evidence for Quantum Theory

Classical mechanics works extremely well for large objects that are moving much slower than the velocity of light. Once objects start to move very fast, we need to modify Newton's equations by relativistic equations. On the other hand, for objects that are very small, quantum theory becomes necessary. If one attempts to extend Newton's laws to domains that are far from daily experience, they start to fail and give incorrect results. Historically, at the turn of the nineteenth century, this failure of Newtonian physics became very evident in the studies of the atom. What experimental evidence do we have that classical physics is invalid, and that, to date, quantum theory is the most accurate explanation of how nature behaves? Classical physics is what intuitively follows from our five senses, and we have no reason to naively extend the world apprehended by our five senses to microscopic domains of which we have no direct experience.

As it turns out, most of the experimental evidence for quantum theory runs counter to one's day to day experiences. One of the fist achievements of quantum theory was the explanation of the structure and stability of atoms, and of the periodic table of elements. Strange phenomena such as super-conductivity, super-fluidity and so on are more macroscopic manifestations of quantum behaviour. Instead of quoting results from experiments far removed from daily life, suffice it to say that most of what goes under the name of high technology is a direct result of the workings of quantum mechanics, and most modern conveniences that we take for granted today would be virtually impossible without it. Observations of radiation from a blackbody and its radiation (measured by spectroscopic lines) provided the first experimental evidence for quantum theory. Every time one sees a neon or sodium light, one is seeing quantum theory in practice.

The light from a neon or sodium source is a spectroscopic line. An electric field excites atoms of the neon or sodium atom to a discrete quantum state; the atom then makes a transition by emitting light that is characteristic of the atom, and yields the particular colour of light that one sees. Furthermore, semiconductors and electronic chips in general exist due to quantum theory. Electronic devices, from computers, television, to mobile phones are all based on the semiconductor, and aeroplanes, ships, cars all use semiconductors in an essential manner. More complex technologies such as MRI (Magnetic Resonance Imaging), lasers, physical chemistry, fabrication of new drugs, modern materials science and so on all draw on the principles of quantum theory. It is no exaggeration to predict that twenty first century technology will largely be based on the principles of quantum physics.

Planck's Quantum Hypothesis

A black body which is maintained at a constant temperature T steadily loses energy from its surface in the form of electromagnetic radiation. Since the atoms composing the black body are in contact with a heat bath at temperature T, each atom has approximately kT amount of energy, where k = Boltzmann's constant. Since the atoms are jiggling around due to thermal motion, classical electromagnetic theory then predicts that all wavelength's of radiation, in particular upto infinitely short wavelengths, should be emitted by a black body. This classical prediction for the spectrum of radiation that is emitted by such a black-body is contradicted by experiment. Max Planck, a German physicist, correctly explained the experimentally measured black- body spectrum by making the epoch-making conjecture in 1900 that electromagnetic waves are the macroscopic manifestations of packets of wave-energy called photons. Planck further made the quantum hypothesis that the energy of photons is quantized in the sense that the energy of the photons only comes in discrete packets, the smallest packet called a quantum.

Photons are massless quantum particles, and all phenomena involving electromagnetic radiation can be fully explained by the quantum theory of photons. The phenomenon of electromagnetic radiation is a classical approximation to the quantum theory of photons.

The classical electro-magnetism is a valid approximation when the typical energy of the photon is less than the characteristic energy of the instrument with which the experiment is being performed. Photons can have wavelength from zero to infinity.

For a wave of frequency *f*, or equivalently, of wavelength λ, the quanta of energy are given by (*c* is the velocity of light)

$$E = N\frac{hc}{\lambda}$$

$$= Nhf$$

With N = 1, 2, . . .

We see from the above that the shorter the wavelength of a photon, the greater is its quantum of energy. The constant *h* is an empirical constant of nature, required by dimensional analysis, and is called Planck's constant. Its numerical value is given by

$$h = 6.62618 \times 10^{-34}\,\text{Js}$$

$$= 4.13570 \times 10^{-15}\,\text{eVs}$$

For the sake of convenience, it is customary to work with

$$\hbar \equiv \frac{h}{2\pi}$$

$$= 1.054589 \times 10^{-34}\,\text{Js}$$

$$= 6.58217 \times 10^{-16}\,\text{eVs}.$$

The quantum postulate immediately solves the problem

of the black-body spectrum; radiation with increasingly short (ultra-violet) wavelength is incorrectly predicted by classical physics to make an increasingly large contribution to the energy loss. Due to Planck's quantum postulate, to emit still a single quanta of ultra-violet radiation would require a minimum energy much larger than the typical thermal energy of about kT that is available for emission, and hence would not be present in the radiated spectrum of a black-body. The black-body spectrum obtained from Planck's postulate is confirmed by experiment, and was the first success of quantum theory.

Effect of Temperature on Fermi-Dirac Distribution Function

Fermi-Dirac distribution function is given by,
f(E) = 1/[1+e(E-EF/KT)]
At T = 0K, for EEF, f(E)=0
At T = 0K, for E = EF, f(E) = indeterminate
At T > 0K, for E = EF, f(E) = 1/2

Classification of Semiconductors

In intrinsic semiconductors, the fermilevel lie exactly at the centre of the forbidden energy gap. In n-type semiconductors fermilevel lie near the conduction band. In p-type semiconductors fermilevel lie near the valence band.

Contamination Levels

In extrinsic semiconductors, addition of impurities introduces new allowed quantum energy states in the forbidden energy band. The quantum state which appears as a single energy level is known as impurity level.

Impurity level is called donor level (Ed) in n-type semiconductors and lie just below the conduction band. Impurity level is called acceptor level (Ea) in p- type semiconductor and lie just above the valence band.

Band theory of solids

The atoms in the solid are very closely packed. The nucleus of an atom is so heavy that it considered to be at rest and hence the characteristic of an atom are decided by the electrons. The electrons in an isolated atom have different and discrete amounts of energy according to their occupations in different shells and sub shells. These energy values are represented by sharp lines in an energy level diagram.

During the formation of a solid, energy levels of outer shell electrons got split up. As a result, closely packed energy levels are produced. The collection of such a large number of energy levels is called energy band. The electrons in the outermost shell are called valence electrons. The band formed by a series of energy levels containing the valence electrons is known as valence band.

The next higher permitted band in a solid is the conduction band. The electrons occupying this band are known as conduction electrons.

Conduction band valence band are separated by a gap known as forbidden energy gap. No electrons can occupy energy levels in this band.

When an electrons in the valence band absorbs enough energy, it jumps across the forbidden energy gap and enters the conduction band, creating a positively charged hole in the valence band.the hole is basically the deficiency of an electron.

Classification of solids on the basis of energy bands

Insulator

Insulators are very poor conductors of electricity with resitivity ranging $10^3 - 10^{17}$ Ωm. In this case Eg ≈ 6 eV. For *e.g.* carbon.

Semiconductor Material

A semiconductor material is one whose electrical properties lie between that of insulators and good conductors. Their forbidden band is small and resistivity ranges between 10^{-4} to 10^3 Ωm.

Ge and Si are examples with forbidden energy gap 0.7 eV and 1.1 eV respectively. An appreciable number of electrons can be excited across the gap at room temperature. By adding impurities or by thermal excitation, we can increase the electrical conductivity in semiconductors

Conductor Bond

Here valence band and conduction band overlap and there is no forbidden energy gap. Resistivity ranges between 10=9 to 10^{-4} Ωm. Here plenty of electrons are available for electrical conduction. The electrons from valence band can freely enter the conduction band.

Intrinsic Pure Semiconductor

A pure semiconductor free from any impurity is called intrinsic semiconductor. Here charge carriers (electrons and holes) are created by thermal excitation.

Si and Ge are examples. Both Si and Ge are tetravalent. *i.e.* each has four valence electrons in the outermost shell. Consider the case of Ge.

It has a total of 32 electrons. Out of these 32 electrons, 28 are tightly bound to the nucleus, while the remaining 4 electrons (valence electrons) revolve in the outermost orbit. In a solid, each atom shares its 4 valence electrons with its nearest neighbours to form covalent bonds. The energy needed to liberate an electron from Ge atom is very small, of the order of 0.7 eV.

Thus even at room temperature, a few electrons can detach from its bonds by thermal excitation. When the electron escapes from the covalent bond, an empty space or a hole is created.

The number of free electrons is always equal to the number of holes.

Extrinsic Semiconductor

Extrinsic semiconductors are formed by adding suitable impurities to the intrinsic semiconductor. This process of adding impurities is called doping. Doping increases the electrical conductivity in semiconductors.

The added impurity is very small, of the order of one atom per million atoms of the pure semiconductor. The added impurity may be pentavalent or trivalent. Depending on the type of impurity added, the extrinsic semiconductors can be divided into two classes: n-type and p-type.

n-type Semiconductor

When pentavalent impurity is added to pure semiconductor, it results in n-type semiconducutor. Consider the case when pentavalent Arsenic is added to pure Ge crystal.

The fifth electron of Arsenic atom is not covalently bonded, but it is loosely bound to the Arsenic atom. Now by increasing the thermal energy or by applying electric field, this electron can be easily excited from the valence band to the conduction band.

Thus every Arsenic atom contributes one conduction electron without creating a positive hole. Hence Arsenic is called donor element since it donates free electrons. Since current carriers are negatively charged particles, this type of semiconductor is called n-type semiconductor.

p-type Semiconductor

When trivalent contamination is added to pure semiconductor, it results in p-type semiconducutor. Consider the case when trivalent Boron is added to pure Ge crystal.

There is a deficiency of one electron (hole) in the bonding with the fourth Ge atom. The Ge atom will steal an electron from the neighbouring Ge atom to form a covalent bond. Due to this stealing action, a hole is created in the adjascent atom. This process continues. Impurity atoms that contribute hole in this manner are called acceptors. Since current carriers are positively charged particles, this type of semiconductor is called p-type semiconductor.

Chapter 5

Semiconductors

AN INTRODUCTION TO SEMICONDUCTORS

A semiconductor has electrical conductivity intermediate to that of a conductor and an insulator. Semiconductors differ from metals in their characteristic property of decreasing electrical resistivity with increasing temperature. Semiconductor materials are useful because their behaviour can be manipulated by the addition of impurities, known as doping. The comprehensive theory of semiconductors relies on the principles of quantum physics to explain the motions of electrons through a lattice of atoms.

On the 14th of November, 1876, the high school teacher Ferdinand Braun gave a presentation entitled "Experiments concerning deviations from Ohm's Law in metallic conductors" in front of the illustrious Naturforschende Gesellschaft zu Leipzig. Neither Mr. Braun nor his critical audience were aware of the fact that they were just witnessing the birth of Semiconductor Physics. Indeed, what Ferdinand Braun had discovered by a long series of meticulous experiments, at first sight did not appear too exciting: if one equipped a solid crystal with two metallic contacts and applied an electrical voltage, two basic kinds of behaviour could be observed. Either no measurable electrical current passed through the crystal. Then this crystal obviously was an electrical insulator and, therefore, was no longer of interest for further investigation of its electrical properties. Or, for the second type of crystals, a sizeable current could be measured.

Then this crystal was a metallic conductor and obeyed Ohm's Law. If one doubled the applied voltage, also the observed current was doubled. And if one inverted the electrical voltage applied to the two contacts, also the current was inverted. At least, that was the way it used to be until 1876...

The deviations from Ohm's Law, which Ferdinand Braun reported to the Natural Society at Leipzig, were quite strange, indeed. Instead of using large electrical contacts, Mr. Braun had performed some of his experiments with very fine contact needles. In some crystals he then had observed an electrical current as in a usual conductor, but when he inverted the applied voltage, the current disappeared and the crystal apparently had converted to an insulator. Similarly unexpected was what happened when Braun changed the magnitude of the applied voltage. Then for these strange crystals the current increased much more strongly than allowed by Ohm's Law.

What Ferdinand Braun had discovered was the first semiconductor device ever: a rectifying diode, which could transform alternating current into direct current, and many years later actually was used in the form of point contact diodes in radio receivers or radar units. Unfortunately, the reason for this strange behaviour of his crystals remained entirely mysterious to Ferdinand Braun. The scientific explanation of this phenomenon only was given much later in 1939 by Walter Schottky, who at that time developed a theory for the electronic properties of semiconductor/metal-interfaces. Honouring this work, rectifying metal/semiconductor contacts now are known as Schottky diodes. As for Ferdinand Braun, he received the Nobel Prize for Physics in 1909 and today mainly is remembered for the invention of the cathode ray tube. As a matter of fact, due to the development of vacuum tubes, solid state electronics did not gain any practical importance until the first transistor was built by Bardeen, Brattain, and Shockley in 1947. Since then, however, solid state electronics based on semiconductor devices has revolutionized our world, which no longer can be imagined without this.

So what actually are semiconductors, what makes them

so different from metallic conductors, and why are they so interesting for many applications? The scientific answer to these questions and the development of new semiconductor materials and devices is what semiconductor physics and technology is all about. It takes many years of intensive studies to master the basics of this important part of solid state physics. Here, we will try to convey the most important concepts concerning the unique properties of semiconductors with the help of a simple analogy.

In a regular periodic crystal lattice, electrons as the carriers of electrical current are not allowed to move around freely. Instead, they have to obey certain rules enforced by quantum mechanics. As a consequence, electrons have to occupy so-called "energy bands" which are separated from each other by small or large "band gaps". This situation can be compared to a two-storey building consisting of a ground floor and a first floor. In the language of solid state physics, these two storeys are called "valence band" and "conduction band", respectively. Both floors are covered by a well-ordered array of quadratic tiles, representing the periodic lattice of atoms in a semiconductor crystal. The movement of electrons in a crystal is then analogous to the movement of inhabitants in our building, whose most important purpose it is to transport "charge" from one end of the building to the other end. The inhabitants of our "semiconductor house" have to obey one additional important rule: at no time more than one inhabitant is allowed to occupy the space of a given tile! In the same way, electrons in a solid crystal have to obey the quantum-mechanical "exclusion principle" formulated by the famous physicist Wolfgang Pauli.

Now that the blueprints of our semiconductor building and the basic rules for its inhabitants have been defined, let us start to occupy this building with people. At first, all inhabitants can be accommodated on the ground floor, where they can move around more or less freely and transport their cargo across the building. This leads to a steady increase of the amount of cargo transported through the building, until the occupancy of the ground floor has increased so much that the inhabitants start to hinder one another on their way. Eventually, the stream of cargo will come to a complete stop, once all tiles in the ground floor are occupied by an inhabitant, so that nobody is able to move any more. Further inhabitants can only occupy the first floor, where they again have sufficient room to move about. As a consequence, the overall cargo stream through the building will again start to increase, reach a maximum, and eventually come to an end when also the first floor is fully occupied.

The fate of electrons in solids is quite similar to what happens to the inhabitants of our semiconductor building. In particular, it is easy to understand why both, electrical conductors as well as insulators exist in nature. Crystals in which energy bands are only partially filled will belong to the group of electrical conductors, since their electrons can move more or less freely through the crystal lattice. If, on the other hand, all energy bands are fully occupied or completely empty, no electrical current can pass through the crystal at all and we are dealing with an electrical insulator. Which situation will be encountered for a given solid crystal depends on how many electrons per atom are available to occupy the energy bands of the crystal. For example, almost all metals are very good electrical conductors due to a half-filled conduction band, whereas metal oxides very often are good insulators with a completely filled valence band and an empty conduction band.

Now, how do semiconductors fit into this picture? As already suggested by their name, semiconductors are solids which are able to pass an electrical current much better than insulators, but at the same time not as efficiently as an electrical conductor. Obviously, semiconductors are solids in which for one reason or the other a few of the many tiles on the ground floor remain empty or a few of the conduction band tiles are occupied, or both. This particular constellation can be achieved via three routes, all of which are of fundamental importance in semiconductor physics.

The situation of an electrical insulator, where all tiles in the ground floor are occupied by exactly one inhabitant and all tiles in the first floor are empty. Thus, no charge transport can occur. To change this state of affairs, which is very unfavourable for device applications, semiconductor physicists have developed the concept of "doping". Contrary to the very negative image in sports, doping in semiconductors can be used to exactly pre-determine the electrical conductivity of a given device by addition of a precisely calculated amount of impurity atoms. In the analogue of our semiconductor building, doping can be achieved by adding special tiles with the following properties. As a first example, so-called "acceptor tiles" can be added to the ground floor. These acceptor tiles have the unpleasant property of swallowing exactly one inhabitant of the fully occupied ground floor, thus creating a "hole" in the overall occupancy. This allows the other inhabitants of the ground floor to move again. The hole created by the acceptor-tiles also will move at the same time, however in the opposite direction as compared to the inhabitants. In the same way, acceptor atoms incorporated into a semiconductor crystal will create a hole in the occupancy of the valence band, which will act as a "missing electron" and, thus, as a positively charged particle in electrical transport. Therefore, doping of a semiconductor crystal with acceptor atoms is referred to as "p-type" doping ("p" as in positive). The second possibility to induce controlled electrical conduction in an insulator is the doping with donor impurities. In our semiconductor building, such "donor tiles" bring along one additional inhabitant, who has to occupy a free tile in the first floor, since all tiles of the ground floor are already occupied. Accordingly, donor atoms added to a semiconductor crystal will provide additional electrons in the conduction band, which contribute to electronic charge transport in the expected way ("n-type" doping by additional negatively charged electrons).

In summary, it is indeed the possibility of doping with additional donor or acceptor atoms which distinguishes semiconductors from insulators or conductors as a third class of materials. Conductors will always pass electrical current with little resistance and independent of chemical details, no matter what. In the same way, insulators will always block electrical current. In contrast, semiconductors will either behave more like an insulator or more like a metal, depending on the level of doping. This provides semiconductors with the unique property to rectify, switch, or amplify electrical signals and, thus, to manipulate electrical current as it passes through the semiconductor crystal.

There is yet another way to produce additional holes in the valence band or electrons in the conduction band of a semiconductor without doping, namely by providing external energy in the form of heat or light. We all know from our own experience that it takes energy to walk up the stairs from the ground floor to the first floor. The same holds for the electrons in a semiconductor: electrons in the conduction band (first floor) have a higher energy than electrons in the valence band (ground floor). This difference in energy is determined by the band gap of the semiconductor. Since electrons are lazy, they prefer to stay on the ground floor. In order to move up to the first floor, they have to be stimulated by an external influence. One possibility is provided by the thermal movement of the atoms. At low temperatures, atoms are frozen at their lattice sites, but at higher temperatures they start to wiggle more and more and to push the electrons around. In the analogue of our semiconductor building, the thermal motion of the atoms can be visualized by a staircase leading from the ground floor to the first floor. The thermal motion of the atoms will push the electrons upwards step by step. The larger the band gap of the semiconductor, the longer the staircase and the smaller the number of electrons which actually make it all the way up to the first floor. However, in every well-planned building, there is also another possibility to reach the upper floors more easily: an elevator. In semiconductors, the job of the elevator is done by the elementary particles of light, the photons. If such a flash of light hits a semiconductor, it can directly elevate an electron from the valence band up to the conduction band. The stronger the light beam that falls onto the semiconductor, the more often the photon elevator will make the trip between the two floors, each time taking an electron with it. But also the other direction of electron transport is possible: electrons in the conduction band can return to the valence band, if there is a hole to accommodate the returning electron. This process is called "recombination". To do this, the electrons can either take the staircase down, giving their energy back to the atoms, or they can take the photon elevator. Then, each time the elevator doors open in the valence band and an electron recombines with a hole, an elementary flash of light is emitted by the semiconductor. The energy of the emitted photon is the same as the band gap of the semiconductor. Semiconductors with a small band gap emit red photons, whereas semiconductors with a large band gap emit blue photons.

Semiconductors and Light

This interaction between electrons and photons in semiconductors provides the basis of optoelectronics, another very important application area. The fundamental optoelectronic devices are solar cells and light-emitting diodes (LEDs). In a solar cell, light enters the semiconductor from the outside and, via the photon elevator, lifts electrons from the valence into the conduction band. The excited electrons leave the semiconductor as an electrical current. In an LED, on the other hand, electrons are injected into the conduction band of the semiconductor through one contact and extracted from the valence band through a second contact, leaving holes behind. When the injected electrons recombine with these holes, they emit light.

This short introduction into the basic properties and electronic processes of semiconductors should show why semiconductors are so important for electronics. They differ from metals and insulators through the fact that they can be doped, thus enabling complete control over their electrical conductivity necessary for tailor-made diodes and transistors. In addition we have seen how the existence of a band gap between the valence and the conduction band can be used for the absorption and emission of light. Unfortunately, we also have to pay a price for this flexibility. Since small amounts of foreign impurity atoms can considerable alter the electrical properties of semiconductors, the preparation and deposition of semiconductors requires ultra-pure environments and utmost care. And to emit or absorb light efficiently at different wavelengths, new semiconducting compounds with complex chemical compositions have to be synthesized, investigated, and optimized.

A Semiconductor Chip

But semiconductors are worth such an effort! Be it in computer sciences, the control of industrial processes, energy technology, information technology, consumer electronics, medical diagnostics, illumination technology or in airplanes, cars, appliances, phones, or watches: semiconductor devices are omnipresent and indispensable. Today, the direct annual market volume of semiconductor devices is about 300 Billion Euro, and the financial impact of semiconductors as a key enabling technology in many other markets is by far larger, still. Also in the future, semiconductors will be a part of our daily life, hopefully with a positive impact. A very visible example in the true sense of the words is the rapid progress in solid state lighting. Here, highly efficient LEDs are beginning to replace the old vacuum tube technology, much in the same way as 50 years ago solid state transistors have replaced vacuum tubes in analogue and digital signal processing. We all witness personally the current progress in computer processors, where Moore's law is still alive and well. And last but not least semiconductors will help to provide the world population with clean and sustainable energy. The current prediction is that in the year 2010 alone, solar cells with an accumulated electrical power of 20 Gigawatt will be installed, the equivalent of about 20 nuclear power plants.

ESSENCE OF A SEMICONDUCTOR

A semiconductor can be considered a material having a conductivity ranging between that of an insulator and a metal. A crucial property of semiconductors is the band gap; a range of forbidden energies within the electronic structure of the material. Semiconductors typically have bandgaps ranging between 1 and 4 eV, whilst insulators have larger bandgaps, often greater than 5 eV. The thermal energy available at room temperature, 300 K, is approximately 25 meV and is thus considerably smaller than the energy required to promote an electron across the bandgap. This means that there are a small number of carriers present at room temperature, due to the high energy tail of the Boltzmann-like thermal energy distribution. It is the ability to control the number of charge carriers that makes semiconductors of great technological importance.

Semiconducting materials are very sensitive to impurities in the crystal lattice as these can have a dramatic effect on the number of mobile charge carriers present. The controlled addition of these impurities is known as doping and allows the tuning of the electronic properties, an important requirement for technological applications. The properties of a pure semiconductor are called 'intrinsic', whilst those resulting from the introduction of dopants are called 'extrinsic'. This introduction of dopants results in the creation of new, intra-band, energy levels and the generation of either negative (electrons) or positive (holes) charge carriers. More detail on doping can be found on the electronic bandstructure webpage.

CHARGE CARRIERS IN SEMICONDUCTORS

When an electric field is applied to a metal, negatively charged electrons are accelerated and carry the resulting current. In a semiconductor the charge is not carried exclusively by electrons. Positively charged holes also carry charge. These may be viewed either as vacancies in the otherwise filled valence band, or equivalently as positively charged particles.

Since the Fermi-Dirac distribution is a step function at absolute zero, pure semiconductors will have all the states in the valence bands filled with electrons and will be insulators at absolute zero. This is depicted in the E-k diagram below; shaded circles represent filled momentum states and empty circles unfilled momentum states. In this diagram k, rather than *k*, has been used to denote that the wave vector is actually a vector, *i.e.*, a tensor of the first rank, rather than a scalar.

If the band gap is sufficiently small and the temperature is increased from absolute zero, some electrons may be thermally excited into the conduction band, creating an electron-hole pair. This is as a result of the smearing out of the Fermi-Dirac distribution at finite temperature. An electron may also move into the conduction band from the valence band if it absorbs a photon that corresponds to the energy difference between a filled state and an unfilled state.

If an electric field is now applied to the material, all of the electrons in the solid will feel a force from the electric field. However, because no two electrons can be in the exact same quantum state, an electron cannot gain any momentum from the electric field unless there is a vacant momentum state adjacent to the state being occupied by the electron. The electron in the conduction band can gain momentum from the electric field, as can an electron adjacent to the vacant state left behind in the valence band. Both of these electrons are shown moving to the right.

The vacant site in the valence band which has moved to the left can be viewed as being a particle which carries positive electric charge of equal magnitude to the electron charge. This is therefore a hole. It should be appreciated that these schematics do not represent electrons 'hopping' from site to site in real space, because the electrons are not localised to specific sites in space. These schematics are in momentum space. As such, holes should not be thought of as moving through the semiconductor like dislocations when metals are plastically deformed – it suffices to view them simply as particles which carry positive charge.

The opposite process to the creation of an electron-hole pair is called recombination. This occurs when an electron drops down in energy from the conduction band to the valence band. Just as the creation of an electron-hole pair may be induced by a photon, recombination can produce a photon. This is the principle behind semiconductor optical devices such as light-emitting diodes (LEDs), in which the photons are light of visible wavelength.

Intrinsic and Extrinsic Semiconductors

In most pure semiconductors at room temperature, the population of thermally excited charge carriers is very small. Often the concentration of charge carriers may be orders of magnitude lower than for a metallic conductor. For example, the number of thermally excited electrons cm^{-3} in silicon (Si) at 298 K is 1.5×10^{10}. In gallium arsenide (GaAs) the population is only 1.1×10^{6} electrons cm^{-3}. This may be compared with the number density of free electrons in a typical metal, which is of the order of 10^{28} electrons cm^{-3}.

Given these numbers of charge carriers, it is no surprise that, when they are extremely pure, silicon and other semiconductors have high electrical resistivities, and therefore low electrical conductivities. This problem can be overcome by doping a semiconducting material with impurity atoms. Even very small controlled additions of impurity atoms at the 0.0001% level can make very large differences to the conductivity of a semiconductor.

It is easiest to begin with a specific example. Silicon is a group IV element, and has 4 valence electrons per atom. In pure silicon the valence band is completely filled at absolute zero. At finite temperatures the only charge carriers are the electrons in the conduction band and the holes in the valence band that arise as a result of the thermal excitation of electrons to the conduction band. These charge carriers are called *intrinsic* charge carriers, and necessarily there are equal numbers of electrons and holes. Pure silicon is therefore an example of an intrinsic semiconductor.

If a very small number of atoms of a group V element such as phosphorus (P) are added to the silicon as substitutional atoms in the lattice, additional valence electrons are introduced into the material because each phosphorus atom has 5 valence electrons. These additional electrons are bound only weakly to their parent impurity atoms (the bonding energies are of the order of hundredths of an eV), and even at very low temperatures these electrons can be promoted into the conduction band of the semiconductor. This is often represented schematically in band diagrams by the addition of 'donor levels' just below the bottom of the conduction band, as in the schematic below.

The presence of the dotted line in this schematic does not mean that there now exist allowed energy states within the band gap. The dotted line represents the existence of additional electrons which may be easily excited into the conduction band. Semiconductors that have been doped in this way will have a surplus of electrons, and are called n-type semiconductors. In such semiconductors, electrons are the majority carriers.

Conversely, if a group III element, such as aluminium (Al), is used to substitute for some of the atoms in silicon, there will be a deficit in the number of valence electrons in the material. This introduces electron-accepting levels just above the top of the valence band, and causes more holes to be introduced into the valence band. Hence, the majority charge carriers are positive holes in this case. Semiconductors doped in this way are termed p-type semiconductors.

Doped semiconductors (either n-type or p-type) are known as extrinsic semiconductors. The activation energy for electrons to be donated by or accepted to impurity states is usually so low that at room temperature the concentration of majority charge carriers is similar to the concentration of impurities. It should be remembered that in an extrinsic semiconductor there is an contribution to the total number of charge carriers from intrinsic electrons and holes, but at room temperature this contribution is often very small in comparison with the number of charge carriers introduced by the controlled impurity doping of the semiconductor.

Calculation of the Intrinsic Carrier Density

Intrinsic semiconductors are almost always non-degenerate, so that the expressions for the electron and hole densities in non-degenerate semiconductors apply. Labelling the Fermi energy of intrinsic material E_i, we can then write two relations between the intrinsic carrier density and the intrinsic Fermi energy, namely:

$$n_i = N_C e^{(E_i - E_C)/kT} = N_V e^{(E_V - E_i)/kT}$$

It is possible to eliminate the intrinsic Fermi energy from both equations, simply by multiplying both equations and taking the square root. This provides an expression for the intrinsic carrier density as a function of the effective density of states in the conduction and valence band and the bandgap energy $E_g = E_c - E_v$.

$$n_i = \sqrt{N_C N_V}\, e^{-(E_C - E_V)/2kT}$$

A numeric calculation of the intrinsic carrier density for Ge, Si and GaAs as well as its temperature dependence.

The Mass Action Law

It turns out that the product of the electron and hole density, in a non-degenerate semiconductor is always equal to the square of the intrinsic carrier density, and not only for intrinsic semiconductors. Multiplying the expressions for the electron and hole densities in a non-degenerate semiconductor yields:

$$n - p = N_C N_V e^{(E_V - E_C)/kT} = n_i^2$$

This property is referred to as the *mass action law*. It is a powerful relation which enables to quickly find the hole density if the electron density is known or *vice-versa*.

Calculation of the Intrinsic Fermi Energy

The intrinsic electron and hole density can be solved for the intrinsic Fermi energy, yielding:

$$E_i = \frac{E_C + E_V}{2} + \frac{1}{2} kT \ln\left(\frac{N_V}{N_C}\right)$$

The intrinsic Fermi energy is typically close to the *midgap* energy, half way between the conduction and valence band edge. The intrinsic Fermi energy can also be expressed as a function of the effective masses of the electrons and holes in the semiconductor. The effective density of states in the conduction and valence band, yielding:

$$E_i = \frac{E_C + E_V}{2} + \frac{3}{4} kT \ln\left(\frac{m_h^*}{m_e^*}\right)$$

Function of the Intrinsic Parameters

Dividing the expression for the carrier densities, by the one for the intrinsic density allows to write the carrier densities as a function of the intrinsic density and the Fermi energy, or:

$$n = n_i e^{(E_F - E_i)/kT}$$

and

$$p = n_i e^{(E_i - E_F)/kT}$$

We will use primarily these two equations to find the electron and hole density in a semiconductor. The same relations can also be rewritten to obtain the Fermi energy from either carrier density, namely:

$$E_F = E_i + kT \ln \frac{n}{n_i}$$

and

$$E_F = E_i + kT \ln \frac{p}{n_i}$$

Temperature Dependence of the Intrinsic Carrier Density

The temperature dependence of the intrinsic carrier density is dominated by the exponential dependence on the energy bandgap. In addition one has to consider the temperature dependence of the effective densities of states and that of the energy bandgap. A plot of the intrinsic carrier density versus temperature. The temperature dependence of the effective masses was not included since it is small compared to the others.

Extrinsic Semiconductors

The conductivity of an intrinsic semiconductor depends

exponentially on temperature and that at room temperature intrinsic semiconductors are rather poor conductors. It is possible to dope semiconductors with impurity atoms that improve the conductivity dramatically and makes the conductivity nearly constant as a function of temperature near room temperature. Doped semiconductors are called extrinsic semiconductors.

Doped Semiconductors

For a doped semiconductor, the density of electrons in the conduction band is,

$$n = N_c(300)\left(\frac{T}{300}\right)^{\frac{3}{2}} \exp\left(\frac{E_f - E_c}{k_B T}\right).$$

the density of holes in the valence band is,

$$p = N_v(300)\left(\frac{T}{300}\right)^{\frac{3}{2}} \exp\left(\frac{E_v - E_f}{k_B T}\right),$$

the density of ionized donors is,

$$N_d^+ = \frac{N_d}{1 + 2\exp\left(\frac{E_f - E_d}{k_B T}\right)},$$

and the density of ionized acceptors is,

$$N_a^- = \frac{N_a}{1 + 4\exp\left(\frac{E_a - E_f}{k_B T}\right)}.$$

The factor of 4 is valid in the formula for the acceptors if the semiconductor has a light hole and a heavy hole band as Si and Ge do. The four quantities n, p, N_d, and N_a can only be determined if the Fermi energy, E_f, is known. Typically, E_f must first be determined from the charge neutrality condition,

$$n + N_a^- = p + N_d^+.$$

The Fermi energy can be found by solving the charge neutrality condition numerically. One way to do this is to programme the formulas for n, p, N_d^+, and N_a^- in a spreadsheet. Then choose a temperature and calculate n, p, N_d^+, N_a^- for every value of the Fermi energy between E_v and E_c. For one of these E_f values, the charge neutrality condition will be satisfied.

When $n + N_a^-$ and, $p + N_d^+$ are ploted as a function of E_F, the Fermi energy is where the two lines cross. A plot like the one below can be generated by pressing the button below the plot.

The Fermi energy can be calculated as a function of temperature by determining where $n + N_a^- = p + N_d^+$ for every temperature. A plot like the one below can be generated by pressing the button below the plot.

Normally it is not necessary to determine E_f numerically and the following approximation is sufficient.

n-type $N_d > N_a$:

$n = N_d - N_a$

$p = n_i^2/n$

$E_f = E_c - k_B T \ln(N_c/(N_d - N_a))$

p-type $N_a > N_d$:

$p = N_a - N_d$

$n = n_i^2/p$

$E_f = E_v + k_B T \ln(N_v/(N_a - N_d))$

Effect of Temperature on Extrinsic Semiconductors

With the increase in temperature, the concentration of minority carriers starts increasing. Eventually, a temperature is reached called the critical temperature (85° C in case of germanium and 200° C in case of silicon) when the number of covalent bonds that are broken is very large and the number of holes is approximately equal to number of electrons. The extrinsic semiconductor now behaves essentially like an intrinsic semi-conductor.

Movement of Charge Carriers

There are two mechanisms by which holes and electrons move through a semiconductor crystal. These are diffusion and drift causing diffusion current and drift current.

In semiconductors concentrations of charge carriers (either electrons or holes) tend to distribute themselves uniformly throughout a semiconductor crystal. The charge carrier movement that results is called the diffusion current. When available charges move under the influence of an influence of an applied electric field, the drift current results in. Drift and diffusion occur simultaneously in a semiconductor.

Conductivity of Extrinsic Semiconductors

Under thermal equilibrium the product of concentration of free electrons, n and the concentration of holes, p is constant and is independent of the amount of doping by donor and acceptor impurities. This is known as mass-action law.

So $n.p. = n_i^2$

Where n_i is the intrinsic concentration and is a function of temperature. For an intrinsic semiconductor $n = p = n_i$

If N_D is the concentration of donor atoms there will be N_D immobile positive charges per unit volume contributed by donor ions as the donor atoms are ionized. Thus positive charge density will be $N_D + p$.

Similarly as the acceptor atoms are ionized at room temperature there will be N_A immobile negative charges per unit volume and total negative charge density will be N_{A-} +n where $N-_A$ is the concentration of acceptor atoms. Since the semiconductor is neutral, the magnitude of positive charge density will be equal to the magnitude of negative charge density

i.e. $N_D + p = N_A + n$

In n-type semiconductors there is no acceptor doping *i.e.* $N_A = 0$. Also the number of electrons is much greater than the number of holes *i.e.* n

So $n = N_D$

i.e. in n-type semiconductors, the free electron concentration is approximately equal to the density of donor atoms.

Now the concentration of holes in n-type semiconductors will be given by the expression

$P = n_i^2/ n = N_I^2/ N_D$ $(p.n = n_i^2)$

Similarly in case of p-type semiconductor

$P = N_A$

and $n = n_i^2 / N_A$

Total conductivity in semiconductor is given by the expression

$\sigma = \sigma_n + \sigma_p = ne\mu_e + pe\mu_h = e(n\mu_e + p\mu_h)$

In case of n type semiconductor hole concentration p_n is negligible and electron concentration $n_n = N_D$. So conductivity in n-type semiconductor,

$\sigma = eN_A\mu_e$

Total current density due to drift of electrons and holes on application of electric field E J = Current density due to hole drift, Jh + Current density due to electron drift,

$_{Je} = Epe\mu_h + Ene\mu_e + Ee$

The carrier currents are also due to concentration gradients in the doped material which leads to the diffusion of carriers from high concentration region to low concentration region.

The current density due to hole diffusion,

$J_h = -e\, D_h\, dp/dx$

And the current density due to hole diffusion,

$J_e = e\, D_e\, dn/dx$

Where D_{h-} and D_e and mobility's and are related by Einstein relations

$D_h / \mu_h = D_e / \mu_e = KT/ e = T/ 11600 = v_M$

Where K is Boltzmann's constant and Vm is 25 mV at room temperature of 25°C.

Effect of Temperature on Extrinsic Semiconductor

Transtutors is the best place to get answers to all your doubts regarding effect of temperature on extrinsic semiconductors. You can submit your school, college or university level homework or assignment to us and we will make sure that you get the answers you need which are timely and also cost effective. Our tutors are available round the clock to help you out in any way with electrical engineering.

Transtutors has a vast panel of experienced electrical

engineering tutors who specialize in effect of temperature on extrinsic semiconductors and can explain the different concepts to you effectively. You can also interact directly with our electrical engineering tutors for a one to one session and get answers to all your problems in your school, college or university level Industrial management. Our tutors will make sure that you achieve the highest grades for your electrical engineering assignments. We will make sure that you get the best help possible for exams such as the AP, AS, A level, GCSE, IGCSE, IB, Round Square etc.

Semiconductor Structure

Semiconductors, such as Silicon (Si) are made up of individual atoms bonded together in a regular, periodic structure to form an arrangement whereby each atom is surrounded by 8 electrons. An individual atom consists of a nucleus made up of a core of protons (positively charged particles) and neutrons (particles having no charge) surrounded by electrons. The number of electrons and protons is equal, such that the atom is overall electrically neutral. The electrons surrounding each atom in a semiconductor are part of a covalent bond. A covalent bond consists of two atoms "sharing" a single electron. Each atom forms 4 covalent bonds with the 4 surrounding atoms. Therefore, between each atom and its 4 surrounding atoms, 8 electrons are being shared. The structure of a semiconductor is shown in the figure below.

CONDUCTION IN SEMICONDUCTORS

The bond structure of a semiconductor determines the material properties of a semiconductor. One key effect are the energy levels which the electrons can occupy and how they move about the crystal lattice. The electrons in the covalent bond formed between each of the atoms in the lattice structure are held in place by this bond and hence they are localized to the region surrounding the atom. These bonded electrons cannot move or change energy, and thus are not considered "free" and cannot participate in current flow, adsorption, or other physical processes of interest in solar cells. However, only at absolute zero are all electrons in this "stuck," bonded arrangement. At elevated temperatures, especially at the temperatures where solar cells operate, electrons can gain enough energy to escape from their bonds. When this happens, the electrons are free to move about the crystal lattice and participate in conduction. At room temperature, a semiconductor has enough free electrons to allow it to conduct current. At or close to absolute zero a semiconductor behaves like an insulator.

When an electron gains enough energy to participate in conduction (is "free"), it is at a high energy state. When the electron is bound, and thus cannot participate in conduction, the electron is at a low energy state. Therefore, the presence of the bond between the two atoms introduces two distinct energy states for the electrons. The electron cannot attain energy values intermediate to these two levels; it is either at a low energy position in the bond, or it has gained enough energy to break free and therefore has a certain minimum energy. This minimum energy is called the "band gap" of a semiconductor. The number and energy of these free electrons, those electrons participating in conduction, is basic to the operation of electronic devices.

The space left behind by the electrons allows a covalent bond to move from one electron to another, thus appearing to be a positive charge moving through the crystal lattice. This empty space is commonly called a "hole", and is similar to an electron, but with a positive charge.

The most important parameters of a semiconductor material for solar cell operation are:

- The band gap;
- The number of free carriers (electrons or holes) available for conduction; and
- The "generation" and recombination of free carriers (electrons or holes) in response to light shining on the material.

Band Gap

The band gap of a semiconductor is the minimum energy required to excite an electron that is stuck in its bound state into a free state where it can participate in conduction. The band structure of a semiconductor gives the energy of the electrons on the y-axis and is called a "band diagram". The lower energy level of a semiconductor is called the "valence band" (E_V) and the energy level at which an electron can be considered free is called the "conduction band" (E_C). The band gap (E_G) is the gap in energy between the bound state and the free state, between the valence band and conduction band. Therefore, the band gap is the minimum change in energy required to excite the electron so that it can participate in conduction.

Once the electron becomes excited into the conduction band, it is free to move about the semiconductor and participate in conduction. However, the excitation of an electron to the conduction band will also allow an additional conduction process to take place. The excitation of an electron to the conduction band leaves behind an empty space for an electron. An electron from a neighbouring atom can move into this empty space. When this electron moves, it leaves behind another space. The continual movement of the space for an electron, called a "hole", can be illustrated as the movement of a positively charged particle through the crystal structure. Consequently, the excitation of an electron into the conduction band results in not only an electron in the conduction band but also a hole in the valence band. Thus, both the electron and hole can participate in conduction and are called "carriers".

The concept of a moving "hole" is analogous to that of a bubble in a liquid. Although it is actually the liquid that moves, it is easier to describe the motion of the bubble going in the opposite direction.

Intrinsic Carrier Concentration

The thermal excitation of a carrier from the valence band to the conduction band creates free carriers in both bands. The concentration of these carriers is called the intrinsic carrier concentration, denoted by n_i. Semiconductor material which has not had impurities added to it in order to change the carrier concentrations is called intrinsic material. The intrinsic carrier concentration is the number of electrons in the conduction band or the number of holes in the valence band in intrinsic material. This number of carriers depends on the band gap of the material and on the temperature of the material. A large band gap will make it more difficult for a carrier to be thermally excited across the band gap, and therefore the intrinsic carrier concentration is lower in higher band gap materials. Alternatively, increasing the temperature makes it more likely that an electron will be excited into the conduction band, which will increase the intrinsic carrier concentration. This translates directly to solar cell efficiency.

Intrinsic Carrier Concentration of Silicon as a Function of Temperature

At 300 K the generally accepted value for the intrinsic carrier concentration of silicon, n_i, is 1.01×10^{10} cm^{-3}. The previously accepted value was 1.45×10^{10}. An empirical fit to the measured data over the range 275 K to 375 K is given by:

$$n_i = 9.38 \times 10^{19} \left(\frac{T}{300}\right)^2 \exp\left(-\frac{6884}{T}\right)$$

While the intrinsic carrier concentration is normally quoted at 300 K, solar cells are usually measured at 25 °C where the intrinsic carrier concentration is 8.6×10^9 cm^{-3}. The above equation is implemented in the mini-calculator below:

Temperature - Intrinsic Carrier Concentration Calculator
Temperature, T = 278 K
Intrinsic Carrier Concentration, n_i = 8.59e9 cm^{-3}

Doping

It is possible to shift the balance of electrons and holes in a silicon crystal lattice by "doping" it with other atoms.

Atoms with one more valence electron than silicon are used to produce "*n*-type" semiconductor material. These *n*-type materials are group V elements in the periodic table, and thus their atoms have 5 valence electrons that can form covalent bonds with the 4 valence electrons that silicon atoms have. Because only 4 valence electrons are needed from each atom (silicon and *n*-type) to form the covalent bonds around the silicon atoms, the extra valence electron present (because *n*-type materials have 5 valence electrons) when the two atoms bond is free to participate in conduction. Therefore, more electrons are added to the conduction band and hence increases the number of electrons present.

Atoms with one less valence electron result in "*p*-type" material. These *p*-type materials are group III elements in the periodic table. Therefore, *p*-type material has only 3 valence electrons with which to interact with silicon atoms. The net result is a hole, as not enough electrons are present to form the 4 covalent bonds surrounding the atoms. In *p*-type material, the number of electrons trapped in bonds is higher, thus effectively increasing the number of holes. In doped material, there is always more of one type of carrier than the other and the type of carrier with the higher concentration is called a "majority carrier", while the lower concentration carrier is called a "minority carrier."

DOPED SEMICONDUCTORS

Doped semiconductors are semiconductors which contain impurities, foreign atoms which are incorporated into the crystal structure of the semiconductor. These impurities can either be unintentional due to lack of control during the growth of the semiconductor or they can be added on purpose to provide free carriers in the semiconductor.

The generation of free carriers requires not only the presence of impurities, but also that the impurities give off electrons to the conduction band in which case they are called *donors* or that they give off holes to the valence band in which case they are called *acceptors* (since they effectively accept an electron from the filled valence band).

A semiconductor doped with impurities which are ionized (meaning that the impurity atoms either have donated or accepted an electron) will therefore contain free carriers. *Shallow impurities* are impurities which require little energy-typically around the thermal energy or less-to ionize. *Deep impurities* require energies larger than the thermal energy to ionize so that only a fraction of the impurities present in the semiconductor contribute to free carriers. Deep impurities which are more than five times the thermal energy away from either band edge are very unlikely to ionize. Such impurities can be effective recombination centres in which electrons and holes fall and annihilate each other. Such deep impurities are also called *traps*. Ionized donors provide free electrons in a semiconductor which is then called *n-type,* while ionized acceptors provide free holes in a semiconductor which we refer to as being a *p-type* semiconductor.

Ionization of Impurities

The ionization of the impurities is dependent on the thermal energy and the position of the impurity level within the energy band gap. Statistical thermodynamics can be used to obtain the probability that the impurity is ionized. The resulting expression is similar to the Fermi-Dirac probability function except for a factor which accounts for the fact that the impurity can only give off one hole or one electron and also accounts for the degeneracy of the valence band.

Shallow impurities readily ionize so that the free carrier density equals the impurity concentration. For donors this implies that the electron density equals the donor concentration, or:

$$N_d^+ \cong N_d$$

While for accepters the hole density equals the acceptor concentration, or:

$$N_a^- \cong N_a$$

If a semiconductor contains both shallow donors and shallow acceptors it is called *compensated* since equal amounts of donors and acceptors compensate each other, yielding no free carriers. The presence of shallow donors and shallow acceptors in a semiconductor cause the electrons given off by the donor to fall into the acceptor state which ionizes the acceptor without yielding a free electron or hole. The resulting carrier density in compensated material which contains both shallow donors and shallow acceptors is approximately equal to the difference between the donor and acceptor concentration if the donor concentration is larger, yielding n-type material, or:

$$N \cong N_d^+ - N_a^-, \text{ if } N_d^+ - N_a^- >> n_i$$

If the acceptor concentration is larger than the donor concentration, the hole density of the resulting p-type material equals the difference between the acceptor and donor concentration, or:

$$p \cong N_d^+ - N_a^-, \text{ if } N_d^+ - N_a^- >> n_i$$

Charge in the Semiconductor

The charge density in a semiconductor depends on the free electron and hole density and on the ionized impurity densities. Ionized donors have given off an electron and are then positively charged, while ionized acceptors have accepted an electron and are negatively charged. The total charge density is therefore given by:

$$\rho = q\left(p - n + N_d^+ - N_a^-\right).$$

Calculation of the Free Carrier Density

The reader is referred to the general analysis and the graphical solution for a more complete treatment of the problem.

Analysis of Non-degenerate Semiconductors

The calculation of the electron density starts by assuming that the semiconductor is neutral so that there is a zero charge density in the material. The hole concentration in equilibrium is written as a function of the electron density by using the mass action law. This yields the following relation between the electron density and the ionized impurity densities:

$$n = \frac{n_i^2}{n} + N_d^+ - N_a^-$$

Solving this quadratic equation yields a solution for the electron density, namely:

$$n = \frac{N_d^+ - N_a^-}{2} + \sqrt{\left(\frac{N_d^+ - N_a^-}{2}\right)^2 + n_i^2}$$

The same derivation can be repeated for holes, rather than electrons and yields:

$$p = \frac{N_a^- - N_d^+}{2} + \sqrt{\left(\frac{N_a^- - N_d^+}{2}\right)^2 + n_i^2}$$

The above expressions yield the free carrier densities for compensated semiconductors assuming that all donors and acceptors are ionized.

From the carrier densities one then obtains the Fermi energies using:

$$E_F = E_i + kT \ln \frac{n}{n_i}$$

or

$$E_F = E_i + kT \ln \frac{p}{n_i}$$

The Fermi energies in n-type and p-type silicon at 300 K as a function of doping density is shown in the figure below:

The figure illustrates how the fermi energies vary with doping density: starting from the intrinsic energy at low doping densities, the fermi energy varies linearly when plotting the density on a logarithmic scale up to a doping density of 10^{18} cm^{-3}. This simple dependence requires that the semiconductor is neither intrinsic nor degenerate and that all the dopants are ionized. For compensated material one uses the net doping density, $|N_d - N_a|$.

General Analysis

A more general analysis takes also into account the fact that the ionization of the impurities is not 100%, but instread is given by the impurity distribution functions.

The analysis still begins by assuming that there is no net charge in the semiconductor. This condition is referred to as *charge neutrality*. This also means that the total density of positively charged particles (holes and ionized donors) must equals the total density of negatively charged particles (electrons and ionized acceptors) yielding:

$$p + N_d^+ = n + N_a^-$$

The electron and hole densities are then written as a function of the Fermi energy using the expressions for non-degenerate semiconductors, while the ionized impurity densities equal the impurity density multiplied with the probability of occupancy for the acceptors and one minus the probability of occupancy for the donors, yielding:

$$n_i \exp\left(\frac{E_i - E_F}{kT}\right) + \frac{N_D}{1 + 2.e^{(E_F - E_D)/kT}}$$

$$= n_i \exp\left(\frac{E_F - E_i}{kT}\right) + \frac{N_A}{1 + 4.e^{(E_A - E_F)/kT}}$$

Graphical Solution

A graphical solution to the equation above can be obtained by plotting both sides of the equation as a function of the Fermi energy as illustrated in the figure below.

The figure shows the positive and negative charge densities as well as the electron and hole densities as a function of the Fermi energy for silicon containing 10^{16} donors and 10^{14} acceptors. The arrow indicates the intersection of both curves. This intersection provides the Fermi energy and the electron density in the presence of both donors and acceptors.

Temperature Dependence and Carrier Freeze-out

Operation of devices over a wide temperature range requires a detailed knowledge of the carrier density as a function of temperature. While at intermediate temperatures the carrier density approximately equals the net doping, $|N_A - N_D|$, it increases at high temperatures for which the intrinsic density approaches the net doping density and decreases at low temperatures due to incomplete ionization of the dopants.

At high temperatures the carrier density simply equals the intrinsic carrier concentration or:

$$n = n_i = \sqrt{N_C N_V} \exp\left(-\frac{E_g}{2kT}\right), \text{ for } T \geq \frac{E_g}{k \ln N_C N_V - 2k \ln | N_D - N_A |}$$

while at low temperatures the carrier density is dominated by the ionization of the donors. For non-degenerate semiconductors the density at low temperature equals:

$$n = \frac{(N^* + N_A)}{2} + \sqrt{\frac{(N^* + N_A)^2}{4} + N^*(N_D - N_A)},$$

$$\text{for } T \leq \frac{E_g}{k \ln N_C N_V - 2k \ln | N_D - N_A |}$$

where

$$N^* = \frac{N_C}{2} \exp\left(-\frac{E_C - E_D}{kT}\right).$$

The temperature dependence is related to an activation energy by fitting the carrier density versus $1/T$ on a semi-logarithmic scale to a straight line of the form $n(T)$ = C x exp $(-E_A/kT)$, where C is a constant. At high temperatures this activation energy equals half the bandgap energy or $E_A = E_g/2$.

The temperature dependence at low temperatures is somewhat more complex as it depends on whether or not the material is compensated. Calculated for silicon containing both donors and acceptors. At a 70 K the electron density is below the donor density but still larger than the acceptor density.

Under such conditions the activation energy equals half of the ionization energy of the donors or $E_A = (E_C - E_D)/2$. At lower temperatures where the electron density is lower than the acceptor density, the activation energy equals the ionization energy or $E_A = (E_C - E_D)$. This behaviour is explained by the fact that the Fermi energy in compensated material is fixed at the donor energy since the donors levels are always partially empty as electrons are removed from the donor atoms to fill the acceptor energy levels. If the acceptor density is smaller than the electron density, the Fermi energy does change with temperature and the activation energy approaches half of the ionization energy.

Lightly doped semiconductors suffer from freeze-out at relatively high temperature. Higher-doped semiconductor freeze-out at lower temperatures. Highly-doped semiconductors do not contain a single donor energy levels, but rather an impurity band which overlaps with the conduction or valence band. The overlap of the two bands results in free carriers even at zero Kelvin. Degenerately doping a semiconductor therefore eliminates freeze-out effects.

EINSTEIN'S EQUATION

To state Einstein's equation in simple English, we need to consider a round ball of test particles that are all initially at rest relative to each other. As we have seen, this is a sensible notion only in the limit where the ball is very small. If we start with such a ball of particles, it will, to second order in time, become an ellipsoid as time passes. This should not be too surprising, because any linear transformation applied to a ball gives an ellipsoid, and as the saying goes, "everything is linear to first order". Here we get a bit more: the relative velocity of the particles starts out being zero, so to first order in time the ball does not change shape at all: the change is a second-order effect.

Let $V(t)$ be the volume of the ball after a proper time t has elapsed, as measured by the particle at the centre of the ball. Then Einstein's equation says:

$$\frac{\ddot{V}}{V}\bigg|_{t=0} = -\frac{1}{2}\begin{pmatrix} \text{flow of } t\text{-momentum in } t \text{ direction} + \\ \text{flow of } x\text{-momentum in } x \text{ direction} + \\ \text{flow of } y\text{-momentum in } y \text{ direction} + \\ \text{flow of } z\text{-momentum in } z \text{ direction} \end{pmatrix}$$

where these flows are measured at the centre of the ball at time zero, using local inertial coordinates. These flows are the diagonal components of a 4 × 4 matrix T called the 'stress-energy tensor'. The components $T_{\alpha\beta}$ of this matrix say how much momentum in the α direction is flowing in the β direction through a given point of spacetime, where α, β = t, x, y, z. The flow of t-momentum in the t-direction is just the energy density, often denoted ρ. The flow of x-momentum in the x-direction is the 'pressure in the x direction' denoted P_x, and similarly for y and z. It takes a while to figure out why pressure is really the flow of momentum, but it is eminently worth doing. Most texts explain this fact by considering the example of an ideal gas.

In any event, we may summarize Einstein's equation as follows:

$$\frac{\ddot{V}}{V}\bigg|_{t=0} = -\frac{1}{2}(\rho + P_x + P_y + P_z).$$

This equation says that positive energy density and positive pressure curve spacetime in a way that makes a freely falling ball of point particles tend to shrink. Since $E = mc^2$ and we are working in units where c = 1, ordinary mass density counts as a form of energy density. Thus a massive object will make a swarm of freely falling particles at rest around it start to shrink. In short: *gravity attracts.*

We promised to state Einstein's equation in plain English, but have not done so yet. Here it is:

> Given a small ball of freely falling test particles initially at rest with respect to each other, the rate at which it begins to shrink is proportional to its volume times: the energy density at the centre of the ball, plus the pressure in the *x* direction at that point, plus

the pressure in the y direction, plus the pressure in the z direction.

Before we begin, it is worth noting an even simpler formulation of Einstein's equation that applies when the pressure is the same in every direction:

> Given a small ball of freely falling test particles initially at rest with respect to each other, the rate at which it begins to shrink is proportional to its volume times: the energy density at the centre of the ball plus three times the pressure at that point.

The Einstein Field Equations

When expressed mathematically, Einstein's gravitation theory yields a set of formulas known collectively as the Einstein Field Equations. In a nutshell, this equation describes the properties of a gravitational field surrounding a given mass. Stated simply, the equation describes how an object curves space and how the curvature, in turn, stretches or squeezes matter in three spatial directions: north-south, east-west and up-down.

However, applying the equations is no easy task. Mathematically, General Relativity is built upon ten so-called "coupled hyperbolic-elliptic nonlinear partial differential equations" which take many pages to write down (and a deep breath just to say!). For a mathematician, the difficulties lie in the fact that the equations are nonlinear and coupled also and in their sheer number of terms. After he published his famous paper in 1916, Einstein later conceded that the mathematical difficulties of his General Theory of Relativity were a "very serious" impediment to its further development. So serious, in fact, that it took nearly 75 years before the best minds in the field could come close to solving the equations stated by the theory. Now, high performance computers permit more accurate modelling of the distortions of space-time by massive objects, including black holes.

Spherical Symmetry

The first person to apply Einstein's general theory was

the German astrophysicist Karl Schwarzschild. It was 1916, and the First World War was still raging. Just a few days after reading Einstein's newly published theory while stationed at the Russian front, Schwarzschild began to figure out its consequences for the gravitational fields of stars.

For his first attempt, Schwarzschild simplified the problem by considering a perfectly spherical star at rest, ignoring the effects of the star's interior. He sent his preliminary solution of the star's spacetime curvature to Einstein, who reported the results on Schwarzschild's behalf at a physics meeting in January. The curvature of spacetime predicted by the solution became known as the Schwarzschild geometry and had profound implications on future research into gravitation and cosmology.

A few weeks later, Schwarzschild sent a second paper, this time describing the spacetime curvature inside a star. Tragically, Schwarzschild died a few months later of an illness he contracted while at the Russian front.

Schwarzschild was describing a singularity, a region of infinite spacetime curvature that is postulated to lie within what has more recently been termed a black hole. Einstein considered the "Schwarzschild singularity" and black holes as bizzarre constructs, resisting the logic of his own theory right up to his death in 1955.

However, though debate continues on the nature of singularities, since the 1960s there has been mounting indirect evidence that black holes might exist in places where, for example, a collapsed star's intense gravitational field allows nothing, including light, to escape. In that sense, the star disappears from the visible universe and forms what is now called a black hole.

Had Schwarzschild lived, he would have likely developed more elaborate scenarios of spacetime curvature. Nevertheless, his early achievement was not topped for nearly 50 years, when the simple, spherical geometry of his solution was finally expanded to consider the gravitational effects of a spinning star.

Now, in the 1990s, astrophysicists are using supercomputers to extend the calculations to more complex spacetime geometries, including spinning objects that no longer retain their simple, spherical symmetry. Such objects typically exhibit "axisymmetry"—symmetry about one axis (like a football)—or no symmetry at all. The mathematics, however, becomes very difficult to state, let alone solve analytically.

HALL EFFECT

Electrical currents are affected by magnetic fields. When a magnetic field is applied perpendicular to the flow of current, the field causes resistance in the current. This is a manifestation of the Lorentz force, which pushes the negatively charged electrons in the current in a direction dictated by the left hand rule. This movement of electrons results in a weak but measurable potential difference, orvoltage, perpendicular both to the current flow and the applied magnetic field. This is known as the Hall effect, named after American physicist Edwin Hall, who discovered the phenomenon in 1879. This effect is particularly pronounced in thin metals, and is easily observable in a low-density plasma (an electrically conductive ionized gas), such as a fluorescent light, as in this tutorial.

The ends of the Hall Effect Tube (a vacuum with a trace of neon gas) are connected to a Battery. A smaller tube intersects with the larger tube; attached to its ends are electrodes that are connected to a Voltmeter to detect voltage. Notice that the neon in the tube is fluorescing (emitting light) due to the excitation of the electrical current supplied from the battery. This current is reflected in the flow of electrons, depicted here as small yellow particles. Adjust the Magnet Position slider to move the strong permanent magnet closer to the Hall Effect Tube. Check the voltmeter; the Hall effect causes a Hall voltage perpendicular to the main current. Observe how the flow of electrons responds to the magnetic field. Experiment with the blue Flip Magnet and Flip Battery buttons to see how this affects the potential difference.

A similar effect is seen in semiconductors, where the Hall effect plays a large role in the design of integrated circuits on semiconductor chips. In most conductors, such as metals, the Hall effect is very small because the density of conduction in electrons is very large and the drift speed (charged particle erraticism) is extremely small, even for the highest obtainable current densities. The Hall effect is therefore considered unimportant in most electric circuits and devices and is not mentioned in many texts on electricity and magnetism. However, in semiconductors and in most laboratory plasmas, the current density is many orders of magnitude smaller than in metals, and the Hall effect is correspondingly larger and is often easily observable. Some devices for measuring magnetic fields make use of semiconductors as the sensing elements and are called Hall probes.

DIRECT AND INDIRECT BAND GAP SEMICONDUCTORS

The band gap represents the minimum energy difference between the top of the valence band and the bottom of the conduction band, However, the top of the valence band and the bottom of the conduction band are not generally at the same value of the electron momentum. In a direct band gap semiconductor, the top of the valence band and the bottom of the conduction band occur at the same value of momentum, as in the schematic below.

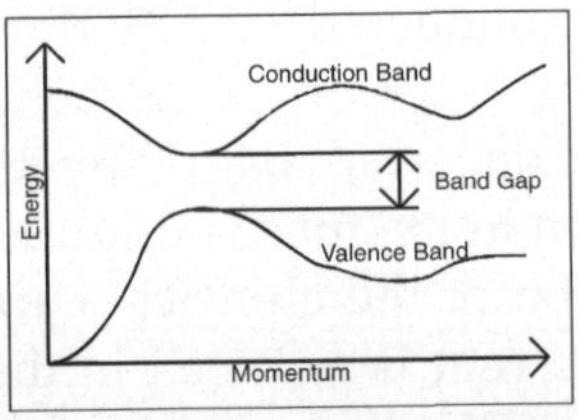

In an indirect band gap semiconductor, the maximum energy of the valence band occurs at a different value of momentum to the minimum in the conduction band energy:

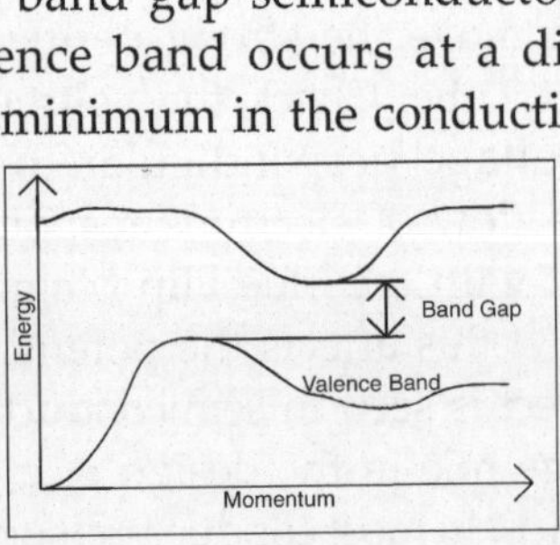

The difference between the two is most important in optical devices. The charge carriers in semiconductors, a photon can provide the energy to produce an electron-hole pair.

Each photon of energy E has momentum $p = \frac{E}{c}$, where c is the velocity of light. An optical photon has an energy of the order of 10^{-19} J, and, since $c = 3 \times 10^8$ ms^{-1}, a typical photon has a very small amount of momentum.

A photon of energy E_g, where E_g is the band gap energy, can produce an electron-hole pair in a direct band gap semiconductor quite easily, because the electron does not need to be given very much momentum. However, an electron must also undergo a significant change in its momentum for a photon of energy E_g to produce an electron-hole pair in an indirect band gap semiconductor. This is possible, but it requires such an electron to interact not only with the photon to gain energy, but also with a lattice vibration called a phonon in order to either gain or lose momentum.

The indirect process proceeds at a much slower rate, as it requires three entities to intersect in order to proceed: an electron, a photon and a phonon. This is analogous to chemical reactions, where, in a particular reaction step, a reaction between two molecules will proceed at a much greater rate than a process which involves three molecules.

The same principle applies to recombination of electrons and holes to produce photons. The recombination process is much more efficient for a direct band gap semiconductor than for an indirect band gap semiconductor, where the process must be mediated by a phonon.

As a result of such considerations, gallium arsenide and other direct band gap semiconductors are used to make optical devices such as LEDs and semiconductor lasers, whereas silicon, which is an indirect band gap semiconductor, is not. A number of different semiconducting compounds and their band gaps, and it also specifies whether their band gaps are direct or indirect.

Chapter 6

Superconductivity

The initial discovery of superconductive materials was made in 1911. Before 1986, the critical temperatures for all known superconductors did not exceed 23 Kelvin (23K or –418°F; 0K is absolute zero or –459°F). Before the discovery and development of HTS materials, the use of superconductivity had not been practical for widespread commercial applications, except for magnetic resonance imaging ("MRI") and superconducting magnetic energy storage ("SMES") applications, principally because commercially available superconductors (*i.e.* LTS materials) are made superconductive only when these materials are cooled to near 0K. Although it is technologically possible to cool LTS materials to a temperature at which they become superconductive, broad commercialisation of LTS materials has been inhibited by the high cost associated with the cooling process. For example, liquid helium, which can be used to cool materials to about 4K (-452°F), and which has been commonly used to cool LTS materials, is expensive and relatively costly to maintain.

In 1986, a breakthrough in superconductivity occurred when two scientists, Dr. K. Alex Muller, who is currently under contract as a consultant to ASC, and Dr. J. Georg Bednorz, at an IBM laboratory in Zurich, Switzerland, identified a ceramic oxide compound which was shown to be superconductive at 36K (–395°F). This discovery earned them a Nobel Prize for Physics in 1987, which is one of four Nobel Prizes that have been awarded for work on superconductivity. A series of related ceramic oxide compounds which have higher critical temperatures were subsequently discovered, including those being used by American Superconductor.

INTRODUCTION TO SUPERCONDUCTIVITY

Zero Resistance

Superconductors lose all resistance to the flow of direct electrical current and nearly all resistance to the flow of alternating current when cooled below a critical temperature, which is different for each superconducting material.

Perfect Conductor of Electricity

A superconductor is a perfect conductor of electricity; it carries direct current with 100% efficiency because no energy is dissipated by resistive heating. Once induced in a superconducting loop, direct current can flow undiminished forever. Superconductors also conduct alternating current, but with some slight dissipation of energy.

Critical Temperature

Superconducting materials known today, including both high temperature superconductor ("HTS") and low temperature superconductor ("LTS") materials, need to be cooled to cryogenic temperatures in order to exhibit the property of superconductivity.

HTS vs LTS

The differences between high and low temperature superconductors can best be explained using the figure below. This graph illustrates the complete loss of resistance to the flow of electricity through wires of an LTS material (niobium-titanium alloy) and an HTS material (bismuth-based, copper oxide ceramic) at the critical temperature T_c which is different for each superconducting material. The specific HTS material in this chart has no electrical resistance below 108K (–265°F) as opposed to the specific LTS material in this chart, which has no electrical resistance below 10K (–441°F).

Conditions Required for a Material to Exhibit Superconducting Behaviour:

- The material must be cooled below a characteristic temperature, known as its superconducting transition or critical temperature (T_c).
- The current passing through a given cross-section of the material must be below a characteristic level known as the critical current density (J_c).
- The magnetic field to which the material is exposed must be below a characteristic value known as the critical magnetic field (H_c).

These conditions are interdependent, and define the environmental operating conditions for the superconductor.

Advantages of Superconducting Wire

Superconducting wires provide significant advantages over conventional copper wires because they

- Conduct electricity with little or no resistance and associated energy loss
- Can transmit much larger amounts of electricity than conventional wires of the same size

HISTORICAL BACKGROUND

Major advances in low-temperature refrigeration were made during the late 19th century. Superconductivity was first discovered in 1911 by the Dutch physicist, Heike Kammerlingh Onnes. Onnes dedicated his scientific career to exploring extremely cold refrigeration. On July 10, 1908, he successfully liquified helium by cooling it to 452 degrees below zero Fahrenheit (4 Kelvin or 4 K). Onnes produced only a few millilitres of liquid helium that day, but this was to be the new beginnings of his explorations in temperature regions previously unreachable. Liquid helium enabled him to cool other materials closer to absolute zero (0 Kelvin), the coldest temperature imaginable. Absolute zero is the temperature at which the energy of material becomes as small as possible.

In 1911, Onnes began to investigate the electrical properties of metals in extremely cold temperatures. It had been known for many years that the resistance of metals fell when cooled below room temperature, but it was not known what limiting value the resistance would approach, if the temperature were reduced to very close to 0 K. Some scientists, such as William Kelvin, believed that electrons flowing through a conductor would come to a complete halt as the temperature approached absolute zero. Other scientists, including Onnes, felt that a cold wire's resistance would dissipate. This suggested that there would be a steady decrease in electrical resistance, allowing for better conduction of electricity. At some very low temperature point, scientists felt that there would be a levelling off as the resistance reached some ill-defined minimum value allowing the current to flow with little or no resistance. Onnes passed a current through a very pure mercury wire and measured its resistance as he steadily lowered the temperature. Much to his surprise there was no levelling off of resistance, let alone the stopping of electrons as suggested by Kelvin. At 4.2 K the resistance suddenly vanished. Current was flowing through the mercury wire and nothing was stopping it, the resistance was zero. According to Onnes, "Mercury has passed into a new state, which on account of its extraordinary electrical properties may be called the superconductive state". The experiment left no doubt about the disappearance of the resistance of a mercury wire. Kamerlingh Onnes called this newly discovered state, Superconductivity.

Onnes recognized the importance of his discovery to the scientific community as well as its commercial potential. An electrical conductor with no resistance could carry current any distance with no losses. In one of Onnes experiments he started a current flowing through a loop of lead wire cooled to 4 K. A year later the current was still flowing without significant current loss. Onnes found that the superconductor exhibited what he called persistent currents, electric currents that continued to flow without an electric potential driving them. Onnes had discovered superconductivity, and was awarded the Nobel Prize in 1913.

Whenever a new scientific discovery is made, researchers must strive to explain their theories. By 1933 Walther Meissner and R. Ochsenfeld discovered that superconductors are more than a perfect conductor of electricity, they also have an interesting magnetic property of excluding a magnetic field. A superconductor will not allow a magnetic field to penetrate its interior. It causes currents to flow that generate a magnetic field inside the superconductor that just balances the field that would have otherwise penetrated the material.

This effect, called the Meissner Effect, causes a phenomenon that is a very popular demonstration of superconductivity. The magnetic field lines from a magnet levitating above a superconductor. The Meissner Effect will occur only if the magnetic field is relatively small. If the magnetic field becomes too great, it penetrates the interior of the metal and the metal loses its superconductivity.

In 1957 scientists began to unlock the mysteries of superconductors. Three American physicists at the University of Illinois, John Bardeen, Leon Cooper, and Robert Schrieffer, developed a model that has since stood as a good mental picture of why superconductors behave as they do. The model is expressed in terms of advanced ideas of the science of quantum mechanics, but the main idea of the model suggests that electrons in a superconductor condense into a quantum ground state and travel together collectively and coherently. In 1972, Bardeen, Cooper, and Schrieffer received the Nobel Prize in Physics for their theory of superconductivity, which is now known as the BCS theory, after the initials of their last names.

In 1986, Georg Bednorz and Alex Müller, working at IBM in Zurich Switzerland, were experimenting with a particular class of metal oxide ceramics called perovskites. Bednorz and Müller surveyed hundreds of different oxide compounds. Working with ceramics of lanthanum, barium, copper, and oxygen they found indications of superconductivity at 35 K, a startling 12 K above the old record for a superconductor. Soon researchers from around the world would be working with the new types of superconductors. In February of 1987, a perovskite ceramic material was found to superconduct at 90K. This discovery was very significant because now it became possible to use liquid nitrogen as a coolant. Because these materials superconduct at significantly higher temperatures they are referred to as High Temperature Superconductors. Since then scientists have experimented with many different forms of perovskites producing compounds that superconduct at temperatures over 130 K. Currently, many governments, corporations and universities are investing large sums of money for research in High Temperature Superconductors. The ease of cooling new superconductors has greatly influenced vast efforts in the development of new materials, material fabrication, and changing theory of the behaviour of superconductors at relatively high temperatures. In addition, electrical power applications for the high temperature superconductors are expected to now be practical, thanks to the increased machine reliability and decreased cost associated with the cooling of such devices at temperatures greater than 20 K. The history of superconductors is only just now beginning.

APPLICATIONS OF SUPERCONDUCTORS

Soon after Kamerlingh Onnes discovered superconductivity, scientists began dreaming up practical applications for this strange new phenomenon. Powerful new superconducting magnets could be made much smaller than a resistive magnet, because the windings could carry large currents with no energy loss. Generators wound with superconductors could generate the same amount of electricity with smaller equipment and less energy. Once the electricity was generated it could be distributed through superconducting wires. Energy could be stored in superconducting coils for long periods of time without significant loss.

The recent discovery of high temperature superconductors brings us a giant step closer to the dream of early scientists. Applications currently being explored are mostly extensions of current technology used with the low temperature superconductors. Current applications of high temperature superconductors include; magnetic shielding devices, medical imaging systems, superconducting quantum interference devices (SQUIDS), infrared sensors, analog signal processing devices, and microwave devices. As our understanding of the properties of superconducting material increases, applications such as; power transmission, superconducting magnets in generators, energy storage devices, particle accelerators, levitated vehicle transportation, rotating machinery, and magnetic separators will become more practical.

The ability of superconductors to conduct electricity with zero resistance can be exploited in the use of electrical transmission lines. Currently, a substantial fraction of electricity is lost as heat through resistance associated with traditional conductors such as copper or aluminium. A large scale shift to superconductivity technology depends on whether wires can be prepared from the brittle ceramics that retain their superconductivity at 77 K while supporting large current densities. The field of electronics holds great promise for practical applications of superconductors. The miniaturization and increased speed of computer chips are limited by the generation of heat and the charging time of capacitors due to the resistance of the interconnecting metal films. The use of new superconductive films may result in more densely packed chips which could transmit information more rapidly by several orders of magnitude. Superconducting electronics have achieved impressive accomplishments in the field of digital electronics. Logic delays of 13 picoseconds and switching times of 9 picoseconds have been experimentally demonstrated. Through the use of basic Josephson junctions scientists are able to make very sensitive microwave detectors, magnetometers, SQUIDs and very stable voltage sources.

The use of superconductors for transportation has already been established using liquid helium as a refrigerant. Prototype levitated trains have been constructed in Japan by using superconducting magnets.

Superconducting magnets are already crucial components of several technologies. Magnetic resonance imaging (MRI) is playing an ever increasing role in diagnostic medicine. The intense magnetic fields that are needed for these instruments are a perfect application of superconductors. Similarly, particle accelerators used in high-energy physics studies are very dependant on high-field superconducting magnets. The recent controversy surrounding the continued funding for the Superconducting Super Collider (SSC) illustrates the political ramifications of the applications of new technologies.

New applications of superconductors will increase with critical temperature. Liquid nitrogen based superconductors has provided industry more flexibility to utilize superconductivity as compared to liquid helium superconductors. The possible discovery of room temperature superconductors has the potential to bring superconducting devices into our everyday lives.

High-temperature superconductors are recent innovations from scientific research laboratories. New commercial innovations begin with the existing technological knowledge generated by the research scientist. The work of commercialization centres on the development of new products and the engineering needed to implement the new technology. Superconductivity has had a long history as a specialized field of physics. Through the collaborative efforts of government funded research, independent research groups and commercial industries, applications of new high-temperature superconductors will be in the not so distant future. Time lags however, between new discoveries and practical applications are often great. The discovery of the laser in the early 60's has only recently been appreciated today through applications such as laser surgery, laser optical communication, and compact disc players. The rapid progress in the field of superconductivity leads one to believe that applications of superconductors is limited only by one's imagination and time.

THERMAL PROPERTIES OF SUPERCONDUCTORS

Superconductivity is a startling departure from the properties of normal (*i.e.,* nonsuperconducting) conductors of electricity. In materials that are electric conductors, some of the electrons are not bound to individual atoms but are free to move through the material; their motion constitutes an electric current. In normal conductors these so-called conduction electrons are scattered by impurities, dislocations, grain boundaries, and lattice vibrations (phonons). In a superconductor, however, there is an ordering among the conduction electrons that prevents this scattering. Consequently, electric current can flow with no resistance at all. The ordering of the electrons, called Cooper pairing, involves the momenta of the electrons rather than their positions. The energy per electron that is associated with this ordering is extremely small, typically about one thousandth of the amount by which the energy per electron changes when a chemical reaction takes place. One reason that superconductivity remained unexplained for so long is the smallness of the energy changes that accompany the transition between normal and superconducting states. In fact, many incorrect theories of superconductivity were advanced before the BCS theory was proposed.

Hundreds of materials are known to become superconducting at low temperatures. Twenty-seven of the chemical elements, all of them metals, are superconductors in their usual crystallographic forms at low temperatures and low (atmospheric) pressure. Among these are commonly known metals such as aluminium, tin, lead, and mercury and less common ones such as rhenium, lanthanum, and protactinium. In addition, 11 chemical elements that are metals, semimetals, or semiconductors are superconductors at low temperatures and high pressures. Among these are uranium, cerium, silicon, and selenium. Bismuth and five other elements, though not superconducting in their usual crystallographic form, can be made superconducting by preparing them in a highly disordered form, which is stable at extremely low temperatures. Superconductivity is not exhibited by any of the magnetic elements chromium, manganese, iron, cobalt, or nickel.

Most of the known superconductors are alloys or compounds. It is possible for a compound to be superconducting even if the chemical elements constituting it are not; examples are disilver fluoride (Ag_2F) and a compound of carbon and potassium (C_8K). Some semiconducting compounds, such as tin telluride (SnTe), become superconducting if they are properly doped with impurities.

Since 1986 some compounds containing copper and oxygen (called cuprates) have been found to have extraordinarily high transition temperatures, denoted T_c. This is the temperature below which a substance is superconducting. The properties of these high-T_c compounds are different in some respects from those of the types of superconductors known prior to 1986, which will be referred to as classic superconductors. For the most part, the high-T_c superconductors are treated explicitly towards. The properties possessed by both kinds of superconductors will be described, with attention paid to specific differences for the high-T_c materials. A further classification problem is presented by the superconducting compounds of carbon (sometimes doped with other atoms) in which the carbon atoms are on the surface of a cluster with a spherical or spheroidal crystallographic structure. These compounds, discovered in the 1980s, are called fullerenes (if only carbon is present) or fullerides (if doped). They have superconducting transition temperatures higher than those of the classic superconductors. It is not yet known whether these compounds are fundamentally similar to the cuprate high-temperature superconductors.

THE MEISSNER EFFECT

One of the properties of superconductors most easy to demonstrate, and also the most dazzling, is the Meissner Effect. Superconductors are strongly diamagnetic. That is to say that they will repel a magnet. Imagine a 'perfect' conductor of electricity that simply has no resistance to the flow of an electric current. If a conductor of electricity is moved into a magnetic field, Faraday's Law of Induction would lead us to expect an induced electrical current in the conductor and its associated magnetic field which would oppose the applied field. The induced electrical current would not dissipate in a `perfect' conductor, and thus the associated magnetic field would also continue to oppose the applied field. Conversely, if the `perfect' conductor was already in a magnetic field, and then that applied field was removed, the same physical law would indicate that an electrical current and its associated magnetic field would appear in the conductor which would attempt to oppose the removal of the applied field. If we were to do an experiment in which we placed a magnet on top of a material that by some process then became a `perfect' conductor, we would see no physical effect on the magnet. However, were we to attempt to remove the magnet, only then would we feel an opposing force.

A superconductor is fundamentally different from our imaginary 'perfect' conductor. Contrary to popular belief, Faraday's Law of induction alone does not explain magnetic repulsion by a superconductor. At a temperature below its Critical Temperature, Tc, a superconductor will not allow any magnetic field to freely enter it. This is because microscopic magnetic dipoles are induced in the superconductor that oppose the applied field. This induced field then repels the source of the applied field, and will consequently repel the magnet associated with that field. This implies that if a magnet was placed on top of the superconductor when the superconductor was above its Critical Temperature, and then it was cooled down to below Tc, the superconductor would then exclude the magnetic field of the magnet. This can be seen quite clearly since magnet itself is repelled, and thus is levitated above the superconductor. For this experiment to be successful, the force of repulsion must exceed the magnet's weight. This is indeed the case for the powerful rare earth magnets supplied with our kits. One must keep in mind that this phenomena will occur only if the strength of the applied magnetic field does not exceed the value of the Critical Magnetic Field, Hc for that superconductor material. This magnetic repulsion phenomena is called the Meissner Effect and is named after the person who first discovered it in 1933. It remains today as the most unique and dramatic demonstration of the phenomena of superconductivity.

On account of the polycrystalline nature of a typical ceramic superconductor, the Meissner Effect appears to be a bulk phenomena. This can be demonstrated by stacking two or more superconductor disks. With the addition of each disk, the magnet will be levitated higher. This result is particularly advantageous if the Meissner Effect is being demonstrated to an audience with the help of an overhead projector.

Another interesting observation is that the levitated magnet does not slide off the superconductor. This seemingly stable equilibrium is actually a manifestation of Flux Pinning, a phenomena uniquely associated with Type II superconductors, of which our high temperature ceramic superconductors are examples. Here lines of magnetic flux associated with a magnet can penetrate the bulk of the superconductor in the form of magnetic flux tubes. These flux tubes are then pinned to imperfections or impurities in the crystalline matrix of the superconductor thereby pinning the magnet.

In other words, what is happening is that you are initially forcing the magnetic field to exist in these non superconducting regions, by "squeezing" it though the cracks between the superconducting crystals. These regions of the material are surrounded by superconducting material. Think of a gallon jug, filled with water, that has a small pin hole in the bottom. The jug is the superconductor, the water is the magnetic field. This superconducting material will not allow a magnetic field to pass though it, in much the same way the jug will not allow the water to pass though it. However, the tiny non superconducting regions will allow the magnetic field to pass though, in the same way the pin hole in the jug allows the water to pass though. When you lift the magnet up, the force of gravity acting on the pellet (F=ma first semester physics stuff), is not great enough to force the trapped magnetic field to pass though the superconducting material, hence, like a weight on a string, you can lift the pellet. The string in this case is the magnetic field, and the weight is the superconductor.

Meissner Effect Demonstration

The procedure below, will guide the experimenter through a demonstration of the Meissner Effect in a cookbook fashion, step by step.

The shallow dish-like depression in the styrofoam container for the kit, or a third of an inch high portion of the bottom of a styrofoam coffee cup, can be used for holding liquid nitrogen for the experiment. To project a sharp image of the Meissner Effect with an overhead projector, use a very small dish so that the levitated magnet is less than an inch from its glass plate.

Procedure:

- *Action*: Carefully pour a small amount of liquid nitrogen into the dish or styrofoam cup until the liquid is about a quarter of an inch deep.
  Result: The liquid boils furiously for a short while. Wait until it stops boiling.
- *Action*: Using the provided tweezers, carefully place the black superconductor disk flat in the liquid until its top is just flush with the surface of the liquid nitrogen.
  Result: Again, the nitrogen boils around the disk. Wait until this boiling stops too.
- *Action*: Again using the tweezers, pick up the provided magnet, and attempt to balance it on top of the superconductor disk.
  Result: Instead of settling down onto the surface of the superconductor, the magnet will simply 'float' a few millimetres above the superconductor.This is a demonstration of the Meissner Effect.

Precautions:

- When pouring liquid nitrogen please be careful to prevent any splashing.
- Conduct the experiments in a well-ventilated room.
- Do not touch any items immersed in the liquid nitrogen with your hand until they have warmed to room temperature. Use the provided tweezers to add and remove items from the liquid nitrogen.

This experiment can also be conducted by placing the magnet on top of the superconductor before it is cooled in liquid nitrogen. As predicted by the Meissner Effect, the magnet will levitate when the temperature of the superconductor falls below its Critical Temperature. As explained earlier, there is no material other than a superconductor which could have shown this effect.

If you carefully set the magnet rotating, you will observe that the magnet continues to rotate for a long time. This is a crude demonstration of a frictionless magnetic bearing using the Meissner Effect. The rotational speed of a cube-shaped magnet can be increased by using a plastic drinking straw to blow a stream of air at one of the edges or corners of the cube. Another way to increase the magnet's rotational speed is to cut out a small rectangular hole in a piece of paper. The hole is positioned over the levitated magnet such that half of the magnet projects above the plane of the paper. A stream of air directed along the upper surface of the paper will cause the magnet to rotate rapidly.

The cubical magnet naturally is slowed by the resistance of air. Consequently, it can be expected to stop after a while. A cylindrical magnet will rotate for much longer since it is rotationally streamlined. However, the cubical magnet makes this demonstration much more graphic. A research group at Cornell University has demonstrated a frictionless superconducting bearing that can turn at a rate of one million rotations per minute. A bearing constructed in this manner, using the Meissner Effect is much more convenient and safe than a conventional magnet bearing because of the 'self-centring' nature of the Meissner Effect on account of flux pinning.

All Kits from Colorado Superconductor Inc. are equipped to demonstrate the Meissner Effect. The Comparison Kits contain both a yttrium-based ($YBa_2Cu_3O_7$) and a bismuth-based ($Bi_2Sr_2Ca_2Cu_3O_{10}$) superconductor. Both superconductors exhibit the Meissner Effect, however, if the disks are carefully removed from the liquid nitrogen bath, while magnet is still levitated, the bismuth-based material will continue levitating the magnet for a considerably longer time than the yttrium-based superconductor. This is because the bismuth-based superconductor has a significantly higher Critical Temperature than to the yttrium-based one.

The Critical Temperature Kit and the Critical Temperature Comparison Kit both use the Meissner Effect to measure the Critical Temperature of superconductors.

TYPE I AND TYPE II SUPERCONDUCTORS

Depending upon their behaviour in an external magnetic field, superconductors are divided into two types:

Type I superconductors

Type I superconductors are those superconductors which loose their superconductivity very easily or abruptly when placed in the external magnetic field. As you can see from the graph of intensity of magnetization (M) versus applied magnetic field (H), when the Type I superconductor is placed in the magnetic field, it suddenly or easily looses its superconductivity at critical magnetic field (Hc) (point A).

After Hc, the Type I superconductor will become conductor.

Type I superconductors are also known as soft superconductors because of this reason that is they loose their superconductivity easily.

Type I superconductors perfectly obey Meissner effect.

Example of Type I superconductors: Aluminium (Hc = 0.0105 Tesla), Zinc (Hc = 0.0054)

Type II Superconductors

Type II superconductors are those superconductors which loose their superconductivity gradually but not easily or abruptly when placed in the external magnetic field. As you can see from the graph of intensity of magnetization (M) versus applied magnetic field (H), when the Type II superconductor is placed in the magnetic field, it gradually looses its superconductivity. Type II superconductors start to loose their superconductivity at lower critical magnetic field (Hc1) and completely loose their superconductivity at upper critical magnetic field (Hc2).

The state between the lower critical magnetic field (Hc1) and upper critical magnetic field (Hc_2) is known as vortex state or intermediate state.

After Hc_2, the Type II superconductor will become conductor.

Type I superconductors are also known as hard superconductors because of this reason that is they loose their superconductivity gradually but not easily. Type I superconductors obey Meissner effect but not completely.

Example of Type I superconductors: NbN (Hc = 8×10^6 Tesla), $Babi_3$ (Hc = 59×10^3 Tesla)

Application of Type II superconductors: Type II superconductors are used for strong field superconducting magnets.

A.C. AND D.C. JOSEPHSON EFFECTS IN A BOSE-EINSTEIN CONDENSATE

In our laboratory we were able to create the conditions to generate and observe both the a.c. and d.c. Josephson effects in a BEC of rubidium atoms. Here we present the experiment, its results, and some of the theory behind it.

a.c. and d.c. Josephson Effects

When two superconductors are joined together, separated only by a thin insulating barrier, some new phenomena arise. First, if a voltage is applied across the junction, a small oscillating current starts flowing back and forth through the junction, without equilibrating the two sides. This is known as the a.c. Josephson effect. Second, if a constant current is made to flow through the junction, no voltage drop is detected across it, as long as the current stays below some critical value. This is known as the d.c. Josephson effect. Accordingly, the setup of a superconductor-insulator-superconductor is known as a Josephson junction.

The phenomena of the a.c. and d.c. Josephson effects manifest because of the quantum nature of each superconductor as a whole. Quantum mechanics usually apply to systems at the microscopic level. However, in superconductors, the many electrons in the metal "condense" into the same quantum state, creating a macroscopic quantum entity. B.D. Josephson originally predicted the effect in 1962 for superconductors relying on this fact. However, it is possible in principle to observe the a.c. and d.c. Josephson effects in any two macroscopic quantum systems separated by a tunnelling barrier.

In 1997, the a.c. Josephson effect was observed in superfluid ^3He. Superfluid ^3He is another example of a system where quantum phenomena manifest macroscopically. In ^3He, it is the helium atoms that form the quantum state, and the current is not of electrical type, but the flow of atoms through a thin hole separating two helium reservoirs. The d.c. Josephson effect in superfluid ^3He, and both a.c. and d.c. effects in superfluid ^4He, have not yet been observed.

Bose-Einstein Condensate

Bose-Einstein condensate (BEC) is a state of matter where, due to the laws of quantum mechanics, all the particles constituting the matter are coerced into a single quantum state of the lowest energy, reshaping themselves as a single entity.

This new form of matter was predicted by Satyendra Nath Bose and Albert Einstein in 1925. In the following years, it was established that superfluids and superconductors are a form of BECs, but an 'ideal' BEC of weakly-interacting atoms, corresponding to the original theory, required extremely low temperatures, less than millionth of a degree above the absolute zero. Only in 1995 were scientists able to produce a BEC from a gas of dilute atoms, 70 years after its prediction.

Bose-Einstein condensates provide a rich ground for the testing of fundamental physics, of which this research is an instance.

Bose-Einstein condensates comprise a new physical system for observing the a.c. and d.c. Josephson effects, Apart from superconductors and superfluids. Being a distinct quantum state, a BEC is a macroscopic entity of definite *quantum phase*. This property, also called coherence, is the key to Josephson-like behaviour.

In a typical apparatus for studying BECs, a large number of atoms (several millions) are collected inside a magnetic trap that confines them. Subsequently the atoms are cooled by various means to a temperature below the critical temperature for the transition to condensate phase to occur, around 100 nano-Kelvin. After creating the condensate, a smaller number of atoms remain (in our apparatus, approximately 100,000 atoms). The BEC is further probed only with magnetic or optical forces, since any contact with material bodies will cause the temperature to quickly rise, destroying the condensate.

The Pendulum Equations

The a.c. and d.c. Jospephson effects can actually be described by three very simple equations that have direct mechanical analogs. Before introducing the equations we need to specify the quantities involved.

Each condensate is characterized by the number of atoms it contains, N, and by its chemical potential, μ. The chemical potential plays the role of potential in electrical systems. A difference in chemical potential between two systems means that the systems can equilibrate by flow of atoms from the higher-potential system to the lower-potential one. Because a condensate is a (macroscopic) quantum state, it has a defined phase φ.

We denote the two condensates 1 and 2, and define the *relative population imbalance* as $\eta = (N_1 - N_2)/(N_1 + N_2)$, with $-1 < \eta < 1$. Also, the *chemical potential difference* is defined as $\Delta\mu = \mu_1 - \mu_2$. Finally, the *phase difference* between the condensates $\varphi = \varphi_1 - \varphi_2$ has a major role in the dynamics of the Josephson junction.

The physics of Josephson junction is governed by three simple equations.

$$\dot{\eta} = \omega_J \sin\varphi$$

$$\dot{\varphi} = -\frac{\Delta\mu}{\hbar} \quad \Delta\mu = \hbar\omega_C\left(\eta - \eta_{equil}\right)$$

is the current flow through the tunnelling barrier, $\hbar$ is Planck's constant, η_{equil} is the equilibrium value of η, and the ω's are parameters that characterize the physical system.

The first of these equations conveys the sinusoidal nature of the Josephson current. The second relates the rate of change of phase difference to the chemical potential difference. The third connects potential difference with population imbalance.

The three equations can be combined into

$$\ddot{\varphi} = -\omega_P^2 \sin\varphi + \omega_C \dot{\eta}_{equil}$$

with $\omega_P = \sqrt{\omega_J \omega_C}$. This is the equation of motion for the phase difference φ.

The a.c. Josephson Effect

For the a.c. Josephson effect, consider the first two equations with an *applied* constant chemical potential difference $\Delta\mu$. Then $\varphi = -\frac{\Delta\mu}{\hbar}t$ and $\eta = \frac{\hbar\omega_J}{\Delta\mu}\cos\left(\frac{\Delta\mu}{\hbar}t\right)$. The relative population imbalance oscillates with frequency $\Delta\mu/h$ with amplitude inversely proportional to $\Delta\mu$.

More generally, if the external potential is static, then $\dot{\eta}_{equil} = 0$ and the equation of motion for φ reduces to $\ddot{\varphi} = -\omega_P^2 \sin\varphi$ which describes the motion of a classical pendulum with angle φ. The a.c. Josephson effect corresponds to the case of the pendulum executing complete rotations with always-increasing angle, with an oscillation period of $(\Delta\mu/h)^{-1}$.

In contrast, in a bulk macroscopic quantum system, the current is proportional to the gradient of the phase, and we would expect the relation $\dot{\eta} \propto \varphi$. Such a system would show no oscillating current because φ increases at a constant rate. Note that the a.c. Josephson effect is very different from the plasma oscillations, also indicated in the above figure, for which the pendulum oscillates about zero with $-\pi < \varphi < \pi$. These plasma oscillations exist even for small-angle oscillations, for which also $\dot{\eta} \alpha \varphi$, as in a bulk macroscopic quantum system. The a.c. Josephson effect has no analogue in a bulk system.

The d.c. Josephson Effect

The equation of motion for φ can be rewritten as

$$\frac{\hbar N}{2\omega_C}\ddot{\varphi} = -\frac{\partial U}{\partial \varphi}$$

with $U = \frac{\hbar N}{2}\left[\omega_J\left(1-\cos\varphi\right) - \dot{\eta}_{equil}\varphi\right]$

The mechanical analogy here is a point particle with "mass" $\hbar N / 2\omega_C$ and "position" φ moving in an external "washboard" potential U. Mechanically, $\dot{\eta}_{equil}$ controls the tilt of the washboard. Since atoms flow in order to reach equilibrium value η_{equil}, this tilt is analogous to an applied current.

As long as the applied current $\dot{\eta}_{equil}$ is smaller than ω_J, the particle sits in a local minimum of the washboard: the phase difference φ remains constant and there is no chemical potential difference $\Delta\mu$. When the applied current reaches the critical value ω_J, the tilt is too high and the particle is free to fall down the slope–the phase difference φ starts increasing, resulting in a non-zero chemical potential difference.

The Josephson junction thus exhibits two different states, depending on current: a "supercurrent" state, where current flows with no potential difference across the junction, and a "normal" state, with normal current flowing alongside supercurrent, causing a finite potential difference. This behaviour is usually illustrated in a V-I (or $\Delta\mu$-I) curve, for voltage vs. current:

Observing the a.c. and d.c. Josephson Effects in a BEC

We have successfully observed both the a.c. and d.c. Josephson effects in a BEC of ^{87}Rb atoms by containing two BECs in a double-well potential. The barrier is sufficiently thin to allow coupling (tunnelling) between the two condensates.

In order to realize the double-well potential, atoms are first gathered in a magnetic trap. Then a thin "sheet" of laser light divides the trap into two regions. The laser is specially frequency-tuned to repel the atoms, effectively creating a potential barrier. The atoms are now evaporatively-cooled to the stage of forming two Bose-Einstein condensates in the two wells.

Observing The a.c. Josephson Effect

In the a.c. Josephson effect, a constant average chemical potential difference is maintained between the two BECs. By the Josephson equations, a sinusodial current through the barrier is established, with atoms flowing back and forth between the condensates. The chemical potentials do not equilibrate – this is known as macroscopic quantum self-trapping (MQST).

We create an initial chemical potential difference by starting from an asymmetric double-well, and then shifting the barrier to the middle, resulting in a symmetric double-well configuration with different number of atoms in each well. The shift is done very quickly so as not to allow the atoms to 'pass' through the barrier.

We observe the Josephson oscillations *in-situ* by using non-destructive phase-contrast imaging. This allows taking multiple images without destroying the cloud. Imaging pulses are sent through the atomic cloud to the camera once per frame. The imaging process integrates the atom density of the cloud along the imaging direction. Thus the resulting image is a map of the column density of the cloud.

The imaging camera is a CCD array of 1024 × 256 pixels. The CCD array is logically divided into 16 strips of 64 × 256 pixels each, all covered except the first one. After taking each image, the entire array is shifted one strip, thus exposing the next strip for the next image. After 16 (or so) images are taken, the entire CCD array is read out and stored in an image file.

There are 14 frames with 0.33 msec between each frame. The left cloud is bigger than the right one because of the chemical potential difference. The image is a plot of an integration of the image along its y axis. This is the second integration performed on the cloud.

From these plots, we can extract the chemical potential difference $\Delta\mu$ and the relative population imbalance η as a function of time. The a.c. Jospehson effect is manifest through oscillations in ηin a frequency equal to $\Delta\mu$ (in units of Planck's constant, h). The upper curve is for $\Delta\mu$ = 750 Hz × h, and the lower curve is for $\Delta\mu$ = 450 Hz × h. The curves show an oscillating behaviour, an it can be seen that the curve with the higher chemical potential difference is also of higher frequency.

We can extract the frequencies of the plots with varying delta mu by inspecting their Fourier transform.

We can then plot the frequency as a function of $\Delta\mu$ and verify that the relation is as predicted. The plot below shows our main result for the a.c. Josephson effect in a BEC medium. We can see that measuring $\Delta\mu$ and the frequency in the same units excellently agrees with the theoretical prediction.

Observing The d.c. Josephson Effect

In the d.c. Josephson effect, current flows through the barrier with no chemical potential difference between the two sides. The d.c. Josephson effect has so far been observed only in superconducting systems. Observing it a BEC medium requires a method to create flow of atoms from one side of the junction to the other, in various magnitudes, and to measure the chemical potentials.

We do this by slowly shifting the barrier from an off-centre position to the centre of the trap, ending with a symmetric potential. In the d.c. Josephson effect, the atoms do not 'feel' the barrier and are allowed to tunnel through it without resistance. The magnitude of the atom current is proportional to the velocity of the barrier. The critical current, the flow of atoms will not incur a difference in the chemical potentials, which will remain at its initial value of zero (equilibrium).

At the end of the experiment we reach a symmetric trap configuration, where condensates of equal chemical potential have the same size. We can measure the chemical potential difference by comparing the sizes of the condensates, and repeat the experiment at various atomic currents by moving the barrier with different velocity each time.

The d.c. Josephson effect is demonstrated by plotting the characteristic I-$\Delta\mu$ curve of the system — the dependence of the chemical potential difference on the current.

The behaviour predicted by the Josephson equations, with a critical current value of about 30 sec^{-1}.

BCS SUPERCONDUCTIVITY THEORY

In 1957, Bardeen, Cooper and Schrieffer (BCS) proposed a theory that explained the microscopic origins of superconductivity, and could quantitatively predict the properties of superconductors. Prior to this, there was Ginzburg-Landau theory, suggested in 1950, which was a macroscopic theory. This will not be dealt with here, but Ginzburg-Landau theory can be derived from BCS theory.

Cooper Pair Formation

Mathematically, BCS theory is complex, but relies on an earlier 'discovery' by Cooper (1956), who showed that the ground state of a material is unstable with respect to pairs of 'bound' electrons. These pairs are known as *Cooper pairs* and are formed by electron-phonon interactions-an electron in the cation lattice will distort the lattice around it, creating an area of greater positive charge density around itself. Another electron at some distance in the lattice is then attracted to this charge distortion (phonon)-the electron-phonon interaction.

Cooper Pairs-BCS Theory Supercurrent Carriers

The Cooper pairs within the superconductor are what carry the supercurrent, but why do they experience such perfect conductivity?

Mathematically, because the Cooper pair is more stable than a single electron within the lattice, it experiences less resistance (although the superconducting state cannot be made up entirely of Cooper pairs as this would lead to the collapse of the state).

Physically, the Cooper pair is more resistant to vibrations within the lattice as the attraction to its partner will keep it 'on course'-therefore, Cooper pairs move through the lattice relatively unaffected by thermal vibrations (electron-phonon interactions) below the critical temperature. Play the animations below by clicking the 'play' icon in the corner to compare Cooper pair superconduction and normal conduction.

High Temperature Superconduction

However, BCS theory predicted a theoretical maximum to T_c of around 30-40K, as above this, thermal energy would cause electron-phonon interactions of an energy too high to allow formation of or sustain Cooper pairs. 1986 saw the discovery of high temperature superconductors which broke this limit (the highest known today is in excess of 150K) - it is in debate as to what mechanism prevails at higher temperatures, as BCS cannot account for this.

High T_c Superconductivity Theory

With the discovery of materials that went superconducting at temperatures above the theoretical limit imposed by BCS theory, there was (and still is) much debate as to what the mechanism of superconduction in these compounds might be.

One explanation involves the use of holes within the superconductor-many high T_c superconductors are compounds such as $YBa_2Cu_3O_{7-x}$ or $La_{(2-x)}Sr_xCuO_4$, where the metal ion (in these cases, copper) will be partially oxidised; obviously, each metal ion cannot be physically partially oxidised, rather, the lattice will be comprised of a ratio of Cu^{2+} to Cu^{3+} ions, depending on x.

This means that there are 'holes' of positive charge (Cu^{3+} ions) within the lattice. This type of superconductor is hence referred to as a *p-type superconductor*; Compounds can also be doped to insert extra electrons into the lattice (*i.e.* a reduction), *e.g.* $La_2CuO_{(4+x)}$-this is called an *n-type superconductor*.

Although the positive 'holes' are usually stabilised by surrounding counterions, the highly charged ions will still ideally want to reduce (*e.g.* Cu^{3+} to Cu^{2+}), however, they cannot gain an electron from neighbouring (Cu^{2+}) ions, as this does not solve the problem.

When a current is applied to the superconductor, the electrons travel along the ion planes in the lattice. As an electron passes a hole in a neighbouring plane, it will push negative charge from orbitals on a reduced cation towards the hole (due to electrostatic repulsion), by distorting the lattice.

The oxidised cation (Cu^{3+}) then reduces, and the reduced ion (Cu^{2+}) oxidises-effectively, the hole moves backwards (as an electron moves forwards). This 'extra' current that is caused by the normal current is the supercurrent.

The theory is supported by the fact that T_c varies with the amount of doping (x)-too many or too few holes destroys the effect.

Uses of Superconductors

Efficient Electricity Transportation

Superconductors have many uses-the most obvious being as very efficient conductors; if the national grid were made of superconductors rather than aluminium, then the savings would be enormous-there would be no need to transform the electricity to a higher voltage (this lowers the current, which reduces energy loss to heat) and then back down again. Superconducting magnets are also more efficient in generating electricity than conventional copper wire generators-in fact, a superconducting generator about half the size of a copper wire generator is about 99% efficient; typical generators are around 50% efficient.

The US Department of Energy are actively encourages the use of superconductors as energy efficient devices. At the moment, the problem lies with the critical temperature-unless a material is found that can superconduct above 300K, some sort of cooling system needs to be employed, which would be expensive, although companies are developing prototypes-in December 1998, Pirelli Wire built a test 150ft cable that transmitted electricity using high temperature superconducting materials.

Magnetic Levitation

So-called 'MagLev' trains such as the Yamanashi MLX01 train show above have been under development in Japan for the past two decades-the train floats above the track using superconducting magnets; this eliminates friction and energy loss as heat, allowing the train to reach such high speeds.

Magnetic Resonance Imaging (MRI)

MRI is a technique developed in the 1940s that allows doctors to see what is happening inside the body without directly performing surgery. The development of superconductors has improved the field of MRI as the superconducting magnet can be smaller and more efficient than an equivalent conventional magnet.

Synchrotrons and Cyclotrons (Particle Colliders)

Particle Colliders like CERN's Large Hadron Collider (LHC) are like very large running tracks that are used to accelerate particles (*i.e.* eletrons, positrons, hadrons and more) to speeds approaching the speed of light before they are collided with one another or other atoms, usually to split them (this was how many sub-nuclear particles such as taus and neutrinos were discovered).

They do this by cycling the particle using magnetic fields, continually increasing the speed of the particle. The first project to use superconducting magnets was the proton-antiproton collider at Fermilab.

Fast Electronic Switches

Type II superconductors can be used to as very fast electronic switches (as they have no moving parts), due to the way in which a magnetic field can penetrate into the superconductor-this has allowed Japanese researchers to build a 4-bit computer microchip (compared to today's 32-bit and

64-bit processors) operating at about 500 times the speed of current processors, where heat output is currently a major problem with typical speeds approaching the 1GHz mark. An article in Superconductor Week focuses upon the efforts of NASA, DARPA and others to build a 'petaflop' (a thousand-trillion floating point operations per second-compared to today's 'teraflop' (1 trillion Flops per sec) computers) computer using superconductor technology.

Chapter 7

Crystal Structures

A crystalline solid is a substance which is composed of a basic unit which is repeated in three dimensions (3D) in an ordered fashion. The basic 3D repeating pattern is called the unit cell and can be composed of atoms, ions, or molecules. The collection of particles which make up the unit cell must meet three requirements:

- They must indicate the coordination number
- They must be consistent with the empirical formula
- They must generate the crystal structure when repeated in three dimensions.

These particles can also be considered as uniform, hard spheres which may form different structures depending on how they are packed.

One of the controlling aspects of the packing of spheres is how they are arranged within each layer. In some layers all of the spheres are touching and each sphere is surrounded by six others. This is the most efficient way to pack spheres and is called closest packing. Layers can also be fashioned from spheres which do not make such efficient use of the available space; in these layers one sphere will be in contact with only four other spheres. The least efficient packing of sphere layers occurs when no contact at all exists between the spheres. The arrangement of the spheres in two dimensional sheets represents only one aspect of the overall crystal structure; how the two dimensional sheets are stacked must also be considered. Two different types of closest packed structures can be generated depending on how close-packed layers of spheres are stacked. The hexagonal close-packed structure is built by placing one layer of spheres in the depressions formed by a first layer and then adding a third directly above the first. A hexagonal prism in generated by the repeating pattern defined by the hexagonal unit cell.

UNIT CELL

The crystal structure of a material or the arrangement of atoms within a given type of crystal structure can be described in terms of its unit cell. The unit cell is a small box containing one or more atoms, a spatial arrangement of atoms. The unit cells stacked in three-dimensional space describe the bulk arrangement of atoms of the crystal. The crystal structure has a three-dimensional shape. The unit cell is given by its lattice parameters, which are the length of the cell edges and the angles between them, while the positions of the atoms inside the unit cell are described by the set of atomic positions (x_i, y_i, z_i) measured from a lattice point.

Miller Indices

Vectors and atomic planes in a crystal lattice can be described by a three-value Miller index notation (ℓmn). The ℓ, m, and n directional indices are separated by 90°, and are thus orthogonal. In fact, the ℓ component is mutually perpendicular to the m and n indices.

By definition, (ℓmn) denotes a plane that intercepts the three points a_1/ℓ, a_2/m, and a_3/n, or some multiple thereof. That is, the Miller indices are proportional to the *inverses* of the intercepts of the plane with the unit cell (in the basis of the lattice vectors).

If one or more of the indices is zero, it simply means that the planes do not intersect that axis (*i.e.*, the intercept is "at infinity").

Considering only (ℓmn) planes intersecting one or more lattice points (the *lattice planes*), the perpendicular distance d

between adjacent lattice planes is related to the (shortest) reciprocal lattice vector orthogonal to the planes by the formula:

$$d = 2\pi / |\mathbf{g}_{\ell mn}|$$

Planes and Directions

The crystallographic directions are fictitious lines linking nodes (atoms, ions or molecules) of a crystal.

Likewise, the crystallographic planes are fictitious *planes* linking nodes. Some directions and planes have a higher density of nodes.

These high density planes have an influence on the behaviour of the crystal as follows:

- *Optical Properties*: Refractive index is directly related to density (or periodic density fluctuations).
- *Adsorption and Reactivity*: Physical adsorption and chemical reactions occur at or near surface atoms or molecules. These phenomena are thus sensitive to the density of nodes.
- *Surface Tension*: The condensation of a material means that the atoms, ions or molecules are more stable if they are surrounded by other similar species. The surface tension of an interface thus varies according to the density on the surface.
- *Microstructural Defects*: Pores and crystallites tend to have straight grain boundaries following higher density planes.
- *Cleavage*: This typically occurs preferentially parallel to higher density planes.
- *Plastic deformation*: Dislocation glide occurs preferentially parallel to higher density planes. The perturbation carried by the dislocation (Burgers vector) is along a dense direction. The shift of one node in a more dense direction requires a lesser distortion of the crystal lattice.

In the rhombohedral, hexagonal, and tetragonal systems, the basal plane is the plane perpendicular to the principal axis.

Cubic Structures

For the special case of simple cubic crystals, the lattice vectors are orthogonal and of equal length (usually denoted *a*); similarly for the reciprocal lattice. So, in this common case, the Miller indices (ℓ mn) and [ℓ mn] both simply denote normals/directions in Cartesian coordinates. For cubic crystals with lattice constant *a*, the spacing *d* between adjacent (ℓ mn) lattice planes is (from above):

$$d_{\ell mn} = \frac{a}{\sqrt{\ell^2 + m^2 + n^2}}$$

Because of the symmetry of cubic crystals, it is possible to change the place and sign of the integers and have equivalent directions and planes:

- Coordinates in *angle brackets* such as <100> denote a *family* of directions that are equivalent due to symmetry operations, such as [100], [010], [001] or the negative of any of those directions.
- Coordinates in *curly brackets* or *braces* such as {100} denote a family of plane normals that are equivalent due to symmetry operations, much the way angle brackets denote a family of directions.

For face-centred cubic (fcc) and body-centred cubic (bcc) lattices, the primitive lattice vectors are not orthogonal.

However, in these cases the Miller indices are conventionally defined relative to the lattice vectors of the cubic supercell and hence are again simply the Cartesian directions.

Crystallographic Planes and Directions

It is necessary to be able to define planes and directions within crystalline solids.

A labelling system that uses combinations of 3 integers or "indices" to define crystallographic directions and planes is used.

This system is known as the Miller System. It has some similarities with conventional vector systems especially for simple cubic systems.

For more complex crystal structures (such as found in

geology and magnetic/electronic devices) then the Miller system becomes very useful indeed.

Here we are only teaching you the basics and will only consider simple cubic systems.

Crystallographic Directions

A crystallographic direction is basically a vector between two points in the crystal. Any direction can be defined by following a simple procedure. Follow through each of the stages in this example:

Look at the drawing of the unit cell on the right. Crystallographers always draw in 3D, the sense of the axes is the same as your used to but they've been turned so the z-direction goes up the page. A crystallographic direction has been drawn in the unit cell. The vector shown does not pass through the origin of the unit cells co-ordinate system.

Step 1: Position the vector so that it is in convenient position within your chosen co-ordinate system.

Ultimately we need to find out the number of; 'steps' the vector goes along each axis. You may find this easier to visualise if you reposition the vector so that it passes through the origin. However you can miss out this step if you prefer. Look at the picture on the right to see how the example vector has been repositioned.

Step 2: Find the projection of the vector onto each of the three axes in terms of the unit cell dimensions.

Then we must find the projection of the vector onto the three axes in terms of the unit cell dimensions. In the example on the right these are shown by the green, blue and purple arrows as follows...

$X = 1, Y = 1, Z = 0.5$

Alternatively, if you haven't positioned the vector to start at the origin, you can get the same answer by finding the number of 'steps' the vector is along each axis. Remember that whichever method you use the vector is always expressed in terms of the unit cell dimension.

Step 3: To get the Miller Index we express the vector as a set of whole numbers, and enclose in square brackets. To get the Miller Index of the example we multiply through by 2 to get rid of the half, then enclose in square brackets. The crystallographic direction shown by the red vector is [221].

Notation

There are certain conventions used when expressing Crystallographic directions using the Miller system.

Directions are enclosed in square brackets. Negative directions are represented by putting a bar above the appropriate integer, *e.g.*

$$\left[\bar{1}\,\bar{1}\,\bar{1}\right]$$

is the opposite direction to [111].

The choice of negative directions is arbitrary but it is essential to be consistent.

Families of Equivalent Directions

Due to the symmetry of crystal structures the spacing and arrangement of atoms may be the same in several directions. These are known as equivalent directions. A group of equivalent directions is known as a family of directions. Families of directions are written in angular brackets. These families of directions will become important when we consider slip directions.

For example consider the FCC unit cell shown opposite. The arrangement of atoms lying diagonally across a face is always the same. So all the directions running diagonally across a face are equivalent. In this case they are all part of the <101> family of directions, you could list each direction in turn and see they all have a similar form.

In FCC structures there are two other significant families of directions.

Crystallographic Planes

Crystallographic planes can be represented in a comparable way to crystallographic directions by using 3 indices. As when finding a direction you must ensure the plane is in a convenient position in your co-ordinate system. You then need to follow these steps:

Step 1: Find the points of intersection of the plane and the axes in terms of the unit cell dimensions. Where a plane is parallel to an axis its intercept is considered infinite.

In the example you can see how the intersections with the axes have been worked out. Because the plane does not cut the y axis it's intercept is considered to be infinite.

Step 2: Take the reciprocals of the intercepts:

$$X=\frac{1}{1}y-\frac{1}{\infty}z=\frac{1}{0.5}$$

Step 3: Convert to smallest possible whole integers:> x = 1 y = 0 z = 2

Step 4: The indices are enclosed in brackets:

As with crystallographic directions negative values are represented by putting a bar above the appropriate integers.

Families of Equivalent Planes

Due to the symmetry of crystal structures the spacing and arrangement of atoms may be the same in several planes. These are known as equivalent planes, and a group of equivalent planes are known as a family of planes. Families of planes are written in curly brackets. For example think about a FCC crystal structure. The arrangement of atoms on each face is the same, so the planes describing each face are equivalent. In this case they are all part of the {001} family of planes. Close-packed planes are tightly packed planes of atoms. They are very significant in understanding the behaviour of dislocations, which you will learn about in the next unit. In FCC unit cells the {111} planes are all close packed. In BCC unit cells there are no fully close-packed planes, although there are close packed directions on the {110} planes.

Hexagonal Crystals

Crystallographic directions and planes in hexagonal crystals are expressed using a more complicated 4 axis co-ordinate system known as the Miller-Bravis system. Whilst it is not necessary to cover this in any depth for this course you should be aware that it exists.

BRAVAIS LATTICES

When the crystal systems are combined with the a variety of possible lattice centerings, we arrive at the Bravais lattices. They describe the geometric arrangement of the lattice points, and thereby the translational symmetry of the crystal. In three dimensions, there are 14 unique Bravais lattices that are distinct from one another in the translational symmetry they contain. All crystalline materials recognized until now (not including quasicrystals) fit in one of these arrangements. The fourteen three-dimensional lattices, classified by crystal system, are shown above. The Bravais lattices are sometimes referred to as *space lattices*.

The crystal structure consists of the same group of atoms, the *basis*, positioned around each and every lattice point. This group of atoms therefore repeats indefinitely in three dimensions according to the arrangement of one of the 14 Bravais lattices. The characteristic rotation and mirror symmetries of the group of atoms, or unit cell, is described by its crystallographic point group. In geometry and crystallography, a Bravais lattice, studied by Auguste Bravais (1850), is an infinite array of discrete points generated by a set of discrete translation operations described by:

$$\mathbf{R} = n_1\mathbf{a}_1 + n_2\mathbf{a}_2 + n_3\mathbf{a}_3$$

where n_i are any integers and a_i are recognized as the primitive vectors which lie in different directions and span the lattice. This discrete set of vectors must be closed under vector addition and subtraction. For any choice of position vector R, the lattice looks exactly the same.

A crystal is made up of a periodic arrangement of one or more atoms (the *basis*) repeated at each lattice point. Consequently, the crystal looks the same when viewed from any of the lattice points. Two Bravais lattices are often considered equivalent if they have isomorphic symmetry groups. In this sense, there are 14 possible Bravais lattices in three-dimensional space. The 14 possible symmetry groups of Bravais lattices are 14 of the 230 space groups.

DEFECTS AND IMPURITIES

Real crystals feature defects or irregularities in the perfect arrangements described above and it is these defects that critically determine many of the electrical and mechanical properties of real materials. When one atom substitutes for one of the principal atomic components within the crystal structure, alteration in the electrical and thermal properties of the material may ensue. Impurities may also manifest as spin impurities in certain materials.

Research on magnetic impurities demonstrates that substantial alteration of certain properties such as specific heat may be affected by small concentrations of an impurity, as for example impurities in semiconducting ferromagnetic alloys may lead to different properties as first predicted in the late 1960s. Dislocations in the crystal lattice allow shear at lower stress than that needed for a perfect crystal structure.

Unit Cell and Structure of Solids

The structure of solids can be described as if they were three-dimensional analogs of a piece of wallpaper. Wallpaper has a regular repeating design that extends from one edge to the other. Crystals have a similar repeating design, but in this case the design extends in three dimensions from one edge of the solid to the other. We can unambiguously describe a piece of wallpaper by specifying the size, shape, and contents of the simplest repeating unit in the design. We can describe a three-dimensional crystal by specifying the size, shape, and contents of the simplest repeating unit and the way these repeating units stack to form the crystal. The simplest repeating unit in a crystal is called a unit cell. Each unit cell is defined in terms of lattice pointsthe points in space about which the particles are free to vibrate in a crystal.

In 1850, Auguste Bravais showed that crystals could be divided into 14 unit cells, which meet the following criteria.

- The unit cell is the simplest repeating unit in the crystal.
- Opposite faces of a unit cell are parallel.
- The edge of the unit cell connects equivalent points.

The 14 Bravais unit cells are shown in fig. below:

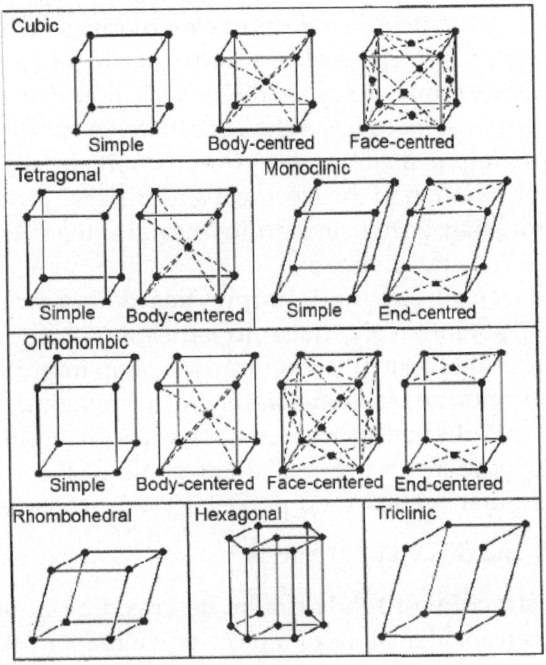

Figure

These unit cells fall into seven categories, which differ in the three unit-cell edge lengths (*a*, *b*, and *c*) and three internal angle. We will focus on the cubic category, which includes the three types of unit cellssimple cubic, body-centred cubic, and face-centred cubicshown in fig. 7.10 below.

These unit cells are important for two reasons. First, a number of metals, ionic solids, and intermetallic compounds crystallize in cubic unit cells. Second, it is relatively easy to do calculations with these unit cells because the cell-edge lengths are all the same and the cell angles are all 90.

The simple cubic unit cell is the simplest repeating unit in a simple cubic structure. Each corner of the unit cell is defined by a lattice point at which an atom, ion, or molecule can be found in the crystal. By convention, the edge of a unit cell always connects equivalent points. Each of the eight corners of the unit cell therefore must contain an identical particle. Other particles can be present on the edges or faces of the unit cell, or within the body of the unit cell. But the minimum that must be present for the unit cell to be classified as simple cubic is eight equivalent particles on the eight corners. The body-centred cubic unit cell is the simplest repeating unit in a body-centred cubic structure. Once again, there are eight identical particles on the eight corners of the unit cell. However, this time there is a ninth identical particle in the center of the body of the unit cell.

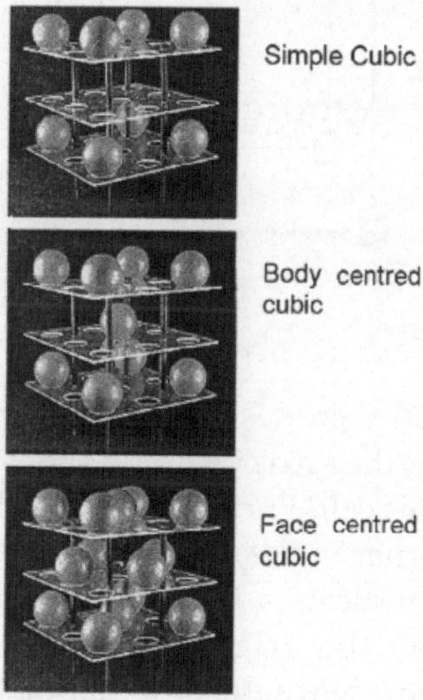

Figure

The face-centred cubic unit cell also starts with identical particles on the eight corners of the cube. But this structure also contains the same particles in the centres of the six faces of the unit cell, for a total of 14 identical lattice points.

The face-centred cubic unit cell is the simplest repeating unit in a cubic closest-packed structure. In fact, the presence of face-centred cubic unit cells in this structure explains why the structure is known as *cubic* closest-packed.

A Three-Dimensional Graph

The lattice points in a cubic unit cell can be described in

terms of a three-dimensional graph. Because all three cell-edge lengths are the same in a cubic unit cell, it doesn't matter what orientation is used for the *a*, *b*, and *c* axes. For the sake of argument, we'll define the *a* axis as the vertical axis of our coordinate system, as shown in fig. below.

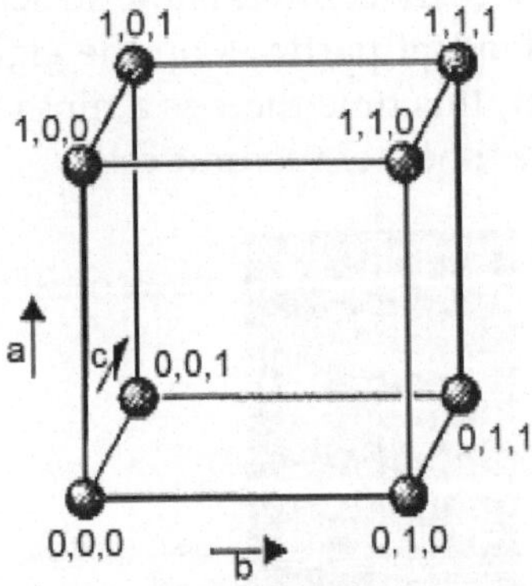

Figure

The *b* axis will then describe movement across the front of the unit cell, and the *c* axis will represent movement towards the back of the unit cell. Furthermore, we'll arbitrarily define the bottom left corner of the unit cell as the origin (0,0,0). The coordinates 1,0,0 indicate a lattice point that is one cell-edge length away from the origin along the *a* axis. Similarly, 0,1,0 and 0,0,1 represent lattice points that are displaced by one cell-edge length from the origin along the *b* and *c* axes, respectively.

Thinking about the unit cell as a three-dimensional graph allows us to describe the structure of a crystal with a remarkably small amount of information. We can specify the structure of cesium chloride, for example, with only four pieces of information.

- CsCl crystallizes in a cubic unit cell.
- The length of the unit cell edge is 0.4123 nm.
- There is a Cl^- ion at the coordinates 0,0,0.
- There is a Cs^+ ion at the coordinates 1/2,1/2,1/2.

Because the cell edge must connect equivalent lattice points, the presence of a Cl^- ion at one corner of the unit cell

(0,0,0) implies the presence of a Cl^- ion at every corner of the cell. The coordinates 1/2,1/2,1/2 describe a lattice point at the center of the cell. Because there is no other point in the unit cell that is one cell-edge length away from these coordinates, this is the only Cs^+ ion in the cell. CsCl is therefore a simple cubic unit cell of Cl^- ions with a Cs^+ in the center of the body of the cell.

Unit Cells: NaCl and ZnS

NaCl should crystallize in a cubic closest-packed array of Cl^- ions with Na^+ ions in the octahedral holes between planes of Cl^- ions. We can translate this information into a unit-cell model for NaCl by remembering that the face-centred cubic unit cell is the simplest repeating unit in a cubic closest-packed structure. There are four unique positions in a face-centred cubic unit cell. These positions are defined by the coordinates: 0,0,0; 0,1/2,1/2; 1/2,0,1/2; and 1/2,1/2,0. The presence of an particle at one corner of the unit cell (0,0,0) requires the presence of an equivalent particle on each of the eight corners of the unit cell. Because the unit-cell edge connects equivalent points, the presence of a particle in the center of the bottom face (0,1/2,1/2) implies the presence of an equivalent particle in the center of the top face (1,1/2,1/2). Similarly, the presence of particles in the centre of the 1/2,0,1/2 and 1/2,1/2,0 faces of the unit cell implies equivalent particles in the centres of the 1/2,1,1/2 and 1/2,1/2,1 faces. Figure 7.12 that there is an octahedral hole in the centre of a face-centred cubic unit cell, at the coordinates 1/2,1/2,1/2. Any particle at this point touches the particles in the centres of the six faces of the unit cell.

If Cl^- ions occupy the lattice points of a face-centred cubic unit cell and all of the octahedral holes are filled with Na^+ ions.

We can therefore describe the structure of NaCl in terms of the following information.

- NaCl crystallizes in a cubic unit cell.
- The cell-edge length is 0.5641 nm.
- There are Cl^- ions at the positions 0,0,0; 1/2,1/2,0; 1/2,0,1/2; and 0,1/2,1/2.

- There are Na^+ ions at the positions 1/2,1/2,1/2; 1/2,0,0; 0,1/2,0; and 0,0,1/2.

Placing a Cl^- ion at these four positions implies the attendance of a Cl^- ion on each of the 14 lattice points that define a face-centred cubic unit. Placing a Na^+ ion in the centre of the unit cell (1/2,1/2,1/2) and on the three unique edges of the unit cell (1/2,0,0; 0,1/2,0; and 0,0,1/2) requires an equivalent Na^+ ion in every octahedral hole in the unit cell.

ZnS crystallizes as cubic closest-packed array of S^{2-} ions with Zn^{2+} ions in tetrahedral holes. The S^{2-} ions in this crystal occupy the same positions as the Cl^- ions in NaCl. The only difference between these crystals is the location of the positive ions.

The structure of ZnS can therefore be described as follows:

- ZnS crystallizes in a cubic unit cell.
- The cell-edge length is 0.5411 nm.
- There are S^{2-} ions at the positions 0,0,0; 1/2,1/2,0; 1/2,0,1/2; and 0,1/2,1/2.
- There are Zn^{2+} ions at the positions 1/4,1/4,1/4; 1/4,3/4,3/4; 3/4,1/4,3/4; and 3/4,3/4,1/4.

Note that only half of the tetrahedral holes are occupied in this crystal because there are two tetrahedral holes for every S^{2-} ion in a closest-packed array of these ions.

Unit Cells: Measuring the Distance Between Particles

Nickel is one of the metals that crystallize in a cubic closest-packed structure. When you consider that a nickel atom has a mass of only 9.75×10^{-23} g and an ionic radius of only 1.24×10^{-10} m, it is a remarkable achievement to be able to describe the structure of this metal. The obvious question is: How do we know that nickel packs in a cubic closest-packed structure? The only way to determine the structure of matter on an atomic scale is to use a probe that is even smaller. One of the most useful probes for studying matter on this scale is electromagnetic radiation.

In 1912, Max van Laue found that x-rays that struck the surface of a crystal were diffracted into patterns that resembled the patterns produced when light passes through a very narrow slit. Shortly thereafter, William Lawrence Bragg, who was just completing his undergraduate degree in physics at Cambridge, explained van Laue's resultswith an equation known as the Bragg equation, which allows us to calculate the distance between planes of atoms in a crystal from the pattern of diffraction of x-rays of known wavelength.

$n\lambda = 2d \sin T$

The pattern by which x-rays are diffracted by nickel metal suggests that this metal packs in a cubic unit cell with a distance between planes of atoms of 0.3524 nm. Thus, the cell-edge length in this crystal must be 0.3524 nm. Knowing that nickel crystallizes in a cubic unit cell is not enough. We still have to decide whether it is a simple cubic, body-centred cubic, or face-centred cubic unit cell. This can be done by measuring the density of the metal.

Unit Cells: Determining the Unit Cell of a Crystal

Atoms on the corners, edges, and faces of a unit cell are shared by more than one unit cell, as shown in the figure below. An atom on a face is shared by two unit cells, so only half of the atom belongs to each of these cells. An atom on an edge is shared by four unit cells, and an atom on a corner is shared by eight unit cells.

Thus, only one-quarter of an atom on an edge and one-eighth of an atom on a corner can be assigned to each of the unit cells that share these atoms.

If nickel crystallized in a simple cubic unit cell, there would be a nickel atom on each of the eight corners of the cell. Because only one-eighth of these atoms can be assigned to a given unit cell, each unit cell in a simple cubic structure would have one net nickel atom.

Simple cubic structure:

8 corners x 1/8 = 1 atom

If nickel formed a body-centred cubic arrangement, there would be two atoms per unit cell, because the nickel atom in the centre of the body wouldn't be shared with any other unit cells.

Body-centred cubic structure:

(8 corners x 1/8) + 1 body = 2 atoms

If nickel crystallized in a face-centred cubic structure, the six atoms on the faces of the unit cell would contribute three net nickel atoms, for a total of four atoms per unit cell.

Face-centred cubic structure:

(8 corners x 1/8) + (6 faces x 1/2) = 4 atoms

Because they have different numbers of atoms in a unit cell, each of these structures would have a different density. Let's therefore calculate the density for nickel based on each of these structures and the unit cell edge length for nickel : 0.3524 nm. In order to do this, we need to know the volume of the unit cell in cubic centimeters and the mass of a single nickel atom. The volume (V) of the unit cell is equal to the cell-edge length (a) cubed.

$V = a^3 = (0.3524\ \text{nm})^3 = 0.04376\ \text{nm}^3$

Since there are 10^9 nm in a meter and 100 cm in a meter, there must be 10^7 nm in a cm.

$$\frac{10^9}{1\text{m}} \times \frac{1\text{m}}{100\text{cm}} = 10^7\ \text{nm / cm}$$

We can therefore convert the volume of the unit cell to cm^3 as follows.

$$4.376 \times 10^{-2}\ \text{nm}^3 \times \left[\frac{1\text{cm}}{10^7\ \text{nm}}\right]^3 = 4.376 \times 10^{-23}\ \text{cm}^3$$

The mass of a nickel atom can be calculated from the atomic weight of this metal and Avogadro's number.

$$\frac{58.69\text{g Ni}}{1\text{mol}} \times \frac{1\text{mol}}{6.022 \times 10^{23}\ \text{atoms}} = 9.746 \times 10^{-23}\ \text{g / atom}$$

The density of nickel, if it crystallized in a simple cubic structure, would therefore be 2.23 g/cm^3, to three significant figures.

Simple cubic structure:

$$\frac{9.746 \times 10^{-23}\ \text{g / unit cell}}{4.376 \times 10^{-23}\ \text{cm}^3\ \text{/ unit cell}} = 2.23\text{g / cm}^3$$

Because there would be twice as many atoms per unit cell if nickel crystallized in a body-centred cubic structure, the density of nickel in this structure would be twice as large.

Body-centred cubic structure:

$$\frac{2\left(9.746\times10^{-23}\ \text{g / unit cell}\right)}{4.376\times10^{-23}\ \text{cm}^3\ /\ \text{unit cell}} = 4.45\ \text{g / cm}^3$$

There would be four atoms per unit cell in a face-centred cubic structure and the density of nickel in this structure would be four times as large.

Face-centred cubic structure:

$$\frac{4\left(9.746\times10^{-23}\ \text{g / unit cell}\right)}{4.376\times10^{-23}\ \text{cm}^3\ /\ \text{unit cell}} = 8.91\ \text{g / cm}^3$$

The experimental value for the density of nickel is 8.90 g/cm^3. The obvious conclusion is that nickel crystallizes in a face-centred cubic unit cell and therefore has a cubic closest-packed structure.

Unit Cells: Calculating Metallic or Ionic Radii

Estimates of the radii of most metal atoms can be found. Where do these data come from? How do we know, for example, that the radius of a nickel atom is 0.1246 nm?

Nickel crystallizes in a face-centred cubic unit cell with a cell-edge length of 0.3524 nm to calculate the radius of a nickel atom. One of the faces of a face-centred cubic unit cell is shown in the fig. below.

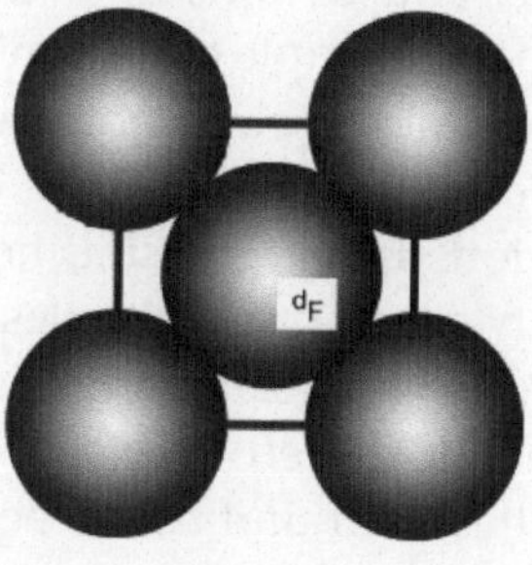

Figure

According to Fig., the diagonal across the face of this unit cell is equal to four times the radius of a nickel atom.

$$d_{face} = 4Y_N$$

The Pythagorean theorem states that the diagonal across a right triangle is equal to the sum of the squares of the other sides. The diagonal across the face of the unit cell is therefore related to the unit-cell edge length by the following equation.

$$d^2_{face} = a^2 + a^2$$

Taking the square root of both sides gives the following result.

$$d_{face} = \sqrt{2}a$$

We now substitute into this equation the relationship between the diagonal across the face of this unit cell and the radius of a nickel atom:

$$4Y_N = \sqrt{2}a$$

Solving for the radius of a nickel atom gives a value of 0.1246 nm:

$$Y_N = \frac{\sqrt{2}a}{4} = \frac{\sqrt{2}(0.3524 \text{ nm})}{4} = 0.1246 \text{ nm}$$

A similar approach can be taken to estimating the size of an ion. Let's start by using the fact that the cell-edge length in cesium chloride is 0.4123 nm to calculate the distance between the centres of the Cs^+ and Cl^- ions in CsCl.

CsCl crystallizes in a simple cubic unit cell of Cl^- ions with a Cs^+ ion in the centre of the body of the cell.

Before we can calculate the distance between the centres of the Cs^+ and Cl^- ions in this crystal, however, we have to recognize the validity of one of the simplest assumptions about ionic solids: The positive and negative ions that form these crystals touch. We can therefore assume that the diagonal across the body of the CsCl unit cell is equivalent to the sum of the radii of two Cl^- ions and two Cs^+ ions.

$$d_{body} = 2\gamma_{Cs^+} + 2\gamma_{Cl^-}$$

The three-dimensional correspondent of the Pythagorean theorem suggests that the square of the diagonal across the body of a cube is the sum of the squares of the three sides.

$$d_{body}^2 = a^2 + a^2 + a^2$$

Taking the square root of both sides of this equation gives the following result.

$$d_{body} = \sqrt{3}a$$

If the cell-edge length in CsCl is 0.4123 nm, the diagonal across the body in this unit cell is 0.7141 nm.

$$d_{body} = \sqrt{3}a = \sqrt{3}(0.4123\,\text{nm}) = 0.7141\,\text{nm}$$

The sum of the ionic radii of Cs^+ and Cl^- ions is half this distance, or 0.3571 nm.

$$\gamma_{Cs^+} + \gamma_{Cl^-} = \frac{d_{body}}{2} = \frac{0.7141\,\text{nm}}{2} = 0.3571\,\text{nm}$$

If we had an estimate of the size of either the Cs^+ or Cl^- ion, we could use the results to calculate the radius of the other ion. The ionic radius of the Cl^- ion is 0.181 nm. Substituting this value into the last equation gives a value of 0.176 nm for the radius of the Cs^+ ion.

$$\gamma_{Cs^+} + \gamma_{Cl^-} = 0.3571\,\text{nm}$$

$$\gamma_{Cs^+} + 0.181\,\text{nm} = 0.3571\,\text{nm}$$

$$\gamma_{Cs^+} = 0.176\,\text{nm}$$

The results of this calculation are in reasonable agreement with the value of 0.169 nm known for the radius of the Cs^+ ion. The discrepancy between these values reflects the fact that ionic radii vary from one crystal to another. The tabulated values are averages of the results of a number of calculations of this type.

LATTICE PARAMETER

The physical properties of solids depends entirely upon the arrangement of the atoms that make up the solid and the distances between them. The arrangement of the atoms in a crystal structure is a combination of the size and shape of the unit-cell and the arrangement of atoms inside the unit-cell.

Unit Cell Size and Shape

The shape of the unit cells is described by the lattice symmetry.

The size of the unit-cell is described in terms of its unit-cell parameters. These are the edge lengths and the angles of the unit-cell. The positions of the X-ray beams diffracted by a crystal structure are related to the size and shape of the unit-cell. We use the Huber diffractometer to measure the positions of X-ray beams diffracted from a crystal to determine the size and shape of the unit-cell.

The process of X-ray *diffraction* by a crystal can be thought as one of *reflection* of the X-rays off planes of atoms within the crystal. With this idea we can derive Bragg's Law:

But with a single-crystal and a four-circle goniometer to orient the crystal, we can also determine the angles through which the crystal is moved to go from one diffraction peak to the next. This information is used with the Bragg angles to determine the unit-cell parameters.

Lattice Parameters at High Pressure

Why High Pressure?

All of our information about the deep Earth is indirect. It comes from geophysical observations. They tell us the density of the Earth at a given depth, but *not* which minerals are present. But the properties of the Earth's interior are dependent on the mineral structures present. We therefore use diamond-anvil cells to measure the lattice parameters of crystals to very high pressures.

This tells us the density of the mineral at high pressure, often expressed as an *Equation of State*. When the density of a mineral, or a combination of minerals, matches the density obtained from geophysical observations then those minerals may be present in the Earth's interior.

We simply load our crystal into a diamond-anvil cell, apply pressure, and measure the angles of the diffracted X-ray beams from the crystal.

Here are two examples of high-pressure studies of the lattice parameters of a crystal.

The sample is spodumene, a clinopyroxene.

The crystal was loaded into a diamond-anvil cell and pressure was applied. We then measured the lattice parameters at many different pressures up to 9 GPa. Each measurement takes about 24 hours.

Away from the phase transition the lattice parameters decrease smoothly with increasing pressure. The volume calculated from the lattice parameters can be used to determine the Equation of State of the sample.

This is the equation of state of albite, which was deliberate by Matt Benusa as part of his senior project on the Huber diffractometer in the Crystallography Laboratory. The small symbols are the actual data, and the estimated uncertainties are smaller than the symbol size.

Up to about 3.5 GPa the volume variation with pressure is normal; the curve is concave upwards indicating that the structure is becoming stiffer as pressure is increased. At higher pressures the solid curve and data points turn over and the structure is clearly becoming softer again. This is very unusual behaviour and is a result of the complex response of the feldspar framework to pressure.

CRYSTAL SYSTEMS

In crystallography, the terms crystal system, crystal family, and lattice system each refer to one of several classes of space groups, lattices, point groups, or crystals. Informally, two crystals tend to be in the same crystal system if they have similar symmetries, though there are many exceptions to this.

Crystal systems, crystal families, and lattice systems are similar but slightly different, and there is widespread confusion between them: in particular the trigonal crystal system is often confused with the rhombohedral lattice system, and the term "crystal system" is sometimes used to mean "lattice system" or "crystal family".

Space groups and crystals are divided into 7 crystal systems according to their point groups, and into 7 lattice systems according to their Bravais lattices. Five of the crystal systems are essentially the same as five of the lattice systems, but the hexagonal and trigonal crystal systems differ from the hexagonal and rhombohedral lattice systems. The six crystal families are formed by combining the hexagonal and trigonal crystal systems into one hexagonal family, in order to eliminate this confusion.

Overview of Lattice System

A lattice system is a class of lattices with the same point group. In three dimensions there are seven lattice systems: triclinic, monoclinic, orthorhombic, tetragonal, rhombohedral, hexagonal, and cubic. The lattice system of a crystal or space group is determined by its lattice but not always by its point group.

A crystal system is a class of point groups. Two point groups are placed in the same crystal system if the sets of possible lattice systems of their space groups are the same. For many point groups there is only one possible lattice system, and in these cases the crystal system corresponds to a lattice system and is given the same name. However, for the five point groups in the trigonal crystal class there are two possible lattice systems for their point groups: rhombohedral or hexagonal. In three dimensions there are seven crystal systems: triclinic, monoclinic, orthorhombic, tetragonal, trigonal, hexagonal, and cubic. The crystal system of a crystal or space group is determined by its point group but not always by its lattice.

A crystal family also consists of point groups and is formed by combining crystal systems whenever two crystal systems have space groups with the same lattice. In three dimensions a crystal family is almost the same as a crystal system (or lattice system), except that the hexagonal and trigonal crystal systems are combined into one hexagonal family. In three dimensions there are six crystal families: triclinic, monoclinic, orthorhombic, tetragonal, hexagonal, and cubic. The crystal family of a crystal or space group is determined by either its point group or its lattice, and crystal families are the smallest collections of point groups with this property.

Table 7.1

<table>
<tr><th>Crystal family</th><th>Crystal system</th><th>Required symmetries of point group</th><th>Point groups</th><th>Space groups</th><th>Bravais lattices</th><th>Lattice system</th></tr>
<tr><td colspan="2">Triclinic</td><td>None</td><td>2</td><td>2</td><td>1</td><td>Triclinic</td></tr>
<tr><td colspan="2">Monoclinic</td><td>1 twofold axis of rotation or 1 mirror plane</td><td>3</td><td>13</td><td>2</td><td>Monoclinic</td></tr>
<tr><td colspan="2">Orthorhombic</td><td>3 twofold axes of rotation or 1 twofold axis of rotation and two mirror planes.</td><td>3</td><td>59</td><td>4</td><td>Orthorhombic</td></tr>
<tr><td colspan="2">Tetragonal</td><td>1 fourfold axis of rotation</td><td>7</td><td>68</td><td>2</td><td>Tetragonal</td></tr>
<tr><td rowspan="3">Hexagonal</td><td rowspan="2">Trigonal</td><td rowspan="2">1 threefold axis of rotation</td><td rowspan="2">5</td><td>7</td><td>1</td><td>Rhombohedral</td></tr>
<tr><td>18</td><td rowspan="2">1</td><td rowspan="2">Hexagonal</td></tr>
<tr><td>Hexagonal</td><td>1 sixfold axis of rotation</td><td>7</td><td>27</td></tr>
<tr><td colspan="2">Cubic</td><td>4 threefold axes of rotation</td><td>5</td><td>36</td><td>3</td><td>Cubic</td></tr>
<tr><td>Total</td><td>7</td><td></td><td>32</td><td>230</td><td>14</td><td>7</td></tr>
</table>

In dimensions less than three there is no essential difference between crystal systems, crystal families, and lattice systems. There are 1 in dimension 0, 1 in dimension 1, and 4 in dimension 2, called oblique, rectangular, square, and hexagonal. The relation between three-dimensional crystal families, crystal systems, and lattice systems is shown in the following table:

Crystal Classes and Structures

The crystal structures of biological molecules (such as protein structures) can only occur in the 11 enantiomorphic point groups, as biological molecules are invariably chiral. The protein assemblies themselves may have symmetries other than those given above, because they are not intrinsically restricted by the Crystallographic restriction theorem. For example the Rad52 DNA binding protein has an 11-fold rotational symmetry (in human), however, it must form crystals in one of the 11 enantiomorphic point groups given above.

Dislocations Crystals

Dislocations are another type of defect in crystals. Dislocations are areas were the atoms are out of position in the crystal structure. Dislocations are generated and move when a stress is applied. The motion of dislocations allows slip – plastic deformation to occur.

Before the discovery of the dislocation by Taylor, Orowan and Polyani in 1934, no one could figure out how the plastic deformation properties of a metal could be greatly changed by solely by forming (without changing the chemical composition). This became even bigger mystery when in the early 1900's scientists estimated that metals undergo plastic deformation at forces much smaller than the theoretical strength of the forces that are holding the metal atoms together. Many metallurgists remained skeptical of the dislocation theory until the development of the transmission electron microscope in the late 1950's. The TEM allowed experimental evidence to be collected that showed that the strength and ductility of metals are controlled by dislocations.

There are two basic types of dislocations, the edge dislocation and the screw dislocation. Actually, edge and screw dislocations are just extreme forms of the possible dislocation structures that can occur. Most dislocations are probably a hybrid of the edge and screw forms but this discussion will be limited to these two types.

Edge Dislocations

The edge defect can be easily visualized as an extra half-plane of atoms in a lattice. The dislocation is called a line defect because the locus of defective points produced in the lattice by the dislocation lie along a line. This line runs along the top of the extra half-plane. The inter-atomic bonds are significantly distorted only in the immediate vicinity of the dislocation line.

Understanding the association of a dislocation is key to understanding why dislocations allow deformation to occur at much lower stress than in a perfect crystal. Dislocation motion is analogous to movement of a caterpillar. The caterpillar would have to exert a large force to move its entire body at once. Instead it moves the rear portion of its body forward a small amount and creates a hump. The hump then moves forward and eventual moves all of the body forward by a small amount.

The dislocation in the top half of the crystal is slipping one plane at a time as it moves to the right from its position in image (a) to its position in image (b) and finally image (c). In the process of slipping one plane at a time the dislocation propagates across the crystal. The movement of the dislocation across the plane eventually causes the top half of the crystal to move with respect to the bottom half. However, only a small fraction of the bonds are broken at any given time. Movement in this manner requires a much smaller force than breaking all the bonds across the middle plane simultaneously.

Screw Dislocations

There is a second basic type of dislocation, called screw dislocation. The screw dislocation is slightly more difficult to visualize. The motion of a screw dislocation is also a result of shear stress, but the defect line movement is perpendicular to direction of the stress and the atom displacement, rather than parallel.

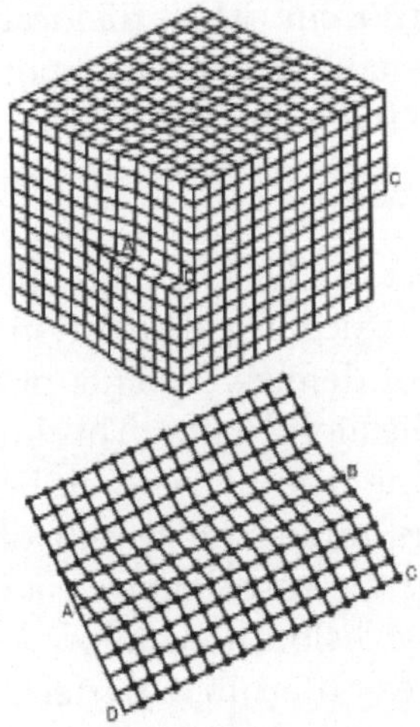

Figure

To visualize a screw dislocation, imagine a block of metal with a shear stress applied across one end so that the metal begins to rip. This is shown in the upper image fig. The atoms represented by the blue circles have not yet moved from their original position. The atoms represented by the red circles have moved to their new position in the lattice and have reestablished metallic bonds. The atoms represented by the green circles are in the process of moving. It can be seen that only a portion of the bonds are broke at any given time. As was the case with the edge dislocation, movement in this manner requires a much smaller force than breaking all the bonds across the middle plane simultaneously.

If the shear force is increased, the atoms will continue to slip to the right. A row of the green atoms will find there way back into a proper spot in the lattice (and become red) and a row of the blue atoms will slip out of position (and become green). In this way, the screw dislocation will move upward in the image, which is perpendicular to direction of the stress. Recall that the edge dislocation moves parallel to the direction of stress

The dislocations move along the densest planes of atoms in a material, because the stress needed to move the dislocation increases with the spacing between the planes. FCC and BCC metals have many dense planes, so dislocations move relatively easy and these materials have high ductility. Metals are strengthened by making it more difficult for dislocations to move. This may involve the introduction of obstacles, such as interstitial atoms or grain boundaries, to "pin" the dislocations. Also, as a material plastically deforms, more dislocations are produced and they will get into each others way and impede movement. This is why strain or work hardening occurs.

In ionically bonded materials, the ion must move past an area with a repulsive charge in order to get to the next location of the same charge. Therefore, slip is difficult and the materials are brittle. Likewise, the low density packing of covalent materials makes them generally more brittle than metals.

Perfect Crystal Defects

A perfect crystal, with every atom of the same type in the correct position, does not exist. All crystals have some defects. Defects contribute to the mechanical properties of metals. In fact, using the term "defect" is sort of a misnomer since these features are commonly intentionally used to manipulate the mechanical properties of a material. Adding alloying elements to a metal is one way of introducing a crystal defect. Nevertheless, the term "defect" will be used, just keep in mind that crystalline defects are not always bad. There are basic classes of crystal defects:

- point defects, which are places where an atom is missing or irregularly placed in the lattice structure. Point defects include lattice vacancies, self-interstitial atoms, substitution impurity atoms, and interstitial impurity atoms
- linear defects, which are groups of atoms in irregular positions. Linear defects are commonly called dislocations.
- planar defects, which are interfaces between homogeneous regions of the material. Planar defects include grain boundaries, stacking faults and external surfaces.

It is significant to note at this point that plastic deformation in a material occurs due to the movement of dislocations (linear defects). Millions of dislocations result for plastic forming operations such as rolling and extruding. It is also important to note that any defect in the regular lattice structure disrupts the motion of dislocation, which makes slip or plastic deformation more difficult. These defects not only include the point and planer defects mentioned above, and also other dislocations. Dislocation movement produces additional dislocations, and when dislocations run into each other it often impedes movement of the dislocations.

DISLOCATION

In materials science, a dislocation is a crystallographic defect, or irregularity, within a crystal structure. The presence of dislocations strongly influences many of the properties of materials. The theory was originally developed by Vito Volterra in 1905 but the term 'dislocation' was not coined until later by the late Professor Sir Frederick Charles Frank of the Physics Department at the University of Bristol. Some types of dislocations can be visualized as being caused by the termination of a plane of atoms in the middle of a crystal. In such a case, the surrounding planes are not straight, but instead bend around the edge of the terminating plane so that the crystal structure is perfectly ordered on either side. The analogy with a stack of paper is apt: if a half a piece of paper is inserted in a stack of paper, the defect in the stack is only noticeable at the edge of the half sheet.

There are two primary types: *edge dislocations* and *screw dislocations. Mixed dislocations* are intermediate between these.

Mathematically, dislocations are a type of topological defect, sometimes called a soliton. The mathematical theory explains why dislocations behave as stable particles: they can be moved about, but maintain their identity as they move.

Two dislocations of opposite orientation, when brought together, can cancel each other (this is the process of annihilation), but a single dislocation typically cannot "disappear" on its own.

Dislocation Geometry

Two main types of dislocation exist: edge and screw. Dislocations found in real materials typically are *mixed*, meaning that they have characteristics of both.

A crystalline material consists of a regular array of atoms, arranged into lattice planes (imagine stacking oranges in a grocery, each of the trays of oranges are the lattice planes). One approach is to begin by considering a 3-d representation of a perfect crystal lattice, with the atoms represented by spheres. The viewer may then start to simplify the representation by visualising planes of atoms instead of the atoms themselves.

Edge Dislocations

An edge dislocation is a defect where an extra half-plane of atoms is introduced mid way through the crystal, distorting nearby planes of atoms. When enough force is applied from one side of the crystal structure, this extra plane passes through planes of atoms breaking and joining bonds with them until it reaches the grain boundary. A simple schematic diagram of such atomic planes can be used to illustrate lattice defects such as dislocations. The dislocation has two properties, a line direction, which is the direction running along the bottom of the extra half plane, and the Burgers vector which describes the magnitude and direction of distortion to the lattice. In an edge dislocation, the Burgers vector is perpendicular to the line direction.

The stresses caused by an edge dislocation are complex due to its inherent asymmetry. These stresses are described by three equations:

$$\sigma_{xx} = \frac{-\mu b}{2\pi(1-\nu)} \frac{y(3x^2 + y^2)}{(x^2 + y^2)^2}$$

$$\sigma_{yy} = \frac{\mu b}{2\pi(1-\nu)} \frac{y(x^2 - y^2)}{(x^2 + y^2)^2}$$

$$\tau_{xy} = \frac{\mu b}{2\pi(1-\nu)} \frac{x(x^2 - y^2)}{(x^2 + y^2)^2}$$

where μ is the shear modulus of the material, b is the Burgers vector, ν is Poisson's ratio and x and y are coordinates.

These equations suggest a vertically oriented dumbbell of stresses surrounding the dislocation, with compression experienced by the atoms near the "extra" plane, and tension experienced by those atoms near the "missing" plane.

Screw Dislocations

A *screw dislocation* is much harder to visualize. Imagine cutting a crystal along a plane and slipping one half across the other by a lattice vector, the halves fitting back together without leaving a defect. If the cut only goes part way through the crystal, and then slipped, the boundary of the cut is a screw dislocation. It comprises a structure in which a helical path is traced around the linear defect (dislocation line) by the atomic planes in the crystal lattice. Perhaps the closest analogy is a spiral-sliced ham. In pure screw dislocations, the Burgers vector is parallel to the line direction. Despite the difficulty in visualization, the stresses caused by a screw dislocation are less complex than those of an edge dislocation. These stresses need only one equation, as symmetry allows only one radial coordinate to be used:

$$\tau_r = \frac{-\mu b}{2\pi r}$$

where μ is the shear modulus of the material, b is the Burgers vector, and r is a radial coordinate. This equation suggests a long cylinder of stress radiating outward from the cylinder and decreasing with distance. Please note, this simple model results in an infinite value for the core of the dislocation at r = 0 and so it is only valid for stresses outside of the core of the dislocation. If the Burgers vector is very large, the core may actually be empty resulting in a micropipe, as commonly observed in silicon carbide.

Mixed Dislocations

In many materials, dislocations are found where the line direction and Burgers vector are neither perpendicular nor parallel and these dislocations are called *mixed dislocations,* consisting of both screw and edge character.

Observation of Dislocations

When a dislocation line intersects the surface of a metallic material, the associated strain field locally increases the relative susceptibility of the material to acidic etching and an etch pit of regular geometrical format results.

If the material is strained (deformed) and repeatedly re-etched, a series of etch pits can be produced which effectively trace the movement of the dislocation in question.

Transmission electron microscopy can be used to observe dislocations within the microstructure of the material. Thin foils of metallic samples are prepared to render them transparent to the electron beam of the microscope.

The electron beam suffers diffraction by the regular crystal lattice planes of the metal atoms and the differing relative angles between the beam and the lattice planes of each grain in the metal's microstructure result in image contrast (between grains of different crystallographic orientation).

The less regular atomic structures of the grain boundaries and in the strain fields around dislocation lines have different diffractive properties than the regular lattice within the grains, and therefore present different contrast effects in the electron micrographs. (The dislocations are seen as dark lines in the lighter, central region of the micrographs on the right). Transmission electron micrographs of dislocations typically utilize magnifications of 50,000 to 300,000 times (though the equipment itself offers a wider range of magnifications than this).

Some microscopes also permit the in-situ heating and/or deformation of samples, thereby permitting the direct observation of dislocation movement and their interactions. Note the characteristic 'wiggly' contrast of the dislocation lines as they pass through the thickness of the material. Note also that a dislocation cannot end within a crystal; the dislocation lines in these images end at the sample surface. A dislocation can only be contained within a crystal as a complete loop. Field ion microscopy and atom probe techniques offer methods of producing much higher magnifications (typically 3 million times and above) and permit the observation of dislocations at an atomic level.

Where surface relief can be resolved to the level of an atomic step, screw dislocations appear as distinctive spiral features - thus revealing an important mechanism of crystal growth: where there is a surface step, atoms can more easily add to the crystal, and the surface step associated with a screw dislocation is never destroyed no matter how many atoms are added to it. (By contrast, traditional optical microscopy, which is not appropriate for the *direct* observation of dislocations, typically offers magnifications up to a maximum of only around 2000 times).

After chemical etching, small pits are formed where the etching solution preferentially attacks the sample surface around the dislocations intercepting this surface, due to the more highly strained state of the material. Thus, the image features indicate points at which dislocations intercept the sample surface. In this way, dislocations in silicon, for example, can be observed *indirectly* using an interference microscope. Crystal orientation can be determined by the shape of the etch pits associated with the dislocations (in the case of the illustration below; 100 elliptical, 111 - triangular/ pyramidal).

Sources of Dislocations

Dislocation density in a material can be increased by plastic deformation by the following relationship: $\tau \propto \rho^{1/2}$. Since the dislocation density increases with plastic deformation, a mechanism for the creation of dislocations must be activated in the material. Three mechanisms for dislocation formation are homogeneous nucleation, grain boundary initiation, and interfaces between the lattice and the surface, precipitates, dispersed phases, or reinforcing fibres.

The creation of a dislocation by homogeneous nucleation is a result of the rupture of the atomic bonds along a line in the lattice. A plane in the lattice is sheared, resulting in 2 oppositely faced half planes or dislocations. These dislocations move away from each other through the lattice. Since homogeneous nucleation forms dislocations from perfect crystals and requires the simultaneous breaking of many bonds, the energy required for homogeneous nucleation is high. For instance the stress required for homogeneous nucleation in copper has been shown to be

$$\frac{\tau_{hom}}{G} = 7.4 \times 10^{-2}$$

where G is the shear modulus of copper (46 GPa).

Solving for τ_{hom}, we see that the required stress is 3.4 GPa, which is very close to the theoretical strength of the crystal. Therefore, in conventional deformation homogeneous nucleation requires a concentrated stress, and is very unlikely. Grain boundary initiation and interface interaction are more common sources of dislocations.

Irregularities at the grain boundaries in materials can produce dislocations which propagate into the grain. The steps and ledges at the grain boundary are an important source of dislocations in the early stages of plastic deformation. The surface of a crystal can produce dislocations in the crystal. Due to the small steps on the surface of most crystals, stress in certain regions on the surface is much larger than the average stress in the lattice.

The dislocations are then propagated into the lattice in the same manner as in grain boundary initiation. In monocrystals, the majority of dislocations are formed at the surface. The dislocation density 200 micrometres into the surface of a material has been shown to be six times higher than the density in the bulk. However, in polycrystalline materials the surface sources cannot have a major effect because most grains are not in contact with the surface.

The interface between a metal and an oxide can greatly increase the number of dislocations created. The oxide layer puts the surface of the metal in tension because the oxygen atoms squeeze into the lattice, and the oxygen atoms are under compression. This greatly increases the stress on the surface of the metal and consequently the amount of dislocations formed at the surface. The increased amount of stress on the surface steps results in an increase of dislocations.

DISLOCATIONS, SLIP AND PLASTICITY

Until the 1930s, one of the enduring challenges of materials science was to explain plasticity in microscopic terms. A naive attempt to calculate the shear stress at which neighbouring atomic planes *slip* over each other in a perfect crystal suggests that, for a material with shear modulus G, shear strength τ_m is given approximately by:

$$\tau_m = \frac{G}{2\pi}.$$

As shear modulus in metals is typically within the range 20 000 to 150 000 MPa, this is difficult to reconcile with shear stresses in the range 0.5 to 10 MPa observed to produce plastic deformation in experiments.

In 1934, Egon Orowan, Michael Polanyi and G. I. Taylor, roughly simultaneously, realised that plastic deformation could be explained in terms of the theory of dislocations. Dislocations can move if the atoms from one of the surrounding planes break their bonds and rebond with the atoms at the terminating edge. In effect, a half plane of atoms is moved in response to shear stress by breaking and reforming a line of bonds, one (or a few) at a time. The energy required to break a single bond is far less than that required to break all the bonds on an entire plane of atoms at once. Even this simple model of the force required to move a dislocation shows that plasticity is possible at much lower stresses than in a perfect crystal. In many materials, particularly ductile materials, dislocations are the "carrier" of plastic deformation, and the energy required to move them is less than the energy required to fracture the material. Dislocations give rise to the characteristic malleability of metals.

When metals are subjected to "cold working" (deformation at temperatures which are relatively low as compared to the material's absolute melting temperature, T_m, *i.e.*, typically less than 0.3 T_m) the dislocation density increases due to the formation of new dislocations and dislocation multiplication. The consequent increasing overlap between the strain fields of adjacent dislocations gradually increases the resistance to further dislocation motion. This causes a hardening of the metal as deformation progresses. This effect is known as strain hardening (also "work hardening"). Tangles of dislocations are found at the early stage of deformation and appear as non well-defined boundaries; the process of dynamic recovery leads eventually to the formation of a cellular structure containing boundaries with misorientation lower than 15° (low angle grain boundaries). In addition, adding pinning points that inhibit the motion of dislocations, such as alloying elements, can introduce stress fields that ultimately strengthen the material by requiring a higher applied stress to overcome the pinning stress and continue dislocation motion.

The effects of strain hardening by accumulation of dislocations and the grain structure formed at high strain can be removed by appropriate heat treatment (annealing) which promotes the recovery and subsequent recrystallisation of the material.

The combined processing techniques of work hardening and annealing allow for control over dislocation density, the degree of dislocation entanglement, and ultimately the yield strength of the material.

Dislocation Climb

Dislocations can slip in planes containing both the dislocation and the Burgers Vector. For a screw dislocation, the dislocation and the Burgers vector are parallel, so the dislocation may slip in any plane containing the dislocation. For an edge dislocation, the dislocation and the Burgers vector are perpendicular, so there is only one plane in which the dislocation can slip. There is an alternative mechanism of dislocation motion, fundamentally different from slip, that allows an edge dislocation to move out of its slip plane, known as dislocation climb. Dislocation climb allows an edge dislocation to move perpendicular to its slip plane.

The driving force for dislocation climb is the movement of vacancies through a crystal lattice. If a vacancy moves next to the boundary of the extra half plane of atoms that forms an edge dislocation, the atom in the half plane closest to the vacancy can "jump" and fill the vacancy. This atom shift "moves" the vacancy in line with the half plane of atoms, causing a shift, or positive climb, of the dislocation. The process of a vacancy being absorbed at the boundary of a half plane of atoms, rather than created, is known as negative climb. Since dislocation climb results from individual atoms "jumping" into vacancies, climb occurs in single atom diameter increments.

During positive climb, the crystal shrinks in the direction perpendicular to the extra half plane of atoms because atoms are being removed from the half plane. Since negative climb involves an addition of atoms to the half plane, the crystal grows in the direction perpendicular to the half plane. Therefore, compressive stress in the direction perpendicular to the half plane promotes positive climb, while tensile stress promotes negative climb. This is one main difference between slip and climb, since slip is caused by only shear stress.

One additional difference between dislocation slip and climb is the temperature dependence. Climb occurs much more rapidly at high temperatures than low temperatures due to an increase in vacancy motion. Slip, on the other hand, has only a small dependence on temperature.

Chapter 8

Lasers

INTRODUCTION

The name LASER is an acronym for Light Amplification by the Stimulated Emission of Radiation.

In 1917, Albert Einstein first theorized about the process which makes lasers possible called "Stimulated Emission."

BEFORE THE LASER THERE WAS THE MASER

In 1954, Charles Townes and Arthur Schawlow invented the maser (microwave amplification by stimulated emission of radiation), using ammonia gas and microwave radiation-the maser was invented before the (optical) laser.

The technology is very close but does not use a visible light.

On March 24, 1959, Charles Townes and Arthur Schawlow were granted a patent for the maser.

The maser was used to amplify radio signals and as an ultrasensitive detector for space research. In 1958, Charles Townes and Arthur Schawlow theorized and published papers about a visible laser, an invention that would use infrared and/or visible spectrum light, however, they did not proceed with any research at the time.

Many different materials can be used as lasers. Some, like the ruby laser, emit short pulses of laser light. Others, like helium-neon gas lasers or liquid dye lasers emit a continuous beam of light.

Ruby Laser

In 1960, Theodore Maiman invented the ruby laser considered to be the first successful optical or light laser.

Many historians claim that Theodore Maiman invented the first optical laser, however, there is some controversy that Gordon Gould was the first.

Gordon Gould-Laser

Gordon Gould was the first person to use the word "laser". There is good reason to believe that Gordon Gould made the first light laser. Gould was a doctoral student at Columbia University under Charles Townes, the inventor of the maser. Gordon Gould was inspired to build his optical laser starting in 1958. He failed to file for a patent his invention until 1959. As a result, Gordon Gould's patent was refused and his technology was exploited by others. It took until 1977 for Gordon Gould to finally win his patent war and receive his first patent for the laser.

Gas Laser

The first gas laser (helium neon) was invented by Ali Javan in 1960. The gas laser was the first continuous-light laser and the first to operate "on the principle of converting electrical energy to a laser light output." It has been used in many practical applications.

Robert Hall-Semiconductor Injection Laser

In 1962, Robert Hall created a revolutionary type of laser that is still used in many of the electronic appliances and communications systems that we use every day.

Kumar Patel-Carbon Dioxide Laser

The carbon dioxide laser was invented by Kumar Patel in 1964.

Hildreth "Hal" Walker-Laser Telemetry

Hildreth Walker invented laser telemetry and targeting systems.

HISTORY OF LASERS

Laser is the acronym for Light Amplification by Stimulated Emission of Radiation.

Albert Einstein first explained the theory of stimulated emission in 1917, which became the basis of Laser. He postulated that, when the population inversion exists between upper and lower levels among atomic systems, it is possible to realize amplified stimulated emission and the stimulated emission has the same frequency and phase as the incident radiation. However, it was in late 1940s and fifties that scientists and engineers did extensive work to realize a practical device based on the principle of stimulated emission. Notable scientists who pioneered the work include Charles Townes, Joseph Weber, Alexander Prokhorov and Nikolai G Basov.

Initially, the scientists and engineers were working towards the realization of a MASER (Microwave Amplification by the Stimulated Emission of Radiation), a device that amplified microwaves for its immediate application in microwave communication systems. Townes and the other engineers believed it to be possible create an optical maser, a device for creating powerful beams of light using higher frequency energy to stimulate what was to become termed the lasing medium. Despite the pioneering work of Townes and Prokhorov it was left to Theodore Maiman in 1960 to invent the first Laser using ruby as a lasing medium that was stimulated using high energy flashes of intense light.

The development of Lasers has been a turning point in the history of science and engineering. It has produced a completely new type of systems with potentials for applications in a wide variety of fields. During sixties, lot of work had been carried out on the basic development of almost all the major lasers including high power gas dynamic and chemical lasers. Almost all the practical applications of these lasers in defence as well as in industry were also identified during this period. The motivation of using the high power lasers in strategic scenario was a great driving force for the rapid development of these high power lasers. In early seventies, megawatt class carbon dioxide gas dynamic laser was successfully developed and tested against typical military targets. The development of chemical lasers, free electron and X-ray lasers took slightly longer time because of involvement of multidisciplinary approach.

The major steps of advances or breakthroughs in Laser research are given below:

Dates, Contributors and events

- 1917: Einstein, A. - Concept and theory of stimulated light emission
- 1948: Gabor, D. - Invention of holography
- 1951: Charles H Townes, Alexander Prokhorov, Nikolai G Basov, Joseph Weber - The invention of the MASER (Microwave Amplification of Stimulated Emission of Radiation) at Columbia University, Lebedev Laboratories, Moscow and University of Maryland.
- 1956: Bloembergen, N. - Solid-state maser- [Proposal for a new type of solid state maser] at Harvard University.
- 1958: Schawlow, A.L. and Townes, C.H. - Proposed the realization of masers for light and infrared at Columbia University.
- 1960: Maiman, T.H. - Realization of first working LASER based on Ruby at Hughes Research Laboratories.
- 1961: Javan, A., Bennet, W.R. and Herriot, D.R. - First gas laser : Helium- Neon (He-Ne laser) at Bell Laboratories.
- 1961: Fox, A.G., Li, T. - Theory of optical resonators at Bell Laboratories.
- 1962: Hall,R. - First Semiconductor laser (Gallium-Arsenide laser) at General Electric Labs.
- 1962: McClung,F.J and Hellwarth, R.W. - Giant pulse generation / Q-Switching.
- 1962: Johnson, L.F., Boyd, G.D., Nassau, K and Sodden, R.R. - Continuous wave solid-state laser.

- 1964: Geusic, J.E., Markos, H.M., Van Uiteit, L.G. - Development of first working Nd:YAG LASER at Bell Labs.
- 1964: Patel, C.K.N. - Development of CO_2 LASER at Bell Labs.
- 1964: Bridges, W. - Development of Argon Ion LASER a Hughes Labs.
- 1965: Pimentel, G. and Kasper, J. V. V. - First chemical LASER at University of California, Berkley.
- 1965: Bloembergen, N. - Wave propagation in nonlinear media.
- 1966: Silfvast, W., Fowles, G. and Hopkins - First metal vapour LASER - Zn/Cd - at University of Utah.
- 1966: Walter, W.T., Solomon, N., Piltch, M and Gould, G. - Metal vapour laser.
- 1966: Sorokin, P. and Lankard, J. - Demonstration of first Dye Laser action at IBM Labs.
- 1966: AVCO Research Laboratory, USA. - First Gas Dynamic Laser based on CO_2
- 1970: Nikolai Basov's Group - First Excimer LASER at Lebedev Labs, Moscow based on Xenon (Xe) only.
- 1974: Ewing, J.J. and Brau, C. - First rare gas halide excimer at Avco Everet Labs.
- 1977: John M J Madey's Group - First free electron laser at Stanford University.
- 1977: McDermott, W.E., Pehelkin, N.R,. Benard, D.J and Bousek, R.R. - Chemical Oxygen Iodine Laser (COIL).
- 1980: Geoffrey Pert's Group - First report of X-ray lasing action, Hull University, UK.
- 1984: Dennis Matthew's Group - First reported demonstration of a "laboratory" X-ray laser from Lawrence Livermore Labs.
- 1999: Herbelin, J.M., Henshaw, T.L., Rafferty, B.D., Anderson, B.T., Tate, R.F., Madden, T.J., Mankey II, G.C and Hager, G.D. - All Gas-Phase Chemical Iodine Laser (AGIL).

- 2001: Lawrence Livermore National Laboratory - Solid State Heat Capacity Laser (SSHCL).

PROPERTIES OF LASER BEAMS

MONOCHROMATICITY

This property is due to the following two factors. First, only an EM wave of frequency n_0 = (E2-E1)/h can be amplified, n_0 has a certain range which is called linewidth, this linewidth is decided by homogeneous broadening factors and inhomogeneous broadening factors, the result linewidth is very small compared with normal lights. Second, the laser cavity forms a resonant system, oscillation can occur only at the resonance frequencies of this cavity. This leads to the further narrowing of the laser linewidth, the narrowing can be as large as 10 orders of magnitude! So laser light is usually very pure in wavelength, we say it has the property of monochromaticity.

Coherence

For any EM wave, there are two kinds of coherence, namely spatial and temporal coherence.

Let's consider two points that, at time t = 0, lie on the same wave front of some given EM wave, the phase difference of EM wave at the two points at time t = 0 is k0.

If for any time t > 0 the phase difference of EM wave at the two points remains k0, we say the EM wave has perfect coherence between the two points.

If this is true for any two points of the wave front, we say the wave has perfect spatial coherence. In practical the spatial coherence occurs only in a limited area, we say it is partial spatial coherence.

Now consider a fixed point on the EM wave front. If at any time the phase difference between time t and time t+dt remains the same, where "dt" is the time delay period, we say that the EM wave has temporal coherence over a time dt. If dt can be any value, we say the EM wave has perfect temporal coherence. If this happens only in a range 0<dt<t0, we say it

has partial temporal coherence, with a coherence time equal to t0.

We emphasize here that spatial and temporal coherence are independent. A partial temporal coherent wave can be perfect spatial coherent. Laser light is highly coherent, and this property has been widely used in measurement, holography, etc.

Divergence and Directionality

Laser beam is highly directional, which implies laser light is of very small divergence. This is a direct consequence of the fact that laser beam comes from the resonant cavity, and only waves propagating along the optical axis can be sustained in the cavity. The directionality is described by the light beam divergence angle. The relationship between divergence and optical systems.

For perfect spatial coherent light, a beam of aperture diameter D will have unavoidable divergence because of diffraction. From diffraction theory, the divergence angle θd is:

$$\theta_d = \beta \lambda / D$$

where λ and D are the wavelength and the diameter of the beam respectively, β is a coefficient whose value is around unity and depends on the type of light amplitude distribution and the definition of beam diameter. θ_d is called diffraction limited divergence.

If the beam is partial spatial coherent, its divergence is bigger than the diffraction limited divergence. In this case the divergence becomes:

$$\theta = \beta \lambda / (Sc)^{1/2}$$

where Sc is the coherence area.

Brightness

The brightness of a light source is defined as the power emitted per unit surface area per unit solid angle. A laser beam of power P, with a circular beam cross section of diameter D and a divergence angle θ and the result emission solid angle is $\pi \theta^2$, then the brightness of laser beam is:

$B = 4P/(\pi D\theta)^2$

The max brightness is reached when the beam is perfect spatial coherent.

$Bmax = 4P/(\pi \lambda \beta)^2$

In case of limited diffraction

$(\theta_d = \lambda \beta/D, D = \lambda \beta/\theta_d, \theta_d = \theta)$.

BASIC PRINCIPLES OF LASERS

To explain how laser light is generated, we need first to investigate the energy transition phenomena in atoms or molecules. These phenomena include: spontaneous emission, stimulated emission/absorption and nonradiative decay.

According to quantum mechanics, the electrons of atoms can take different energy states, say E1, E2, E3, etc., E1 < E2 < E3 <.... Lower energy level is more stable than higher energy levels, so electrons at high energy levels tend to decay to low energy levels, the energy difference between the two levels can be given out as electromagnetic radiation. This process is called Spontaneous Radiation. The relationship is:

$$E2 - E1 = h\nu_0$$

where E2 is the upper energy level, E1 is the lower energy level, h is Plank's constant, ν_0 is frequency of the radiated EM wave.

That the energy difference between the two levels can decay in forms other than radiative decay or, spontaneous radiation which is called Nonradiative Decay. The energy difference can change into kinetic energy or internal energy through collisions with surrounding atoms, molecules or walls. When external EM waves of frequency n_0 are incident on the material whose atoms initially are at energy level E2 and n_0 is very near to the transition frequency between E2 and E1, there is a finite probability that the incident waves will force the atoms to undergo transition E2 → E1. Each such transition gives out an EM wave (a photon), while the incident wave (incident photon) still exists.

Then we have two photons. The transition process is caused by external excitation, so it is called Stimulated

Radiation. Is stimulated radiation caused by some kind of resonance? Yes, the incident EM should have a frequency very close to that of the atoms, and this resonance makes the fundamental difference between spontaneous radiation and stimulated radiation. In the case of spontaneous emission, the radiation is in all directions and in random phases, while in stimulated radiation, the emitted waves of any atoms are in the same direction and in the same phase with the incident wave.

If the atom is initially at level E1, if this is the ground level, the atom will remain in this level unless got excited. When an EM wave of frequency n_0 is incident on the material, there is a finite probability that the atom will absorb the incident energy and jump to energy level E2. This process is called Stimulated Absorption.

Normally the number of atoms at lower energy levels is larger than atoms at higher levels. Stimulated radiation/ absorption, spontaneous emission and nonradiative decay are going on in the same time. Even if we ignore the decay factors, stimulated absorption still dominates over stimulated radiation, the incident EM wave can not be amplified in this case. Amplification of incident wave is possible only when the number of upper level atoms is greater than that of lower level atoms. This case is called Population Inversion. To get more atoms in upper level than in lower level, we have to raise the atoms from lower level to upper level. This process is called Pumping.

BASIC CONSTRUCTIONS OF LASERS

A basic laser system has two mirrors that are placed parallel to each other to form an optical oscillator so that light can be transmitted back and forth between the mirrors along the optical axis.

Between the mirrors is the active medium that can amplify the light by stimulated emission. Under certain pumping mechanism, the active medium can be excited from lower energy state to upper energy state, population inversion happens. Stimulated emissions give out photons in all directions at first. But the photons are transmitted through the system, only photons whose directions are along the optical axis can last, photons in other directions will either be scattered or absorbed. Soon almost all the photons in the system are oscillating in the optical axis direction. One incident photon can become two photons after every stimulated emission, so under proper conditions, light density is amplified. Usually one of the mirrors is nearly totally reflecting, another is partially reflecting, the partially reflecting mirror will output laser light either in continuous wave (CW) or in pulse. Working laser may give out a lot of heat, this heat can affect the operation quality seriously. So lasers usually have cooling systems.

ELEMENTS AND OPERATION OF A LASER

The laser is a light source that exhibits unique properties and a wide variety of applications. Lasers are used in welding, surveying, medicine, communication, national defence, and as tools in many areas of scientific research. Many types of lasers are commercially available today, ranging in size from devices that can rest on a fingertip to those that fill large buildings. All these lasers have certain basic characteristic properties in common.

The basic properties that distinguish laser light from other light sources and the essential elements required to produce this unique light. The lasing process is examined briefly, and several of the terms used to describe and characterize the process are introduced. The student will become acquainted with the basic safety procedures for the operation of a low-powered helium-neon gas laser and will identify the components of that laser.

Properties Of Laser Light

The light emitted by lasers is different from that produced by more common light sources such as incandescent bulbs, fluorescent lamps, and high-intensity arc lamps. An understanding of the unique properties of laser light may be achieved by contrasting it with the light produced by other, less unique sources.

THE FUTURE OF THE LASER

Modern technology is advancing so quickly that the average person simply cannot keep up with it. Even some scientists are occasionally unaware of discoveries being made in other fields. Lasers are very much a part of this technology explosion. They help in the discovery of new knowledge, which further fuels the explosion while, by advancing communications, they help spread the new knowledge to those who want it.

No one can predict what new and unheard-of discoveries will mark the next century of science. These discoveries no doubt will change the world in ways that cannot even be guessed at. What can be imagined are possible ways that today's technology might be used in the near future. In the case of the laser, consider what projects are in the development stages now and what other projects experts see on the immediate horizon.

REALISTIC IMAGES IN HOMES AND OFFICES

Many experts expect laser-computer advances to lead to the eventual perfection of holography, for example. By some estimates, within twenty years three-dimensional holographic movies will become common.

It will be like watching old-fashioned 3D movies, only without the special glasses. Even holographic television will likely be developed, although it will be very difficult to construct because so much information is needed to form a holographic image.

To transmit the information of a single hologram to a home, it will take a cable with the capacity of five hundred television channels. Once the hologram arrives in someone's living room, the television itself will have to be able to project the hologram, and this will require a screen with more than one thousand times more detail than today's TV screens.

Computing at Light Speed

In the mid-1990s the laser joined in a useful working partnership with the computer, but the laser still only reads, writes, and memorizes for the computer. Some scientists think the laser could go further and bring about a drastic change in the way the computer is designed.

The computer itself consists of wires, chips, connections, and other parts through which electrical signals flow. Experts point out that in the larger supercomputers sometimes too many pieces of information try to get to the same place at the same time. Due to the limitations of the machine parts themselves, the information bits can only move so fast. As a result, bottlenecks form.

These are like miniature traffic jams, only with bits of data instead of cars. The laser might be able to eliminate such bottlenecks by using light instead of electricity to process the information. A laser beam could carry millions of signals without once touching a physical connection. Thus bottlenecks would be eliminated and much more information could flow through the computer. Many technical problems need to be worked out before such an optical computer can be built. But researchers around the world are presently trying to solve these problems.

But many researchers believe these problems will be solved. If so, it will mean that more than entertainment can be piped into a person's home. When the phone rings, for instance, a projected image of the caller could appear in the room, an illusion that would seem perfectly real (except, of course, that the person receiving the call would be able to walk right through the image of the caller).

Once perfected, this amazing technology will not be limited to telephone calls. Business meetings will be held in which only a few or even none of the participants are actually in the meeting room. Similarly, a teacher's hologram might be made to appear in the bedroom of a student who is home sick.

Of course, such a system could be seriously misused. For example, a disreputable government or organization could secretly plant a holograph camera in a person's home and then spy on the person by watching a completely three-dimensional hologram of his or her every movement. At the very least, this could be an embarrassing situation. It is hoped that if such technology becomes common, safeguards will be developed to discourage such invasions of privacy.

Walking Electronics Stores?

Advanced laser-based devices may also transform ordinary people into virtual walking electronics stores. The fact that the beam of a laser can be focused to a microscopic point has already given it the ability to create discs to store vast amounts of information, including video and audio discs of high quality.

Researchers are now working to expand this principle to the miniaturization of electronic devices so that they can be carried or even worn by the average person. A tiny disc programmed with billions of bits of information will become the core of each device. The devices themselves will have to be modified to work with fibre optics or some other system that eliminates conventional metal wires and circuits. This will allow the machines to be extremely small.

The end result will be a tiny unit, probably worn like a standard watch or carried in a pocket or purse. Such a unit will include a telephone, television, radio, tape recorder and player, and a wireless hookup to the Internet.

Instead of using a bulky monitor screen, a tiny laser within the unit will project images from the television, tape player, or Internet onto any blank surface the wearer desires or perhaps in the air in the form of a laser hologram.

Such a gadget will be the direct precursor of the "tricorder," the futuristic device that allows the characters of *Star Trek* to gather, access, and analyse all manner of information.

Brains and Eyes like New

Another *Star Trek* device uses beams of light to heal wounds, broken bones, and internal injuries. In a similar vein, doctors have already begun to use lasers in brain surgery for procedures such as burning away a tumour that has formed within the skull. Some researchers are hopeful that many other types of delicate brain operations will be performed with lasers. Some such treatments may use low-power laser light to cause chemical reactions in selected sections of brain tissue, reactions that might help control certain mental disorders.

The future of lasers in eye surgery already promises to bring about a world in which no one needs eyeglasses or contact lenses. Reshaping the cornea with laser light is now a common medical procedure; but in only a few years doctors will be able to go further and completely reshape the human eye using laser beams.

One beam will precisely measure the eye in three dimensions to pinpoint any problems and feed the information into a computer, which will figure out exactly how the eye should be reshaped. The doctor then will use a different beam to cut the eyeball at various strategic points and another beam to weld the incisions together. Eventually, the eyeball will be shaped correctly, and the person will be able to see with perfect twenty-twenty vision.

The Dream of Unlimited Energy

An even more ambitious and far-reaching future use for the laser will be the production of energy, mainly in the form of electricity to power homes, factories, offices, and machines. Today's major sources of energy are water power; the burning of coal, gas, and oil; and nuclear reactors.

But all these methods may not be enough to supply the energy needs of the future. The population of the world continues to grow rapidly, and more people create a demand for more energy.

Moreover, water power requires building plants near rivers or dams; there are only so many such locations and most are not very near population centres. Meanwhile, supplies of coal, gas, and oil are running out, and nuclear reactors can leak radiation, creating a public danger. Disposing of spent nuclear materials is also a big problem. It is no wonder, then, that no new nuclear plants are presently planned in the United States.

The laser, on the other hand, promises to open up new and seemingly endless stores of energy for humanity's use. Production of energy by lasers will take two forms, the first being the solar-powered satellite. The satellite will be rocketed into a special orbital position where it will always stay above a certain fixed point on Earth's surface.

Once in position the satellite will begin gathering energy from sunlight. The energy will power a large laser that will direct a beam back to Earth where a receiver will collect the beam and convert it into electricity. If enough of these satellites can be put into orbit, a large share of Earth's energy needs will be met.

Some people worry that such a beam might be aimed in the wrong direction and cause death and destruction. As a matter of fact, the military has considered this method for making beam weapons. But ways will be found to adjust the power of the beam so that it will not do any damage. The time and money it will take to get these satellites orbiting will be worthwhile because sunlight is free. And because the sun is expected to shine for several billion more years, sunlight is also nearly inexhaustible.

The Power of the Atom

The other way lasers will produce energy is by facilitating nuclear fusion, the process that makes the sun and other stars shine. Fusion is one of two processes that are normally referred to as atomic, the other being nuclear fission. Both of these processes have been successfully used by scientists to make atomic bombs. (Fission produced the atom bomb, and fusion produced the hydrogen bomb.)

Nuclear fission occurs when a subatomic particle (such as a neutron) hits the centre, or nucleus, of an atom. The nucleus splits, sending out other particles plus a burst of energy. These particles then hit other atoms, the process quickly speeds up, and as more and more atoms are split a chain reaction takes place, releasing vast amounts of energy in the form of heat and light.

This large release of energy destroyed the cities of Hiroshima and Nagasaki in Japan in 1945. These bombings, which killed hundreds of thousands of people, brought an end to World War II. Later, scientists learned how to produce fission on a smaller scale. Since they now could control the process, they called it a controlled reaction. Controlled reactions are created at nuclear power plants where the energy produced is converted into electricity. But such reactions give off large amounts of dangerous radiation, which has prompted scientists to search for other safer sources of energy.

Lasers and Nuclear Fusion

Most nuclear scientists believe that in the future nuclear power will be supplied by fusion, a nuclear reaction in which two atoms are combined. But starting a fusion reaction requires an enormous initial force.

Many scientists think that "laser chains" can supply that force. A laser chain consists of several laser amplifiers over a hundred feet long, which intensify the power of laser beams. The high-powered beams are directed through beam splitters and onto mirrors so that several beams strike a tiny fuel pellet from all sides at once. This causes an explosion powerful enough to trigger a fusion reaction.

The other nuclear process, fusion, occurs when two separate atoms are violently forced together. The structure of the atoms breaks down and a new, heavier atom is formed. In the process, large amounts of energy are released as a by-product.

In the sun and other stars, hydrogen atoms fuse to become helium atoms, and energy in the form of heat and light is released. One great benefit of controlling fusion for energy production is that the process is relatively clean and safe. All that is needed for fuel is a small amount of hydrogen, which can be found in ordinary seawater; so the fuel is cheap and the supply almost endless. In addition, the process does not leak dangerous radiation, as fission does.

Scientists have not yet been able to produce controlled fusion reactions of any consequence. This is because fusion requires a large amount of energy just to get the process going. (In the sun, the trigger is the tremendous heat in the interior of the star itself. The trigger used to ignite a hydrogen bomb is an atom bomb.)

The laser may provide a way to get a safe fusion reaction going. Experiments with lasers and fusion began in the late 1960s, but progress was slow for a long time. A major breakthrough occurred in August 2001 when researchers from Japan and the United Kingdom succeeded in using a laser beam to compress a ball-like pellet of nuclear fuel.

The beam, which generated temperatures of 10 million degrees centigrade, focused on the pellet, creating enormous pressure—about 10 million times that of Earth's atmosphere. The pressure caused the pellet to implode (collapse inward) and release energy.

The energy generated in this experiment is not enough to power machines and houses, so the advent of large-scale controlled fusion still lies in the future. But increasingly advanced lasers may bring that future much closer than ever before dreamed—perhaps in only a few decades rather than centuries, as once predicted.

Searching for ET

An even more futuristic and quite intriguing use for advanced lasers is to aid in the detection of extraterrestrial civilizations on planets orbiting distant stars. The idea of flashing lasers to alert our presence to extraterrestrials is not new. But only recently was a laser built with the high power needed to do the job. According to science reporter Seth Shostak:

> Scientists at Lawrence Livermore National Laboratory, in California, have built a laser capable of putting out light pulses with a power of 1,000 trillion watts, although the pulses are brief: only a trillionth of a second long. It is called Nova and it's not your daddy's laser pointer. Imagine... taking aim at a star system 50 light-years away.... Every pulse... will eventually deliver about 10 photons [of light] per square meter onto the planets of the neighbouring star system.... During the laser

transmitter's short duty cycle, it outshines the Sun by a factor of thirty thousand.

The interstellar laser communicator works both ways, of course. Earth scientists may be able to detect high-energy laser pulses sent out by their alien counterparts. Specially designed light receptors on Earth potentially could detect the telltale photons of an alien laser, proving that an extraterrestrial civilization exists and wants to set up a dialogue.

A World Transformed

In 1905 when Albert Einstein described the then unknown process of stimulated photon emission, he and other scientists did not foresee the invention of the laser and its fantastic number of uses. As has happened so many times in the history of science, one person's idea grew to transform the world. And this transformation will surely continue.

In the twenty-first century and beyond, the laser promises to help raise human civilization to new heights. The supertool will build a storehouse of knowledge and put that knowledge within easy reach of most people. Laser light will illuminate a complex and computerized world, one in which technology allows men and women to live increasingly productive and happy lives. Indeed, the laser may one day harness the fire of the stars to give humanity clean, safe, and abundant energy for generations to come as well as access to alien knowledge that could transform the world in ways not yet imagined.

Bibliography

Christopher J. : *Atomic Physics*, Oxford University Press, 2008.

Datta, S. : *Electronic Transport in Mesoscopic Systems*,Cambridge University Press, Cambridge, 1995.

Doi, M. and S. F. Edwards: *The Theory of Polymer Dynamics*, Oxford University Inc NY, 1986.

Flory, P. : *Principles of Polymer Chemistry*, Cornell University Press, 1953.

Gardiner, C.W. *Handbook of Stochastic Methods*. Springer-Verlag, Berlin/Heidelberg, 2004.

Gedde, U.W.: *Polymer Physics*, Chapman & Hall, 1995

Hahn, T. : *International Tables for Crystallography*, Kluwer Academic, Dordrecht, 1992.

Herzberg, G.: *Molecular Spectra and Molecular Structure*, Van Nostrand Reinhold Company, New York, 1979.

Jha, A.K. : *A Textbook of Applied Physics*, I.K. International Pub, 2009.

Juneja, J.K. : *Comprehensive Objective Physics*, Laxmi Publications, Delhi, 2006.

Kumar, Manoj: *A Comprehensive Text Book of Applied Physics*, Abhishek, Delhi, 2009.

Lahiri, Girish: *Fundamental of Practical Physics*, Mohit Books International, Delhi, 2012.

Mangal, R.P.S.: *Handbook of Plasma Physics*, Dominant, Delhi, 2010.

McCrum, N.G., Buckley, C.P., Bucknall,C.B.: *Principles of Polymer Engineering*, Oxford University Press, 1988

Mehta, Neeraj : *Applied Physics for Engineers*, PHI Learning, Delhi, 2011.

Michael Rubinstein and Ralph H. Colby: *Polymer Physics*, Oxford University Press, London, 2003.

Pierre Gilles De Gennes, *Scaling Concepts in Polymer Physics,* Cornell University Press, Ithaca and London, 1979.

Prakash, Gyan: *Experimental Physics,* Studium Press India, Delhi, 2012.

Sahu, S P : *Basic Nuclear Physics,* Campus Books International, Delhi, 2009.

Shaked, H., P.M. Keane, J.C. Rodriguez, F.F. Owen, R.L. Hitterman, and J.D. Jorgensen, *Crystal Structures of the High-Tc Superconducting Copper-Oxides,* Elsevier Science B.V., Amsterdam, 1994.

Sharma, L.P. : *Principles of Applied Physics,* ALP Books, Delhi, 2011.

Singh, R. B. : *Introduction To Modern Physics,* New Age Publications, Delhi, 2009.

Subrahmaniam, N. : *Atomic and Nuclear Physics,* S. Chand Publisher, Delhi, 2006.

Treloar L.R.G.: *The Physics of Rubber Elasticity,* Clarendon Press, Oxford, 1975

Villars, P. and L.D. Calvert: *Pearson's Handbook of Crystallographic Data for Intermetallic Phases,* ASM International, Materials Park, Ohio, 1991.

Wyckoff, R.W.G. : *Crystal Structures,* John Wiley & Sons, New York, London, 1963.

Yadav, Vinita : *Applied Physics,* Swastik, Delhi, 2007.

Index

D